TREASURY

of

WOMEN'S

QUOTATIONS

CAROLYN WARNER

Foreword by ERMA BOMBECK

PRENTICE HALL
Career & Personal Development
Englewood Cliffs, NJ 07632
A Simon & Schuster Company

Prentice-Hall International (UK) Limited, *London*
Prentice-Hall of Australia Pty. Limited, *Sydney*
Prentice-Hall Canada, Inc., *Toronto*
Prentice-Hall Hispanoamericana, S.A., *Mexico*
Prentice-Hall of India Private Limited, *New Delhi*
Prentice-Hall of Japan, Inc., *Tokyo*
Simon & Schuster Asia Pte. Ltd., *Singapore*
Editora Prentice-Hall do Brasil, Ltda., *Rio de Janeiro*

© 1992 by
PRENTICE-HALL, INC.

10 **9** **8** **7** **6** **5** **4** **3**

Originally published as *The Last Word: A Treasury of Women's Quotes*
ISBN 0-13-517715-4.

This edition published exclusively for Borders Press.

Library of Congress Cataloging-in-Publication Data

Warner, Carolyn
    The last word: a treasury of women's quotes / by Carolyn
Warner.
      p. cm.
    Includes index.
    ISBN 0-13-641689-6
    1. Women—Quotations, maxims, etc.   2. Women—Quotations.
I. Title.
PN6084.W6W37 1992   92-13954
082'.082—dc20   CIP

ISBN 0-13-641689-6 NBZI

PRENTICE HALL
Career & Personal Development
Englewood Cliffs, NJ 07632
A Simon & Schuster Company

Printed in the United States of America

DEDICATION

This book is dedicated
with equal measures of love, respect, and gratitude
to my mother, Mary Tullis Kunde
and to my grandmother, Nellie Hershey Tullis.
They were my life's examples and, to me, they said it all.

FOREWORD

Carolyn Warner and I had a mutual friend who could have been a candidate for the first tongue transplant. The woman loved to talk. When her phone rang, her husband used to yell, "Laura! Someone wants to listen to you."

The story always got a laugh, but more important, it was true. People listened to Laura because she was one of the most "quotable" women they knew.

Being a professional, the first thing I did when Carolyn sent me the manuscript of this book, was to read through it to see how many times my name was mentioned. But as I read, I was struck with the realization that at last women were being given a voice. They had a showcase that mirrored what they are talking about and what they are thinking, what their priorities are, what their moods, concerns, and attitudes are, what they laugh about and what they cry about. Their words could enhance any speaker's presentation.

In earlier times, a book of women's quotes might never have been possible because if women wanted to be successful communicators, their works had to be published under a man's name.

Inquiring minds didn't want to know that George Sand, George Eliot, Ellis, Acton, and Currer Bell were really Amadine Aurore Lucie Dupin Dudevant, Mary Ann Evans, and Anne, Emily, and Charlotte Brontë.

As recently as the 1950's, the late syndicated financial columnist and journalist Sylvia Porter wrote under the name of S. Porter to assure credibility.

We have come some distance since Julia Ward Howe was forbidden by her husband to speak in public meetings and Abigail Adams pleaded (to no avail) with her husband, John, to "Don't forget the ladies," as he set out to pen the Declaration of Independence.

Following my words on these pages is an alphabetical journey of thoughts and emotions of our times from the women who lived them. From Miss Piggy ("Never eat more than you can lift.") to the equally wise Eleanor Roosevelt. From

Mary Kay Ash to Pearl Buck I found myself either nodding in agreement or chuckling out loud.

I am here to attest that Carolyn is one of those rare speakers who does not hyperventilate and blow into a paper bag to remain conscious before she speaks. I personally envy her that. A week before I am to speak, I kick the dog repeatedly, have arguments with my husband, and pray that inclement weather will paralyze transportation in whatever city I'm expected to speak.

On occasion, I have shared the dais with Carolyn, and she is relaxed and ready for a good time. Maybe it's true. In her words, "I don't go up there alone." She takes along the poetry of Maya Angelou, the humor of Dorothy Parker, and the common sense of Ann Landers. Whatever, it works.

What program chairman has not clutched at a podium with sweaty palms and wished someone would have been with her? One comes to mind who introduced me one afternoon, and after presenting my entire life from the day I was conceived, said shakily, "And now I present Irma Rombauer." Not only did Irma Rombauer write cookbooks, but she's been dead for about twenty years.

The road to the speaker's platform hasn't been exactly a yellow brick one for women. It has been paved with prejudice, insensitivity, and low esteem, not to mention the dreaded words, "We are a nonprofit organization and cannot pay a fee, but we are having chicken for lunch."

Inch by inch, mile by mile, chicken by chicken, we are bridging the gap and proving that not only do we have something worthwhile to say—we are saying things that bear repeating.

Most of today's women speakers started out where Carolyn and I began: in the utility room. We didn't speak publicly, but we ironed the shirt of the man who did, typed the speech of the man who did, and laughed at his jokes from the audience when no one else did.

We felt like Barbara Mandrell when she went to the Grand Ole Opry for the first time. Minutes into the performance she leaned over and said to her Daddy, "I don't belong down here in the audience. I belong up there."

Throughout this volume, Carolyn offers expertise on how to make that road to the lectern a little smoother. She tells you how to avoid detours, bad road conditions, and offers some new trails to blaze that are not listed on your traditional map.

In my office, I have a shelf of reference books on women. This volume is long overdue.

I'm not saying this because I'm in it.

I don't even know how many times I am mentioned.

That's not important to me.

Ten times would be a very good guess.

Erma Bombeck

ACKNOWLEDGMENTS

In a compilation of quotations, the author is tempted to repeat in her Acknowledgments the entire Index because, were it not for the women whose words and thoughts constitute this book, there wouldn't be one.

Short of that, there are a number of people, named and unnamed, to whom Acknowledgments are due:

—to my very special husband, Ron, and our children Cathy, Caron, Steven, Connie, Christopher, and Christi, who have so generously and lovingly supported my life and my work;

—to my dear friends Geraldine Emmett, who has given me years of caring and constant encouragement; Erma Bombeck, who is my greatest living example of what can be done if you care enough to do it; and Thelma Green, a very special woman in my life;

—to all the women who have made statements of consequence that have been preserved, and all those whose statements were not written down, or perhaps even heard, by anyone;

—to the women who have been sources of quotations used in this book, but about whom nothing beyond their names is known to us (any reader knowing more is earnestly encouraged to provide additional information);

—to the women who responded to my requests for the quotations that have mattered in their lives;

—to the women leaders, and women's leadership organizations, such as the YWCA of the USA, the Women's Campaign Research Fund, the National Women's Political Caucus, the International Women's Forum, the League of Women Voters, the American Association of University Women, the Center for Women Policy Studies, the Wellesley Center for Research on Women, Charter 100, P.E.O., and many others who have—individually and collectively—encouraged women to think beyond the present and aspire beyond the current;

—to my persistent but sympathetic editor, Tom Power, and my tirelessly encouraging agent, Julie Castiglia;

—to the hundreds of magazines, journals, newspapers, reference and related publications from whose pages a portion of this material and documentation has been confirmed or derived, to the libraries who preserve and protect the written word, and to the librarians who so patiently make it available;

—to a special group of friends and colleagues who have encouraged and assisted me so ably in this effort, especially Marilyn Curry, David Bolger, Bert Emmett, Leanna Hall, Peyton Pollacia, Lee Robert, James Mason, Judy Boylson, Caitlin Wood, and Lisa Huggins.

My gratitude for this book belongs to all of these. The ultimate responsibility for any errors—of omission or commission—rests with me.

AUTHOR'S INTRODUCTION

The best impromptu speeches are the ones written well in advance.

Ruth Gordon

❧

An oft-quoted survey of people's fears reveals that the fear of speaking in public is greater than the fear of death by drowning!

How can this be? There have been a lot of probing psychological studies done on this surprising discovery, and a tremendous amount of "psycho-babble" written about it. The best analogy I've heard to explain this fear was the comedian who said, "When you're up on that stage, it's like you're standing there completely naked, turning around very slowly and asking, 'Well, what do you think?'" This may not be the most elegant example, but it's probably accurate.

When we are standing before an audience we are, in fact, baring our souls and minds, if not our bodies. Whether the audience is an auditorium of thousands or a boardroom of a dozen, a civic gathering or a business presentation, an educational meeting or a political rally, the focus is still the same. *We* are speaking, *others* are listening. We are the center of attention, and all eyes are focused on us.

Over the last fifteen years, I have given from 50 to 200 speeches or presentations a year. In all those years, I will confess to never having been gripped by that cold, deadly feeling that I would rather be drowning than up there in front of an audience talking.

But when people, especially women, would ask me, "Carolyn, how can you do it?" I could never really come up with a satisfying answer.

A couple of years ago, I began searching for some of those answers because the questions about "How can you do it?" began coming more frequently as an increasing number of women were finding communications skills to be more and more necessary.

Having long subscribed to Socrates' belief that "the unexamined life is not worth living," I had not yet applied that concept to my own career as a speaker. Up to that time my platform techniques, like Topsy, "jist growed." But when I did ask myself, I discovered some amazing and interesting things about my own collection of tricks of the trade.

At that point, I decided I also had another communications responsibility: to share some of my own insights with other women who might find the prospect of a watery grave to be more comforting than expressing themselves in public.

I had also wondered why this fear seems to be so widespread among women speakers, only to discover that men have the same problem. The causes have been exhaustively explored and written about. Some of the conclusions reached regarding women who experience this paralyzing fear of speaking are:

- the relatively new status of women in so-called power positions in the workplace;

- a lower competitive level than men;

- an unfamiliarity with the rules of the game;

- fewer opportunities to practice the art of communications;

- the lack of female role models and a good old girl network to smooth the way up the organizational ladder; and

- an unwillingness to appear to be in an out front position.

Well, believe me, it doesn't have to be that way!

I have been speaking in public for many years. I began back in Oklahoma as a teenage political stump speaker. I continued as a high school and college debater, then in radio and early television. Through the subsequent forty years in business, in public office, and on the national platform circuit, I've never stopped talking.

To be sure, there are many reasons why I have never feared the podium. But one of the most significant reasons is because I never go up there *alone*. I always take a variety of people with me—people whose words or thoughts or deeds comfort me, inspire me, stimulate me. One time it might be Helen Keller, another time, Elizabeth Barrett Browning or Golda Meir or Dorothy Parker. It is often Eleanor Roosevelt, and sometimes it is my grandmother, Nellie Hershey Tullis. My mother's aphorisms are there, too.

I have never found a better way to enhance the communications process than by reinforcing the points or concepts I wish to make with timely, memorable quotations from someone whose life, actions, character, fame, or notoriety makes what they have to say worth repeating.

A well-planned speech is comprised of several parts—all of which can include quotations. These parts are:

- an *Introduction* to get the attention of the audience;
- a *Premise* that clearly spells out the purpose of the presentation;
- an *Expository or Information section* that informs the audience about the realities, problems, and challenges facing them;
- an *Illustrative section* (which should overlay every other part of the speech) in which are sprinkled anecdotes, jokes, quotations, and other devices to enliven and validate a premise; and, of course,
- a *Conclusion*, in which the speaker ties together the totality of her remarks.

A wide range of quotations are necessary for the repertoire of a well-rounded speaker. Quotations are able to illustrate in a few words what is difficult to explain in many. They can cause an audience to think about a topic from a different perspective or serve to inspire an audience. In truth, an appropriate quotation can strengthen and enliven *any* part of a presentation.

Often, younger speakers ask about my use of quotations; why I use them and where I find them.

Why use quotations at all? Some people equate the use of quotations to the sort of overblown, flowery rhetoric that hearkens back to the days of long-winded political speeches (and teenage stump speakers!). Or might the use of quotations simply be camouflage for a speaker who has nothing original to say on her own?

"Doesn't the insertion of quotations just drag out my speech, or make it sound somehow old-fashioned?" they ask. My answer, of course, is *Yes*—if all you rely on are the *well-known* ("The only thing we have to fear is fear itself.") or the *trite* ("To thine own self be true."). But, if you pepper your remarks with timely quotations, and timely refers more to the *currency* or appropriateness of the quote than to when it was uttered—be they humorous, thought-provoking, nostalgia-evoking, or downright cynical—you can do wonders for your speaking presence, your message, and especially your listeners.

When you are speaking, sharing, inspiring, motivating, explaining, or leading, quotations can be used to:

- *validate* your own point of view;
- *vary the pace* of your remarks;
- *reinforce* a point;

- *demonstrate* that a mind, perhaps greater than yours, has also expressed your position;
- *illustrate* in a way that you alone might not be able to easily express;
- *evoke emotions* that you might not arouse by using your own words;
- *establish a common bond* with an audience by quoting a person known and respected by your listeners; and yes,
- you use quotations to *get a laugh*. There's absolutely nothing wrong with that.

You use quotations because when utilized appropriately they reinforce the best available thoughts, concepts, ideas, or relevant points of view. Even better, they have already been distilled by some of the world's great minds (or great heroes or villains) into relatively brief, to-the-point, self-contained capsules.

As to the second question: *Where do I find quotations*? The answer is, *everywhere*.

No newspaper, magazine, journal, book, letter or speech has been safe from my ready pen and 3 × 5 cards. A good quotation may appear when and where you least expect it. I find them in the writings of both famous and infamous people. I have found some of the best in poems sent to me by school children, in conversations with interesting people, in speeches I have heard, and in business periodicals that have never pretended to be repositories of quotable quotes.

Finding a good quotation—a statement or saying that distills in a very few words a universal thought or concept—is a matter of reading and listening with that purpose in mind. It may be a somewhat more elegant pursuit than French pigs looking for truffles, but the method is the same: You search for them, find them, and root them out.

Because I have been collecting quotations since I was thirteen years old, my quotation antennae have become sensitive to the point that now I find them everywhere. Anyone can develop the skill to collect good quotations merely by heightening their own awareness.

What keeps me in pursuit of just the right quotation is that I use them now for the same purposes I used them in my youth: to support positions, to entertain, to provoke thought, to enlighten, to illustrate a point, to use the eloquence and wisdom of great men and women to validate in their words the points or principles *I* want to express.

My current inventory of quotations now numbers over 18,000—and I'm not slowing the process down a bit. In fact, the more I speak, the more I pursue good quotes. Because I lecture frequently, I also *hear* a lot of speeches—a *lot* of speeches—and if I remember nothing else, I remember the jokes, the stories, the point-makers that make the difference between an ordinary presentation and a great one.

Two things about a good quotation fascinate me.

- First is its universality. The wise words of an elementary school teacher can be the perfect illustration to use for a roomful of bankers.

- Second is its timeless quality. A bit of wisdom uttered in the Thirties by a farm woman is the best piece of career-planning advice I've ever come across.

A good point to remember is that everyone has the same *quantity* of words to use when making a presentation. It is, however, the *quality* of these words that separates the significant speaker from the perspiring amateur.

As I examined why I lacked the sweaty palms and rapid pulse of the fearful speaker, I realized that having this arsenal of wisdom (my quotation file) literally at my fingertips was one of the major reasons.

Once I know the topic of my presentation and have an understanding of the composition of the audience, my quotations virtually shape my remarks. I don't mean that my remarks are simply a stringing together of pithy quotes. I find that my best received speeches are those in which I judiciously space out my own comments with the carefully selected thoughts of people a great deal wiser than I shall probably ever be.

Some of my presentations may contain only five or six quotations; some may have a dozen or more. The important thing is that I can reinforce any point, illustrate any concept, help my audience to laugh or cry, all by calling upon these invisible friends.

So I concluded that if I am seriously to assist others in developing their own speaking skills, the best place to begin would be to introduce a collection of my friends and make them available to readers, speakers, and writers.

I further decided that as a woman and a woman speaker, I should focus my effort on other women. In writing this book, I am making available several hundred quotations—all of them by women. Virginia Woolf said, "I would venture to guess that Anon, who wrote so many poems without signing them, was often a woman." So you will find in this collection a few *Anon's*.

I have further divided these quotations into forty topic areas. The selections of both quotations and topic areas are purely arbitrary. This was not an exercise in objectivity; I selected the quotations because I *like* them. I have a great appreciation for the clear, succinct, poetic manner in which generations of women have passed down their wisdom to us. Even those that express a thought or feeling or position with which I disagree do so in words as good or better than any I've heard before.

The absence of a usable source of quotations by women to assist women speakers is my motivation for creating this book. The topic areas were selected because they are those subjects which, as a speaker, I have found to be most commonly used.

It is my fond hope that these quotations and topic areas will form a basic library for women speakers. I hope that every woman who uses this book will be motivated to start her own collection of quotable quotes. I will feel that I have helped answer that "How do you do it?" question if other women start looking for quotations that express their own philosophy and feelings, and if they use this book as a point of departure.

With that goal in mind, I encourage every woman to begin her own collection, and together with those presented here, create her own personal quotation library.

The first duty of a lecturer: to hand you after an hour's discourse a nugget of pure truth to wrap up between the pages of your notebooks, and keep on the mantelpiece forever.

                                                                    Virginia Woolf

A NOTE ABOUT THE CHAPTERS AND INDEX

As the reader will note, I have characterized the quotations in different chapters in different ways.

Certain quotations—in topic areas like ABILITY, ACTION, AND ATTITUDE—are *empowering*. They serve to motivate an audience to do something and a speaker to cause something to happen.

Other quotations—as those in areas such as AGE, EDUCATION, OR FAMILY—are designed to *create a mood or feeling*.

Some quotations are designed to *give facts*, to *inform*, to *educate*.

Still others are intended to *humanize* both the speaker and the audience.

While compiling the words of the celebrated and uncelebrated women in this book, I tried to document the birth and death, nationality, and profession of each. Unfortunately, for some of these women I have nothing but a name.

Perhaps my readers can be of help. If you have biographical information on any women in this book for which I have incomplete data, I encourage you to provide your input. I assure you it will be most appreciated.

CONTENTS

Chapter 1

ABILITY

A sobering thought: What if, right at this very moment, I am living up to my full potential?

Jane Wagner

❧

The bottom-line intent of practically all speeches is to encourage and inspire an audience to use their abilities, collective and individual, to advance a purpose or cause. ABILITY is one of the great empowering gifts that a speaker can give an audience.

To be able—in other words, to have ability—implies action. Even if the purpose of a speech is solely to inform, the speaker still has the responsibility to encourage listeners to form opinions or draw conclusions, based on the information given. Although this is essentially a passive activity, it still requires listeners to *do something*—in this case, to use their intellectual abilities to gain insights and information.

In the formation of any speech, the presenter must at the beginning present a need or challenge or problem for her listeners. But to simply state the obvious (or even the obscure) without offering potential solutions is, when you boil away all the rhetoric, simply complaining. And that's not a speech. It may be all your audience wants to hear—simply someone to commiserate with them—but you, as a speaker, have a responsibility to do more.

First, the responsible speaker must apply her skills toward helping listeners recognize that they each possess, as individuals, inherent abilities.

Second, the speaker then must help the audience visualize how those individual abilities can help the organization meet its own collective challenges.

Speakers, in preparing their remarks, must recognize that these are two quite separate responsibilities. It isn't enough to simply cause listeners to acknowledge their own abilities. It's in the taking of that second step—persuading listeners to put those abilities to work for the benefit of the group—that is of greatest value. The attainment of this second step helps meld a collection of individuals into a team, with the ability to do something that will benefit the group as a whole.

Perhaps the greatest difference between the old-style "motivational" speaker and today's more information-oriented presenter lies in the recognition of this second organizational responsibility. Whereas purely motivational speeches often focus on the realization of personal wants, needs, desires, or ambitions (a more or less selfish end if carried no further), these presentations don't go far enough because the real key to a successful speech is in prompting listeners to identify ways in which these newly realized *personal* abilities can benefit their organization.

One of the values of quotations concerning ability lies in the fact that most people have more abilities, or capabilities, than they realize. A timely quotation may trigger an emotional, or even an intellectual, response that may unlock these capacities. "Aha," a listener thinks, "I can do *that*."

It is especially important that you choose quotations from sources to which your listeners can relate. Quotations on ability from a person of renown will be essentially meaningless unless most of the audience know who that person is or why she is considered great.

When speaking to a predominantly female audience, use of a quotation by another woman may be especially encouraging. We identify with those of similar experience and feel that their advice is somehow *more appropriate for us*. With quotations on ability, the speaker is trying to establish some sort of *relational* bond between the attitude conveyed by the quote (or the person who said it) and the person hearing it.

And, it is important that your quotations, as your speech itself, be geared to prompting first the personal, then the group, unlocking of abilities that will result in performance. When you quote someone talking about using her abilities to do something, say to your audience, "You can do that, too."

Give examples of what people can do on an individual basis. Support those examples with appropriate quotations. Then, when you have helped your audience unlock their individual abilities, use other quotations and examples to show how these individual abilities can be put to use for the group as a whole.

Your effort to tap into the talents and resources of your audience isn't always easy. It requires knowing a great deal about the audience and their concerns. But, if you can be the catalyst for your listeners discovering and maximizing the use of their abilities, the payoff for both of you is incredible.

[My mother] said that I must always be intolerant of ignorance but under-standing of illiteracy. That some people, unable to go to school, were more educated and more intelligent than college professors.

Maya Angelou

I know how to do anything—I'm a mom.

Roseanne Barr Arnold

God does not ask your ability or your inability. He asks only your availability.

Mary Kay Ash

It seems to me that those songs that have been any good, I have nothing much to do with the writing of them. The words have just crawled down my sleeve and come out on the page.

Joan Baez

Genius is the gold in the mine; talent is the miner that works and brings it out.

Lady Marguerite Blessington

When I stand before God at the end of my life, I would hope that I would not have a single bit of talent left and could say, "I used everything you gave me."

Erma Bombeck

Neither birth nor sex forms a limit to genius.

Charlotte Brontë

Since when was genius found respectable?

Elizabeth Barrett Browning

An Arabian proverb says there are four sorts of men:
   He who knows not and knows not he knows not: he is a fool—shun him.
   He who knows not and knows he knows not: he is simple—teach him.
   He who knows and knows not he knows: he is asleep—wake him;
   He who knows and knows he knows: he is wise—follow him.

Lady Isabel Burton

If you don't realize there is always somebody who knows how to do something better than you, then you don't give proper respect for others' talents.

Hortense Canady

Those whom the gods would destroy they first call "promising."

Jan Carew

Assuredly men of merit are never lacking at any time, for those are the men who manage affairs, and it is the affairs that produce the men.

Catherine the Great

It is necessary to try to pass one's self always; this occupation ought to last as long as life.

Queen Christina of Sweden

Common sense is perhaps the most equally divided, but surely the most under-employed, talent in the world.

Christiane Collange

Creativity is inventing, experimenting, growing, taking risks, breaking rules, making mistakes, and having fun.

Mary Lou Cook

It's not enough to be good if you have the ability to be better. It is not enough to be very good if you have the ability to be great.

Alberta Lee Cox, grade 8

It is the creative potential itself in human beings that is the image of God.

Mary Daly

A pint can't hold a quart—if it holds a pint it is doing all that can be expected of it.

Margaretta W. Deland

It always seemed to me a sort of clever stupidity only to have one sort of talent—like a carrier pigeon.

George Eliot

Creative minds have always been known to survive any kind of bad training.

Anna Freud

Every person is responsible for all the good within the scope of his abilities, and for no more, and none can tell whose sphere is the largest.

Gail Hamilton

I think most of the people involved in any art always secretly wonder whether they are really there because they're good—or there because they're lucky.

Katharine Hepburn

Anybody can cut prices, but it takes brains to make a better article.

Alice Hubbard

I am only one; but still I am one. I cannot do everything, but still I can do something. I will not refuse to do the something I can do.

Helen Keller

Nothing feeds the center [of being] so much as creative work. The curtain of mechanization has come down between the mind and the hand.

Anne Morrow Lindbergh

What really matters is what you do with what you have.

Shirley Lord

I'd gone through life believing in the strength and competence of others; never in my own. Now, dazzled, I discovered that *my* capacities were real. It was like finding a fortune in the lining of an old coat.

Joan Mills

Besides learning to see, there is another art to be learned—*not to see* what is not.

Maria Mitchell

Genius, without religion, is only a lamp on the outer gate of a palace; it may serve to cast a gleam of light on those that are without, while the inhabitant is in darkness.

Hannah More

If you see a tennis player who looks as if he is working hard, then that means he isn't very good.

Helen Wills Moody

If you're going to write, don't pretend to write down. It's going to be the best you can do, and it's the fact that it's the best you can do that kills you.

Dorothy Parker

Ignorance is no excuse—it's the real thing.

Irene Peter

Thank goodness I was never sent to school; it would have rubbed off some of the originality.

Beatrix Potter

You have to accept whatever comes and the only important thing is that you meet it with the best you have to give.

Eleanor Roosevelt

Any woman who has a great deal to offer the world is in trouble.

Hazel Scott

Talent and worth are the only eternal grounds of distinction. To these the almighty has affixed his everlasting patent of nobility, and these it is which make the bright immortal names to which our children, as well as others, may aspire.

Catherine M. Sedgwick

There is a growing strength in women, but it's in the forehead, not in the forearm.

Beverly Sills

I thought that the chief thing to be done in order to equal boys was to be learned and courageous. So I decided to study Greek and learn to manage a horse.

Elizabeth Cady Stanton

You are the product of your own brainstorm.

Rosemary Konner Steinbaum

One only gets to the top rung on the ladder by steadily climbing up one at a time, and suddenly all sorts of powers, all sorts of abilities which you thought *never* belonged to you—suddenly become within your own possibility and you think, 'Well, I'll have a go, too.'

Margaret Thatcher

It is the mind that makes the body.

Sojourner Truth

I learned . . . that inspiration does not come like a bolt, nor is it kinetic, energetic striving, but it comes into us slowly and quietly and all the time, though we must regularly and every day give it a little chance to start flowing, prime it with a little solitude and idleness.

Brenda Ueland

I found, while thinking about the far-reaching world of the creative black woman, that often the truest answer to a question that really matters can be found very close.

Alice Walker

To tell the truth, old-timers like myself find introspection about creativity to be much less interesting than launching new projects. We artists are like master carpenters; we know our reason for living and we take our skills and motivations for granted.

June Wayne

Fear gives intelligence even to fools.

Anon.

Chapter 2

ACTION

Millions long for immortality who don't know what to do on a rainy afternoon.

Susan Ertz

❧

ACTION is the conversion of ability into conduct. The ability to lead an audience from a focusing of attitudes on both individual and group goals into the development of action plans—both individual and group—is what separates a speaker-leader from a person who simply talks.

So in thinking about action, we want to focus on helping listeners shape these capabilities into concrete responses. As a presenter, you have a wonderful opportunity to be the catalyst that motivates your listeners to *act*.

An ancient Greek philosopher once said, "Give me a lever and a place to stand, and I can move the earth." The speaker's version of that might be, "Give me an understanding of the problem and an action plan, and I can shape events." Understanding without action, is merely an intellectual exercise. But combine understanding *with* action, and you have the lever that can make a difference in any challenge.

In preparing your remarks, it is important to remember that if your audience believed they already had all the insight, knowledge, or skills needed to address their problem and build an action plan to solve it without you, they would have done so.

Whenever I think about motivating people for action, I think about the little prayer that so many people pray when challenged to actually do something about a problem: "Use me, Oh Lord, in Thy work—especially in an advisory capacity."

The world is full of people who are willing, even eager, to be used in an advisory capacity. But these are not the people who will get the work done; these are not the people who will take the personal responsibility or be a part of the group that makes things happen. Instead, these are the people who need to be moved to action.

It is important for the speaker to understand that in seeking to motivate a group to action, it is not necessary to cause each listener to feel overwhelmed with the weight of their individual responsibility. Just the opposite. The skillful speaker will lay out the possibilities for an action plan, building upon the internally identified abilities of her listeners. She will do it in such a way that members of the audience will come to feel that there are things they can do, within the operational confines of their daily lives and work, that can advance their cause.

The ability to inspire groups and individuals to take action is a special challenge and opportunity for a woman speaker. Women have long been perceived as being willing to be used mainly in that aforementioned advisory capacity as passive helpers rather than action-initiators. But passivity is the antithesis of action. No amount of good intentions ever solved a problem or met a need, whether in the business, social, personal, political, religious, educational, or community service sectors. The irony is that in many of these areas, women have been for centuries the chief problem identifiers and solvers!

The secret is to realize that the attitudes, the abilities, and the skills required to solve one set of problems can transfer into other sectors. The solution is to understand that the nature of problem solving is the ability to analyze, to segment the whole into manageable parts, and to build a consensus for action. Women have been engaging in those skills very successfully for many, many years.

The problem-solving approach is also valid for speech preparation itself. I believe the best place to begin is not at the beginning, but in the middle. Generally, in preparing a speech in which I hope to elicit action from a group, I begin by making a list of their problems. Then, next to each problem, I list the specific steps my listeners can take, both individually and as a group, to solve the problem. Whether this exercise produces one page or ten, I have just taken an action that has given me the heart of my speech. I then can develop my Introduction and Conclusion to lead into and out of the action plan that is the focus of my remarks.

Next (and this is the most enjoyable part for me), I search for quotations, examples, stories, poems, proverbs, aphorisms that will best illustrate or advance the various points. I am careful to select items that will be meaningful to my audience and that will help illuminate a point by speaking directly to their hearts or minds, preferably both.

Understand that not every single quotation will have a direct or strong effect on every single person in the audience. If I know I am speaking to a group with some amount of diversity, I will search for quotations that appeal to various types of people in the group. The continuing search for new quotations that will cast a different or more contemporary light on a topic is what keeps my library of quotations a living thing. It is also why each speaker should work to develop her own library of quotations that best fits her and her speaking style.

The trite little tale of the hopelessly lost tourist in New York City asking a man carrying a violin case, "How do I get to Carnegie Hall?" and being told, "Practice!" pretty well describes how to get anywhere or how to achieve anything. It requires one simple activity: action. Do it! It's true for a speech, it's true for a speaker. No one will get anywhere until an action plan is identified and started.

Remember: Quotations about action are not just intended to cause people to think, they are intended to get them to *act*.

❦

Cautious, careful people, always casting about to preserve their reputations . . . can never effect a reform.

Susan B. Anthony

Forgiveness is the key to action and freedom.

Hannah Arendt

There is no such thing as *can't*, only *won't*. If you're qualified, all it takes is a burning desire to accomplish, to make a change. Go forward, go backward. Whatever it takes! But you can't blame other people or society in general. It all comes from your mind. When we do the impossible we realize we are special people.

Jan Ashford

Why not seize the pleasure at once? How often is happiness destroyed by preparation, foolish preparation!

Jane Austen

When duty calls me, I'm prepared
  as though our goals were aimed and shared.
I draw my breath in, shoulders straight,
  and quietly procrastinate.

Alison Wyrley Birch

Justice is a concept. Muscle is the reality.

Linda Blandford

I'm going to have to ride the fence awhile until I find where the gates are.
Eva Bowring

I can think of few important movements for reform in which success was won by any method other than that of an energetic minority presenting the indifferent majority with a *fait accompli*, which was then accepted.
Vera Brittain

Beauty can't amuse you, but brainwork—reading, writing, thinking—can.
Helen Gurley Brown

A life of reaction is a life of slavery, intellectually and spiritually. One must fight for a life of action, not reaction.
Rita Mae Brown

I don't wait for moods. You accomplish nothing if you do that. Your mind must know it has got to get down to earth.
Pearl S. Buck

I am an organization person. I believe in individuals banding together. I don't believe in unilateral actions. Some people don't like organizations. But it is always awesome to me when you can pool a lot of talent and a lot of people who have so many talents. That is when you really can make your program move.
Hortense Canady

No witchcraft, no enemy action had silenced the rebirth of new life in this stricken world. The people had done it themselves.
Rachel Carson

You philosophers are lucky men. You write on paper, and paper is patient. Unfortunate Empress that I am, I write on the susceptible skins of living beings.
Catherine the Great

If you really want something you can figure out how to make it happen.
Cher

Americans need help understanding their world now more than ever. [TV] believes it's filled its obligation to the public because it's presented both sides. But most of what we're living through now has multiple sides, and those sides, if you take the extreme oppositional views, have to be brought together for people to make a decision about how to act on the information.
Hillary Rodham Clinton

One never notices what has been done; one can only see what remains to be done.
Marie Curie

I think even lying on my bed I can still do something.
attributed to Dorothea Dix

You really *can* change the world if you care enough.
Marion Wright Edelman

It is vain to say human beings ought to be satisfied with tranquility: they must have action; and they will make it if they cannot find it.
George Eliot

It is no sin to attempt and fail. The only sin is not to make the attempt.
SuEllen Fried

I am suffocated and lost when I have not the bright feeling of progression.
Margaret Fuller

The first duty of a human being is to assume the right relationship to society—more briefly, to find your real job, and do it.
Charlotte Perkins Gilman

It's easier to act your way into new ways of feeling than to feel yourself into new ways of acting.
Susan Glaser

Pray for the dead and fight like hell for the living.
"Mother" Mary Jones

And the trouble is, if you don't risk anything, you risk even more.
Erica Jong

Don't wait for your "ship to come in," and feel angry and cheated when it doesn't. Get going with something small.
Irene Kassorla

Science may have found a cure for most evils; but it has found no remedy for the worst of them all—the apathy of human beings.
Helen Keller

Don't agonize. Organize.

Florynce Kennedy

The glass ceiling gets more pliable when you turn up the heat!

Pauline R. Kezer

Be bold. If you're going to make an error, make a doozy, and don't be afraid to hit the ball.

Billie Jean King

Procrastination gives you something to look forward to.

Joan Konner

If the world seems cold to you, kindle fires to warm it.

Lucy Larcom

Many older women are inhibited and afraid to act. It is such a waste of human potential.

Frances Lear

Let us never confuse stability with stagnation.

Mary Jean LeTendre

Love is a verb.

Clare Boothe Luce

There are so many things that we wish we had done yesterday, so few that we feel like doing today.

Mignon McLaughlin

Risk! Risk anything! Care no more for the opinion of others, for those voices. Do the hardest thing on earth for you. Act for yourself. Face the truth.

Katherine Mansfield

I have always had a dread of becoming a passenger in life.

Queen Margreth II of Denmark

Stop the habit of wishful thinking and start the habit of thoughtful wishes.

Mary Martin

Never doubt that a small group of thoughtful, committed citizens can change the world. Indeed, it is the only thing that ever has.

Margaret Mead

Idleness among children, as among men, is the root of all evil, and leads to no other evil more certain than ill temper.

Hannah More

Just go out there and do what you've got to do.

Martina Navratilova

The most subtle flattery a woman can receive is that conveyed by actions, not by words.

Susanne Curchod Necker

I postpone death by living, by suffering, by error, by risking, by giving, by losing.

Anaïs Nin

Slaying the dragon of delay is no sport for the short-winded.

Sandra Day O'Connor

Go! Go! Go! It makes no difference where just so you go! go! go! Remember at the first opportunity—go!

Jeannette Rankin

A woman is like a teabag—you can't tell how strong she is until you put her in hot water.

Nancy Reagan

Noble deeds and hot baths are the best cures for depression.

Dodie Smith

Talk without effort is nothing.

Mary W. Stewart

To have ideas is to gather flowers; to think, is to weave them into garlands.

Anne Sophie Swetchine

Do not wait for leaders; do it alone, person to person.

Mother Teresa

You may have to fight a battle more than once to win it.

Margaret Thatcher

The next best thing to winning is losing! At least you've been in the race.

Nellie Hershey Tullis

'Tis this one hour that God has given;
His Now we must obey;
And it will make our earth his heaven
To live today—today.

Lydia Avery Coonley Ward

It's easy to work for somebody else; all you have to do is show up.

Rita Warford

Saddle your dreams afore you ride 'em.

Mary Webb

He who hesitates—is a damn fool.

Mae West

The splendid discontent of God with Chaos, made the world; and from the discontent of man the world's best progress springs.

Ella Wheeler Wilcox

Out of the strain of the Doing,
Into the peace of the Done.

Julia Louise Woodruff

Talk doesn't cook rice.

Chinese proverb

Chapter 3

AGE

Old age is no place for sissies.

Bette Davis

❧

A GE is something that every single member of an audience can relate to. It's a condition that affects us all. Everybody is interested in age: their own, their co-workers, the speaker's, Elizabeth Taylor's. When we are young, we consider ourselves to be essentially age-less. Once we pass, say twenty-nine, it becomes one of our favorite preoccupations. This is certainly true for me, because the older I get the more interesting and relevant I find quotations about age and aging.

There are a number of potent ways a speaker can use quotations about age. It is a marvelous tool for the type of self-deprecating humor that can be one of the speaker's most effective weapons. This is especially true for a woman speaker. Women are supposed to be both sensitive and secretive about their age, so age-related, self-directed humor can have an incredibly disarming effect on an audience.

An older speaker can make light of her age by interjecting a play on Erma Bombeck's comment (in discussing some self-important younger person), "I have a cookie sheet older than him." This sort of self-deprecation communicates to the audience that you don't take yourself too seriously—and certainly don't think that you have all the answers.

An older speaker can use age to humanize herself and to build a real rapport with her listeners. She can warm up a younger group by playing on their respective age differences; she can loosen up an older group by playing in a humorous way with their common preoccupation with aging.

Quotations about age can be a powerful attention-getter when making or illustrating important points. Many people's view of the world is largely shaped by the events that occurred during their formative years. Therefore, by doing some evaluation of your audience, you can draw analogies or illustrations that will strike a responsive chord with them. By indicating to an audience that *you* understand *their* perspective, you have created a frame of reference for the validation of all your points, one that likely will work for you throughout the balance of your remarks.

A speaker may also use quotations that involve using her own age, juxtaposed against that of most of the audience, to make points and to increase audience rapport. For example, a younger speaker can use a quote or a reference that is clearly outside her own age frame of reference that will elicit an instantly sympathetic response from an older audience. By pointing out, for instance, that she was in kindergarten when America's first female astronaut flew on the space shuttle, the speaker can indicate her appreciation of the responsibility of "being the first woman who . . . ," and point out the challenges young people (or young women) face in doing the not-yet-done. The speaker can also pay tribute to older women—regardless of their personal accomplishments—by indicating her awareness of the difficulties women faced in prior years and by thanking these women for the barriers they helped remove for her generation.

Preparing your own chronological chart is an excellent tool, and one that you will refer to continually. Prepare it in five-year increments beginning from your birth. In an opposite column, list three or four significant things that happened during each five-year period. Use local, national, international, natural, company or school events, and so forth. These can then be adapted to suit a particular audience or modified to make a certain point.

If you are older (and I am writing from experience here), you can use quotations or cite examples of things clearly outside the age frame of most of your audience to make a point—and get a laugh at the same time.

One of my favorites is Dorothy Parker's little literary zinger,

"I'd rather flunk my Wasserman test than read a poem by Edgar Guest."

This one works on multiple levels, at least for me. First, Dorothy Parker's wit is largely lost on people under fifty, because most of them never heard of her *or* the Wasserman test. A lot of people laugh because it just *sounds* funny. But I can almost always pick out somebody, usually a nodding woman, who knows about both. So with a vague gesture, I will look in her general direction and say, "You're going to have to explain it to the rest of them." This evokes a second laugh and, by then, the audience has begun to feel that we're all sort of a friendly, sharing family.

Another effective age-related angle is referring to a parent, another relative, or to an older mentor or role model. It is important that the reference be pertinent and not simply an excuse to relate a favorite family anecdote or similar "As my old granddaddy used to say . . ." story.

I sometimes refer to my mother, explaining that, as a former English teacher, she loved good writing and didn't go in for maudlin sentimentality. I will indicate that I am going to close with a poem by an author of whom she was not particularly fond. I'll talk about my mother's feeling on the matter and say, "But Mother isn't giving this speech, I am, and I'm going to close with this poem." Everybody in the audience is either somebody's parent or somebody's child, and the image of a middle-aged woman *daring* to flaunt her mother's literary sensibilities has a wonderful, humanizing effect.

Whether creating a framework for looking back, looking forward, or putting the present in perspective, the creative speaker can use the universal preoccupation with age to humanize herself and her points. If an audience likes you, they will accept almost anything you say. If they don't, even the greatest pearls may not be accepted.

I use this topic area of age in its broadest sense, and I encourage you to begin developing your own collection of quotations—building upon your own age and life experiences.

❦

Such to me is the new image of aging: growth in self and service for all mankind.

Ethel Percy Andrus

I'm not interested in age. People who tell me their age are silly. You're as old as you feel.

Elizabeth Arden

I refuse to admit that I am more than fifty-two, even if that does make my sons illegitimate.

Lady Nancy Astor

We grow neither better nor worse as we get old, but more like ourselves.
Mary Lamberton Becker

You may search my time-worn face,
You'll find a merry eye that twinkles.
I am NOT an old lady
Just a little girl with wrinkles!

Edythe E. Bregnard

I believe the true function of age is memory. I'm recording as fast as I can.

Rita Mae Brown

Perhaps one has to be very old before one learns how to be amused rather than shocked.

Pearl S. Buck

Age is something that doesn't matter, unless you are a cheese.

Billie Burke

A major advantage of age is learning to accept people without passing judgment.

Liz Carpenter

Sure, I'm for helping the elderly. I'm going to be old myself someday. (spoken when she was in her eighties)

Lillian Carter

A woman has the age she deserves.

Coco Chanel

It is a rare and difficult attainment to grow old gracefully and happily.

Lydia M. Child

An archaeologist is the best husband a woman can have; the older she gets, the more interested he is in her.

Agatha Christie

If you want a thing well done, get a couple of old broads to do it.

Bette Davis

The really frightening thing about middle age is the knowledge that you'll grow out of it.

Doris Day

When a noble life has prepared for old age, it is not decline that it reveals, but the first days of immortality.

Mme. de Staël

In youth we learn; in age we understand.

Marie Ebner-Eschenbach

Old men's eyes are like old men's memories; they are strongest for things a long way off.

George Eliot

Being an old maid is like death by drowning—a really delightful sensation after you have ceased struggling.

Edna Ferber

Women are not forgiven for aging. Robert Redford's lines of distinction are my old-age wrinkles.

Jane Fonda

This is a youth-oriented society, and the joke is on them because youth is a disease from which we all recover.

Dorothy Fuldheim

An old man once said, "When I was young, I was poor; when old, I became rich; but in each condition I found disappointment. When I had the faculties for enjoyment, I had not the means; when the means came, the faculties were gone."

Comtesse Catherine de Gasparin

It is often the case with fine natures, that when the fire of the spirit dies out with increasing age, the power of intellect is unaltered or increased. An originally educated judgment grows broader and gentler as the river of life widens out to the everlasting sea.

Margaret Gatty

It is the duty of youth to bring its fresh new powers to bear on Social progress. Each generation of young people should be to the world like a vast reserve force to a tired army. They should lift the world forward. That is what they are for.

Charlotte Perkins Gilman

When you finally learn how to do it, you're too old for the good parts.

Ruth Gordon

The hardest years in life are those between ten and seventy.

Helen Hayes

Someone asked someone who was about my age: "How are you?" The answer was, "Fine. If you don't ask for details."

Katharine Hepburn

Childhood sometimes does pay a second visit to a man; youth never.

Anna Jameson

For the last third of life there remains only work. It alone is always stimulating, rejuvenating, exciting and satisfying.

Käthe Kollwitz

I enjoy my wrinkles and regard them as badges of distinction—I've worked hard for them!

Maggie Kuhn

The great thing about getting older is that you don't lose all the other ages you've been.

Madeleine L'Engle

Once I looked into the mirror and saw my father's tired eyes look back at me; reaching to smooth a vagrant hair, Mother's wrinkled hand. Age came upon me unaware.

Helen Rul Lawler

The reason some men fear older women is they fear their own mortality.

Frances Lear

I have everything I had twenty years ago, only it's all a little bit lower.

Gypsy Rose Lee

All one's life as a young woman one is on show, a focus of attention, people notice you. You set yourself up to be noticed and admired. And then, not expecting it, you become middle-aged and anonymous. No one notices you. You achieve a wonderful freedom. It is a positive thing. You can move about, unnoticed and invisible.

Doris Lessing

Remember that as a teenager you are in the last stage of your life when you will be happy to hear the phone is for you.

Fran Leibowitz

Perhaps middle-age is, or should be, a period of shedding shells; the shell of ambition, the shell of material accumulations and possessions, the shell of the ego.

Anne Morrow Lindbergh

Age is totally unimportant. The years are really irrelevant. It's how you cope with them.

Shirley Lord

There is a fountain of youth: it is your mind, your talents, the creativity you bring to your life and the lives of people you love. When you learn to tap this source, you will truly have defeated age.

Sophia Loren

You just wake up one morning, and you got it! (on old age)

Moms Mabley

The process of maturing is an art to be learned, an effort to be sustained. By the age of fifty you have made yourself what you are, and if it is good, it is better than your youth.

Marya Mannes

Being seventy is not a sin.

Golda Meir

Age doesn't protect you from love. But love, to some extent, protects you from age.

Jeanne Moreau

Would you be young again?
So would not I—
One tear to memory given,
Onward I'd hie.

Carolina Oliphant

I have an unshakable faith in the younger generation of our country [India], and am deeply and humbly grateful that so many of them trust me and turn to me. This has always been a cause of happiness to me, and perhaps it is what keeps me young though the years creep up.

Vijaya Lakshmi Pandit

Thank God I have the seeing eye, that is to say, as I lie in bed I can walk step by step on the fells and rough land seeing every stone and flower and patch of bog and cotton pass where my old legs will never take me again.

Beatrix Potter

We can go into a quiet retirement, which is the traditional stereotype of a 65-year-old, or we can take a risk and put ourselves out where the action is.

Satenig St. Marie

It is quite wrong to think of old age as a downward slope. On the contrary, one climbs higher and higher with the advancing years, and that, too, with surprising strides. Brain-work comes as easily to the old as physical exertion to the child. One is moving, it is true, towards the end of life, but that end is now a goal, and not a reef in which the vessel may be dashed.

George Sand

When men reach their sixties and retire they go to pieces. Women just go right on cooking.

Gail Sheehy

So much had been said and sung of beautiful young girls, why don't somebody wake up to the beauty of old women?

Harriet Beecher Stowe

My forties are the best time I have ever gone through.

Elizabeth Taylor

Unthinking, idle, wild, and young,
I laugh'd and danc'd and talk'd and sung.

Princess Amelie Rives Troubetzkoy

Maturity is:
   the ability to stick with a job until it's finished;
   the ability to do a job without being supervised;
   the ability to carry money without spending it; and
   the ability to bear an injustice without wanting to get even.

Abigail Van Buren

Now that I'm over sixty, I'm veering toward respectability.

Shelley Winters

One of the signs of passing youth is the birth of a sense of fellowship with other human beings as we take our place among them.

Virginia Woolf

The secret of staying young is to live honestly, eat slowly, sleep sufficiently, work industriously, worship faithfully—and lie about your age.

Anon.

It's sad for a girl to reach the age
Where men consider her charmless,
But it's worse for a man to attain the age
Where the girls consider him harmless.

Anon.

Teenagers are people who express a burning desire to be different by dressing exactly alike.

Anon.

Chapter 4

ARTS

Anyone who says you can't see a thought simply doesn't know art.

Wynetka Ann Reynolds

❦

A rt has been called the "objectification of feeling and the subjectification of nature."

The first time I read that definition, I must confess to simply reading the words and thinking they were "doublespeak" at its worst, and wondering, just wondering. Then, I read it again, this time thinking carefully about how one might quantify impressions or feelings; how one could transform the visual or the physical into subjective images.

Slowly, images of great paintings and passages of great writing and snatches of beautiful music came to mind. So did a mental picture of the Grand Canyon. From the transcendent beauty of a Renoir or Monet landscape, to Thoreau's description of Walden Pond, to the emotions evoked by a favorite poem or piece of music, it became clear to me that the ability to generate an emotional or intellectual response to an intangible emotion or a tangible subject is, indeed, characteristic of great art in all its forms.

The skilled speaker can use the evocation of images in much the same way as the artist can—to cause an audience to respond on several levels to the objective and subjective concepts she is using in leading them through any given subject.

Statements about the ARTS or about the artistic or creative processes fall into the category of humanizing quotations. What is the humanizing connection? Basically, the speaker must approach her audience with the affirmation that human life itself is an art form. Each person is a unique creation. And no matter how flawed, what each person has done with her life is also something of an art form in that it, too, is unique.

For example, a successful teacher brings to her profession a combination of individual perceptions, talents, and skills that causes her to be remarkable in her ability to stimulate thinking in her students. A successful businesswoman brings to the job a set of her own distinctive qualities. Just as an artist paints upon a canvas using a chosen palette of colors, so do human beings build a life combining unique sets of *colors* that define who we are.

The realization of uniqueness is one that allows a speaker to humanize her audience, both in her own mind and in the minds of her listeners. Once people see themselves as unique, as special, or as particularly skilled or able, then they can also see themselves as people who are up to a challenge, people who have the *ability* to make a *difference*.

Quotations about the arts are also excellent vehicles for the speaker to help her listeners think about and plan for the future. Art and art forms may be thought of as manifestations of our belief in tomorrow—that someone will be here to see the painting or the scene of natural beauty, to read the words, hear the lyrics, hum the notes after we are gone—just as we enjoy today the creations of past generations. Art may also be considered a vehicle for communicating with those who are yet to come. We cannot reach toward the future or into the past if we lack an appreciation or understanding of what transcends the moment.

Thus, it is the responsibility of the speaker to somehow help her audience, as individuals, see themselves as people who are uniquely qualified to accept the challenges of the moment—and cause those challenges to have some meaning greater than just the task of meeting them. Quotations from the general topic of ARTS are among the best for fulfilling this challenge.

No matter how dry the topic (or the audience, for that matter), it is essential that the speaker inspire her listeners, both as individuals and as a group. It is essential that people have images, thoughts, concepts that they can mentally rally around. Providing this mental inspiration is just as important a responsibility as transmitting facts or information. Because without some sense of vision or inspiration, it is difficult for most people to be motivated toward the realization of a quantifiable or subjective task.

Quotations about the arts are used to elevate the spirit of the listener, to generate feelings of optimism, faith, and confidence. They can provide the speaker with an avenue to unlock the creativity within her listeners.

❦

In life as in the dance: Grace glides on blistered feet.

Alice Abrams

A child her wayward pencil drew
On margins of her book;
Garlands of flower, dancing elves,
Bud, butterfly, and brook,
Lessons undone, and plum forgot,
Seeking with hand and heart
The teacher whom she learned to love
Before she knew t'was Art.

Louisa May Alcott

It's one of the tragic ironies of the theatre that only one man in it can count on steady work—the night watchman.

Tallulah Bankhead

Chamber music—a conversation between friends.

Catherine Drinker Bowen

I'm sorry that our country and the people do not consider the arts as vital to our well-being as, say, medicine. Suffering is unnecessary. It doesn't make you a better artist; it only makes you a hungry one. However, to me the acquisition of the craft of writing was worth any amount of suffering.

Rita Mae Brown

If you can sell green toothpaste in this country, you can sell opera.

Sarah Caldwell

When music fails to agree to the ear, to soothe the ear and the heart and the senses, then it has missed its point.

Maria Callas

I must draw however poor the result, and when I have a bad time come over me, it is a stronger desire than ever.

Annie Carter

[To simplify] is very nearly the whole of the higher artistic process; finding what conventions of form and what detail one can do without—and yet preserve the spirit of the whole.

Willa Cather

Cooking is just as creative and imaginative an activity as drawing, or wood carving, or music. And cooking draws upon your every talent—science, mathematics, energy, history, experience—and the more experience you have the less likely are your experiments to end in drivel and disaster. The more you know, the more you can create.

Julia Child

I think I love and reverence all arts equally only putting my own just above the others; because in it I recognize the union and culmination of my own. To me it seems as if when God conceived the world, that was Poetry; He formed it, and that was Sculpture; He colored it, and that was Painting; He peopled it with living beings, and that was the grand, divine, eternal Drama.

Charlotte Cushman

The truest expression of a people is in its dances and its music. Bodies never lie.

Agnes De Mille

Music is like a soft breeze blowing by.
Music is like the clear blue sky.
Music is a beautiful sound made by people,
It is the sound when spring comes and goes.
Music is the night when it's bright,
It's the sun when it shines.
Music is my light.

Patsy Diaz, age 11

I think of life as a unity. This unity includes mountains, mice, rocks, trees, women and men. It is all one big lump of clay.

Ruth Duckworth

Born as a technology, reared as an industry, and nurtured as an art, the moving image is an unprecedented instrument for education, enlightenment, documentary record, and entertainment. It is the art form of the 20th century—it has the potential to become the literature of the 21st century.

Jean Firstenberg

I don't want life to imitate art. I want life to be art.

Carrie Fisher

Art is part of a rebellion against the realities of its unfulfilled desire.

Emma Goldman

The body is your instrument in dance, but your art is outside that creature, the body. I don't leap and jump anymore. I look at young dancers, and I am envious, more aware of what glories the body contains. But sensitivity is not made dull by age.

Martha Graham

The dance is a poem of which each movement is a word.

Mata Hari

Acting is the most minor of gifts. After all, Shirley Temple could do it when she was four.

Katharine Hepburn

Ever since the first shaggy hunter outlined a running deer with a stick dipped in wood ash or puddled clay or blood, paint has served a vastly more significant and creative purpose—as a vehicle for the human imagination, a creator of illusions, the modest but endlessly pliable means of fixing a glimpse of loveliness for posterity. The true originators in this field have always been the great artists. But close behind these masters of illusion came the masters of the applied arts—designers, architects, decorators, legions of craftsmen whose vocation was to reflect contemporary standards of beauty and harmony.

Jocasta Innes

So, as you go forth into a world of challenge and chaos, I have one last important word of advice for you: BUY OPERA TICKETS!

Ardis Krainik

Art is the objectification of feeling, and the subjectification of nature.

Susanne K. Langer

In times of crisis, it is to art that one can turn to find the center of a society. Societies are not remembered by their battlements, but by their art. Art is an essential reminder of what it is in life that lasts, of why one lives. Art communicates, clarifies, celebrates, mourns and remembers. What else in our lives can do this?

Bella Lewitzky

Art is hard; physics is easy.

Martyl

Broadway has been very good to me—but then I've been very good to Broadway.

Ethel Merman

Rap is poetry set to music. But to me it's like a jackhammer.

Bette Midler

The arts are the signature of a nation.

Joan Mondale

It is the function of art to renew our perception. What we are familiar with we cease to see. The writer shakes up the familiar scene, and, as if by magic, we see a new meaning in it.

Anaïs Nin

If one could only reproduce nature, and always with less beauty than the original, why paint at all?

Georgia O'Keeffe

I found a great salvation through acting. It did a fantastic amount for me—making the person that I really am feel free to be just that.

Lynn Redgrave

Art . . . does not take kindly to facts, is helpless to grapple with theories, and is killed outright by a sermon.

Agnes Repplier

If we are to contribute to a livable society, we must strive to assure that poetry exists to temper technology; that music enlivens and enhances our educational growth; that dance and sculpture challenge our imaginations as much as any new scientific discovery.

Wynetka Ann Reynolds

Art, whose honesty must work through artifice, cannot avoid cheating truth.

Laura Riding

If my husband ever met a woman on the street who looked like one of his paintings he would faint. (speaking of Pablo Picasso)

Jacqueline Roque

Simplicity is the essence of the great, the true, and the beautiful in art.

attributed to George Sand

Rhythm is one of the principal translators between dream and reality. Rhythm might be described as, to the world of sound, what light is to the world of sight. It shapes and gives new meaning. Rhythm was described by Schopenhauer as a melody deprived of its pitch.

Dame Edith Sitwell

Interpretation is the revenge of the intellectual upon art.

Susan Sontag

The first hope of a painter who feels hopeful about painting is the hope that the painting will move, that it will live outside its frame.

Gertrude Stein

Beauty has nothing to do with possession. If possession and beauty must go together, then we are lost souls. A beautiful flower is not to be possessed, it's there to be beheld. You're not going to take a beautiful painting off the museum wall. It's there for your pleasure.

Diana Vreeland

. . . the creative process is an artist's industrial secret. Why clue the competition? When times are hard, the "divine flame" gets one invited to dinner and written about by art historians. Why jeopardize one's insurance?

June Wayne

Any authentic work of art must start an argument between the artist and his audience.

Dame Rebecca West

Strong and convincing art has never risen from theories.

Mary Wigman

There are no teachers, saints, prophets, good people, but the artists.

Virginia Woolf

Museums and galleries are for people. Children need to grow up in them. Art can give you excitement and energy. A painting can do something for your spirit that nothing else can.

Riva Yares

Chapter 5

ATTITUDE

No life is so hard that you can't make it easier by the way you take it.

Ellen Glasgow

❦

I am convinced that ATTITUDE is the key to success or failure in almost any of life's endeavors. Your attitude—your perspective, your outlook, how you feel about yourself, how you feel about other people—determines your priorities, your actions, your values. Your attitude determines how you interact with other people and how you interact with yourself.

Therefore, I have collected all sorts of thoughts from many sources on the subject of ATTITUDE, and I use them frequently. It is very difficult to address an audience, regardless of size or subject, without saying something about attitude. In fact, I can't think of a single presentation of any consequence in which I *do not* include at least one quotation from this selection.

Anything that happens to an organization depends upon the attitudes of its individual members. And the attitude of individuals determines the group attitude that makes one organization or business or enterprise different from another.

A negative attitude among an office work force creates an atmosphere in which productivity is diminished. A positive attitude in a school creates a climate in which learning takes place, almost regardless of other factors.

The *culture* (that is, atmosphere, spirit) of an organization is influenced in more ways than any of us can conceive by the attitudes of its members. So, it is the responsibility of the speaker to do all in her power to help create, and reinforce, a positive attitude on the part of her listeners.

A less experienced speaker might think some people in the audience have a good attitude, and some don't. Will they be receptive to what I have to say?

They aren't even from the same organization; how can what I say help their particular groups?

Whether or not your listeners are all a part of the same organization doesn't really matter. What *is* important is that they are all together in a room, listening to you—and hoping to gain something from what you have to say. For those moments (those five, ten, twenty, thirty, or sixty minutes), they *are* one organization. In the dynamics of the group's response to you, their speaker, they will respond as one organization. *How* they respond is *your* communication challenge.

In this capacity, you are in a real power position. You have been asked to speak because it is believed that you have something to say that the group needs or wants to hear. You certainly haven't been asked to speak because they think you *don't* have something to say.

You can also safely assume that your listeners want to gain something from your presentation. They may want to learn; they may want to laugh. They may want to do both. Whatever *it* is—and it's up to you to know that before you speak—you can be sure that they expect to absorb some of it.

Given this quality of what I call anticipated receptiveness, you have the capacity to change the attitudes of your listeners—to improve perceptions, to shape group opinion; to strengthen positive attitudes and diminish negative ones. If that's not power, then I don't know what power is.

So, use your power well. Select quotations that will reinforce the attitudes you want to help mold. Build your remarks around your motivational and informational targets. Be ready. Start the mental engine that shapes your own attitudes and project that energy into your presentation.

Continue to update your own file so that the authors you quote will include contemporaries. To be an engaging speaker you have to *continually* collect and store the ideas that speak to you. Your sources will be every book, magazine, newspaper column you read and every play, film, television show you see. The words and ideas are out there—everywhere and aplenty.

ॐ

I do not ask for any crown
But that which all may win;
Nor try to conquer any world
Except the one within.
Be Thou my guide until I find
Led by a tender hand,
The happy kingdom in myself
And dare to take command.

Louisa May Alcott

Ride your emotions as the shallop rides the waves; don't get upset among them. There are people who enjoy getting swamped emotionally, just as, incredibly, there are people who enjoy getting drunk.

Mary Austin

If my heart were not light, I would die.

Joanna Baillie

Work is either fun or drudgery. It depends on your attitude. I like fun.

Colleen C. Barrett

Dogs come when they're called; cats take a message and get back to you.

Mary Bly

Striving for excellence motivates you; striving for perfection is demoralizing.

Harriet Braiker

Life appears to me too short to be spent in nursing animosity or registering wrong.

Charlotte Brontë

When you come right down to it, the secret of having it all is loving it all.

Dr. Joyce Brothers

And lips say "God be pitiful,"
Who ne'er said "God be praised."

Elizabeth Barrett Browning

All things are possible until they are proved impossible—even the impossible may only be so, as of now.

Pearl S. Buck

You find yourself refreshed by the presence of cheerful people. Why not make an honest effort to confer that pleasure on others? Half the battle is gained if you never allow yourself to say anything gloomy.

Lydia M. Child

. . . we have a tendency to obscure the forest of simple joys with the trees of problems.

Christiane Collange

Ah! if you only knew the peace there is in an accepted sorrow.

Jeanne de la Motte-Guyton

The more we know, the better we forgive. Whoe'er feels deeply, feels for all that live.

Mme. de Staël

We believe at once in evil, we only believe in good upon reflection. Is not this sad?

Dorothée DeLuzy

Adventure is worthwhile in itself.

Amelia Earhart

He was like a cock who thought the sun had risen to hear him crow.

George Eliot

Take each day as you find it,
If things go wrong, don't mind it,
For each day leaves behind it
A chance to start anew.

Gertrude Ellgas

You've got to take the initiative and play your game . . . confidence makes the difference.

Chris Evert

Take your work seriously, but never yourself.

Dame Margot Fonteyn

Of course, there's no such thing as a totally objective person, except Almighty God, if she exists.

Antonia Fraser

You cannot shake hands with a clenched fist.

Indira Gandhi

I feel, and I live through, all the same things that our citizens live through. I'm a sympathizer with our society—and these are not just words.

Raisa Gorbachev

It's not what you're eating, it's what's eating you.

Janet Greeson

Each person grows not only by her own talents and development of her inner beliefs, but also by what she receives from the persons around her.

Iris Haberli

A discipline I have observed is an attitude of love and reverence to people.

Bessie Head

Security is not the meaning of my life. Great opportunities are worth the risks.

Shirley Hufstedler

The road was new to me, as roads always are going back.

Sarah Orne Jewett

Your world is as big as you make it,
I know, for I used to abide
In the narrowest nest in a corner,
My wings pressing close to my side.

I battered the cordons around me
And cradled my wings on the breeze,
Then soared to the uttermost reaches
With rapture, with power, with ease!

Georgia Douglas Johnson

When one door of happiness closes, another opens; but often we look so long at the closed door that we do not see the one which has been opened for us.

Helen Keller

I discovered I always have choices and sometimes it's only a choice of attitude.

Judith M. Knowlton

Hate is like acid. It can damage the vessel in which it is stored as well as destroy the object on which it is poured.

Ann Landers

If you haven't got anything nice to say about anybody, come sit next to me.

Alice Roosevelt Longworth

Ah, snug lie those that slumber
Beneath Conviction's roof.
Their floors are sturdy lumber,
Their windows weatherproof.
But I sleep cold forever
And cold sleep all my kind,
For I was born to shiver
In the draft from an open mind.

Phyllis McGinley

I'm tough, ambitious, and I know exactly what I want. If that makes me a bitch, okay.

Madonna

We triumph over calumny only by disdaining it.

Françoise d'Aubigné Maintenon

Obstinacy is ever most positive when it is most in the wrong.

Susanne Curchod Necker

I would not have gotten [to Congress] if I had not been more persistent than a hound dog worrying a bone.

Gracie Pfost

Without the ability to be gay and to treat serious things lightly after the serious thinking is done and the decisions reached, I doubt whether any man could long carry the job of being President of the United States.

Eleanor Roosevelt

We have no more right to put our discordant states of mind into the lives of those around us and rob them of their sunshine and brightness then we have to enter their houses and steal their silverware.

Julia Seton

We satisfied ourselves the other day that there was no real ill in life except severe bodily pain; everything else is the child of the imagination, and depends on our thoughts. All other ills find a remedy either from time, or moderation, or strength of mind.

La Marquise de Sévigné

Life has, indeed, many ills, but the mind that views every object in its most cheering aspect, and every doubtful dispensation as replete with latent good, bears within itself a powerful and perpetual antidote.

Lydia H. Sigourney

A happy woman is one who has no cares at all; a cheerful woman is one who has cares but doesn't let them get her down.

Beverly Sills

You can't get spoiled if you do your own ironing.

Meryl Streep

How easy to be amiable in the midst of happiness and success.

Anne Sophie Swetchine

No matter how cynical I get, I can't keep up.

Lily Tomlin

I am firm. You are obstinate. He is a pig-headed fool.

attributed to Katherine Whitehorn

'Tis easy enough to be pleasant, when life flows like a song. But the man worthwhile is the one who will smile when everything goes dead wrong.

Ella Wheeler Wilcox

If you think you are beaten, you are,
If you think that you dare not, you don't,
If you'd like to win, but you think you can't,
It's almost certain you won't.

Anon.

It's a beautiful world to see,
  Or it's dismal in every zone,
The thing it must be in its gloom or its gleam
  Depends on yourself alone.

Anon.

Chapter 6

CHANGE

People change and forget to tell each other.

Lillian Hellman

❦

The only *constant* in life is *CHANGE*. Change permeates everything we are and do. The absence of change is worse than inaction, it is atrophy.

People change. Plans change. Organizations change. Change is natural, it is normal. Yet, the resistance to change is also just as normal and natural a part of human nature as the acceptance of change.

As a speaker, it is your responsibility to be an "explainer" of change, its inevitability and its place in the evolution of individuals and of organizations. A skilled speaker will help her audience not just cope with or accept the fact of change, she will also lead her listeners toward appreciating, toward embracing it. The key is to portray change as part of growth, as a regenerative function. If one were inclined toward the spiritual, one might observe that in a very broad sense, change can be seen as part of the redemptive process.

One of the most difficult aspects of your responsibility as a speaker is that you are almost always serving as an advocate for change, and sometimes even an apologist for change. You are charged with helping the members of a group see beyond the perceived comfort of the status quo to realize the need to do something different. You have the challenge of causing a normal group of human beings to embrace discomfort. It isn't always easy, but achieving it is among the speaker's greatest rewards.

Serving as an advocate for change is so difficult because, to many people, change implies failure—failure of what they are now thinking or doing. What you have to say is a threat, and nobody likes to feel threatened. This challenge is especially great when you are speaking to a volunteer organization, because what most people will immediately think is, you mean we haven't been doing a good job? (Because if we were doing a good job, why do we have to change?)

Your challenge is to help people understand that changing circumstances or needs require a change in behavior or activity. The unwillingness to recognize this has been described as the "trance of nonrenewal."

The key to speaking success is your ability to understand the *psychology of resistance*. You must empathize with your listeners and validate their feelings. You must help them deal with uncertainty and fear, sometimes even with panic.

A related element of your responsibility as a speaker in helping an audience deal with change is to clearly communicate your awareness of the group's emotions. You cannot successfully encourage change if you cannot transmit to your listeners that you *understand* how they feel and, more important, that you *care* how they feel. Once some common ground is established, you will find your audience much more receptive and willing to make that leap of faith required for change. Accepting change is much more a matter of faith than it is of intellect.

A timely, insightful quotation can often be the speaker's best bridge to introducing change, whether change as a concept or change as a specific course of action. It can also be the link in establishing rapport with the audience as they struggle with the change process. The key to both is a good understanding of your audience.

The change-encouraging quotation must be by someone whom the audience both recognizes and respects, and it must be in some way relevant to the nature of the change that is being introduced or encouraged. For example, if you are advocating governmental or organizational change, a salient observation by a respected practitioner such as Margaret Thatcher or Golda Meir can serve to open up the receptivity of your audience. The need for personal change can be validated by the thoughts of any number of philosophers or thinkers. Again, the most important factor is that the quotation be pertinent to your listeners.

I once read that the definition of whether or not a book is great is the degree to which reading it changed your life. The same is true for a speech.

Changing your life, of course, is a matter of definition. It could mean opening your mind to a new concept or causing you to look at the commonplace from a different perspective or with new insight. It doesn't have to be revolutionary to be significant. Your speech may not cause your audience to erect barricades in the streets, or to tear existing barricades down. But it should have the effect of stimulating some bit of thought *about* barricades—literal or figurative.

Your goal is to help your listeners in some way, great or small, modify their perceptions, their thinking, their behavior. It might be significant, it might be trivial—but it is important. One of the greatest gifts you can give your audience is an invitation to meet needed change as a friend rather than as a feared enemy.

That's the risk you take if you change: that people you've been involved with won't like the new you. But other people who do will come along.

Lisa Alther

Modern invention has banished the spinning-wheel, and the same law of progress makes the woman of today a different woman from her grandmother.

Susan B. Anthony

The most radical revolutionary will become a conservative the day after the revolution.

Hannah Arendt

The main dangers in this life are the people who want to change everything . . . or nothing.

Lady Nancy Astor

His hatred of her was the hatred of the old for the new, of the traditional for the innovative, of the dying for the living.

Jean M. Auel

There are two ways of meeting difficulties. You alter the difficulties or you alter yourself to meet them.

Phyliss Bottome

"Yes," I answered you last night;
"No," this morning, sir, I say:
Colors seen by candlelight
Will not look the same by day.

Elizabeth Barrett Browning

Every great mistake has a halfway moment, a split second when it can be recalled and perhaps remedied.

Pearl S. Buck

I learned in my four decades in Washington that one person *can* make a difference.

Liz Carpenter

Only within the moment of time represented by the present century has one species—man—acquired significant power to alter the nature of his world.

Rachel Carson

The universal human yearning for something permanent, enduring, without shadow of change.

Willa Cather

Life is change. Growth is optional. Choose wisely.

Karen Kaiser Clark

The challenges of change are always hard. It is important that we begin to unpack those challenges that confront this nation and realize that we each have a role that requires *us* to change and become more responsible for shaping our own future.

Hillary Rodham Clinton

How many women are ready to admit that they are capable of changing the course of their existence by simply taking time to think? It is easy for them to persuade themselves that the future, luck, chance, and the stars too, are the matters of their fortune. Is it their fault? For centuries fatalism has been passed on to all babies wearing pink booties even as they lie in their bassinets.

Christiane Collange

When we destroy an old prejudice we have need of a new virtue.

Mme. de Staël

Fame is a bee
It has a song
It has a sting
Ah, too, it has a wing.

Emily Dickinson

Vocabulary changes. Two little boys playing and talking. One said, "I found a contraceptive device under the veranda." The other little boy said, "Really! What's a veranda?"

Katie Dusenberry

If you don't like the way the world is, you change it. You have an obligation to change it. You just do it one step at a time.

Marian Wright Edelman

Leisure is gone; gone where the spinning-wheels are gone, and the pack horses, and the slow wagons, and the peddlers who brought bargains to the door on sunny afternoons.

George Eliot

It was not so long ago that people thought that semiconductors were part-time orchestra leaders and microchips were very, very small snack foods.

Geraldine Ferraro

When you can't remember why you're hurt, that's when you're healed. When you have to work real hard to re-create the pain, and you can't quite get there, that's when you're better.

Jane Fonda

When she stopped conforming to the conventional picture of femininity she finally began to enjoy being a woman.

Betty Friedan

You don't have to be afraid of change. You don't have to worry about what's been taken *away*. Just look to see what's been *added*.

Jackie Greer

In my early days I was a sepia Hedy Lamarr. Now I'm black and a woman, singing my own way.

Lena Horne

What we truly and earnestly aspire to be, that in some sense we are. The mere aspiration, by changing the frame of the mind, for the moment realizes itself.

Anna Jameson

Perhaps now and then a castaway on a lonely desert island dreads the thought of being rescued.

Sarah Orne Jewett

We must remember that one determined person can make a significant difference, and that a small group of determined people can change the course of history.

Sonia Johnson

I have not ceased being fearful, but I have ceased to let fear control me. I have accepted fear as a part of life—specifically the fear of change, the fear of the unknown; and I have gone ahead despite the pounding in my heart that says: turn back, turn back, you'll die if you venture too far.

Erica Jong

The heresy of one age becomes the orthodoxy of the next.

Helen Keller

Continuity gives us roots; change gives us branches, letting us stretch and grow and reach new heights.

Pauline R. Kezer

There is no sin punished more implacably by nature than the sin of resistance to change.

Anne Morrow Lindbergh

If we keep on doin' what we always done, we'll keep on gettin' what we always got.

Barbara Lyons

I realized that if what we call human nature can be changed, then absolutely anything is possible. And from that moment, my life changed.

Shirley MacLaine

It's the most unhappy people who most fear change.

Mignon McLaughlin

As the traveler who has once been from home is wiser than he who has never left his own doorstep, so a knowledge of one other culture should sharpen our ability to scrutinize more steadily, to appreciate lovingly, our own.

Margaret Mead

After all my erstwhile dear, my no longer cherished;
Need we say it was not love, just because it perished?

Edna St. Vincent Millay

Changing husbands is only changing troubles.

Kathleen Norris

Today, if you're not confused, you are not thinking clearly.

Irene Peter

Over the last 20 years, we've changed the world just enough to make it radically different, but not enough to make it work.

Anna Quindlen

We either light up with cold, piercing rays of intellect or we burn with passionate flame of emotion. Sometimes, like a coast guard signal, our lamps alternate red and white.

Grace Seton-Thompson

Changes are not only possible and predictable, but to deny them is to be an accomplice to one's own unnecessary vegetation.

Gail Sheehy

My heart is singing for joy this morning. A miracle has happened! The light of understanding has shone upon my little pupil's mind, and behold, all things are changed!

Annie Sullivan

Security is mortal's chiefest enemy.

Dame Ellen Terry

I have fought and kicked and fasted and prayed and cursed and cried myself to the point of existing. It has been like being born again, literally. Just *knowing* has meant everything to me. Knowing has pushed me out into the world, into college, into places, into people.

Alice Walker

We live in an epoch in which the solid ground of our preconceived ideas shakes daily under our certain feet.

Barbara Ward

I took a piece of plastic clay
And idly fashioned it one day,
And as my fingers pressed it, still
It moved and yielded to my will.

I came again when days were past;
The bit of clay was hard at last,
The form I gave it still it bore,
But I could change that form no more!

I took a piece of living clay,
And gently pressed it day by day,
And molded with my power and art
A young child's soft and yielding heart.

Anon.

Chapter 7

CHARACTER

Our strength is often composed of the weakness we're damned if we're going to show.

Mignon McLaughlin

❦

My dictionary defines CHARACTER as the "complex of mental and ethical traits marking a person, group, or nation." It also defines character as "moral excellence and firmness." For the speaker, both definitions apply.

We use quotations about character in many instances to inspire courage or firmness in an audience. We also strive to cause our listeners to develop in themselves, if only about a particular subject or topic, a complex of mental and ethical traits that will allow them to be or do more than they ever imagined. The use of appropriate quotations helps those in the audience refine in their own minds who they are and what their attitudes are—or ought to be.

It is important for a speaker to impress on her listeners that they must create or define their own character. Perhaps my favorite quotation of all time is an old saw first heard from my grandmother, Nellie Hershey Tullis. She told it like this:

Plant a thought, reap an act. Plant an act, reap a habit. Plant a habit, reap a character. Plant a character, reap a destiny.

I have heard it repeated in any number of variations since then, but the point is always the same: thoughts are converted into action; repeated actions eventually become habits; the composite of all these mental and spiritual habits comprise your character. Somebody else said it more succinctly: "Your character is your deliberate creation of yourself."

As a speaker, you are trying to provide encouragement so that people will develop, think, grow into something better. It is the speaker's responsibility to *elevate* her audience—to cause them to feel inspired and encouraged, emboldened and ennobled. There are so many discouragements in our world today, so many "downers" with which people must deal in every aspect of their lives; I can envision few occasions when it is the speaker's duty to add to them.

When using quotations concerning character, it is not the speaker's responsibility to preach. It is the speaker's responsibility to *inspire*—if only for a single decision or specific action—through illustrations of similar thoughts from people who represent both the best and the worst in human nature.

Contrast always clarifies: you may want to quote Mother Teresa in order to clarify evil, or to quote Lady Macbeth to clarify good. One of a speaker's challenges is to assess an audience well enough to be able to select the most effective clarifying quotation and to know her own collection of quotations well enough to be able to select the one that will work best.

The Armed Forces' advertising slogan, "Be All That You Can Be," seems especially appropriate when thinking about encouraging character in an audience. The speaker, whether from the platform or in the board room, should focus on helping her listeners be more than they thought themselves capable of being.

When you, as a speaker, accomplish this, you are also delivering a testament to your own character. When you develop and communicate a spirit of empathy, of concern, of caring with your audience, you are also building or reinforcing those qualities in yourself.

Thus, as a presenter, you need to spend some time considering your own character. Take an inventory of your own "moral excellence and firmness." Then, strive to communicate through your message that your own character is one that is worthy of reflection by your listeners.

The best description of conveying character that I have ever heard: "We are not put on this earth to see through one another, but to see one another through."

Everything nourishes what is strong already.

Jane Austen

Character builds slowly, but it can be torn down with incredible swiftness.

Faith Baldwin

I've never been one who thought the Lord should make life easy; I've just asked Him to make me strong.

Eva Bowring

I wouldn't give you a dime for my seat in the Senate if I couldn't vote according to my convictions and conscience.

Hattie W. Caraway

It matters more what's in a woman's face than what's on it.

Claudette Colbert

When small men cast long shadows the sun is going down.

Venita Cravens

Virtue which has never been attacked by temptation is deserving of no monument.

Mlle. de Scudery

Innocence in genius, and candor in power, are both noble qualities.

Mme. de Staël

There are poor men in this country who can't be bought. The day I found that out, I sent my gold abroad.

Comtesse de Voigrand

We never know how high we are
Till we are called to rise;
And then, if we are true to plan,
Our statures touch the skies.

Emily Dickinson

Most of our platitudes notwithstanding, self-deception remains the most difficult deception. The tricks that work on others count for nothing in that very well-lit back alley where one keeps assignations with oneself: no winning smiles will do here, no prettily drawn lists of good intentions.

Joan Didion

Our deeds determine us, as much as we determine our deeds.

George Eliot

Strength is born in the deep silence of long-suffering hearts; not amid joy.

Felicia Hemans

Without discipline, there is no life at all.

Katharine Hepburn

True delicacy, that most beautiful heart-leaf of humanity, exhibits itself most significantly in little things.

Mary Botham Howitt

Don't compromise yourself. You are all you've got.

Janis Joplin

Small kindnesses, small courtesies, small considerations, habitually practiced in our social intercourse, give a greater charm to the character than the display of great talents and accomplishments.

Mary Ann Kelty

Like other spurious things, fastidiousness is often inconsistent with itself, the coarsest things are done, and the cruelest things said by the most fastidious people.

Mrs. C. M. Kirkland

The one thing that doesn't abide by majority rule is a person's conscience.

Harper Lee

Think wrongly, if you please, but in all cases think for yourself.

Doris Lessing

To give without any reward, or any notice, has a special quality of its own.

Anne Morrow Lindbergh

What you have become is the price you paid to get what you used to want.

Mignon McLaughlin

My ability to survive personal crises is really a mark of the character of my people. Individually and collectively, we react with a tenacity that allows us again and again to bounce back from adversity.

Chief Wilma Mankiller

A slowness to applaud betrays a cold temper of an envious spirit.

Hannah More

Misfortune sprinkles ashes on the head of the man, but falls like dew on the head of the woman, and brings forth gems of strength of which she herself had no conscious possession.

Anna Cora Mowatt

It is no virtue to bear calamities if we do not feel them.

Susanne Curchod Necker

Never grow a wishbone, daughter, where your backbone ought to be.

Clementine Paddleford

Nobility, without virtue, is a fine setting without a gem.

June Porter

Adventure is something you seek for pleasure, or even for profit, like a gold rush or invading a country . . . but experience is what really happens to you in the long run; the truth that finally overtakes you.

Katherine Anne Porter

Character building begins in our infancy and continues until death.

Eleanor Roosevelt

Vanity is the quicksand of reason.

George Sand

Our vanity is the constant enemy of our dignity.

Anne Sophie Swethchine

Character is fate, as the Greeks believed.

Barbara Tuchman

The best index to a person's character is how he treats people who can't do him any good, and how he treats people who can't fight back.

Abigail Van Buren

Flattery is like a base coin: it impoverishes those who receive it.

Mme. Voillez

Virtue must be the result of self-culture; the gods do not take pupils.

Baroness von Krüdener

It's easy to die 'mid the world's applause
For a noble deed, trumpets blaring!
It's the harder part to fight for a cause
And inwardly bleed with no one caring!

Myra Brooks Welch

One ship drives east, and another west
With the self-same winds that blow;
'Tis the set of the sails
And not the gales,
Which decides the way to go.

Ella Wheeler Wilcox

True greatness lies not always
In the winning of worldly fame,
Nor doing our best spurred on by the cheers
And plaudits that follow our name.
But he who can face with a cheery grace
The everyday of life,
With its petty things that rasp and sting,
Is a hero in the strife.

Fannie Herron Wingate

If you do not tell the truth about yourself you cannot tell it about other people.
Virginia Woolf

When wealth is lost, nothing is lost;
When health is lost, something is lost;
When character is lost, all is lost.

German proverb

Dignity does not consist in possessing honors, but in deserving them.
Anon.

Chapter 8

CHOICE

If I didn't start painting, I would have raised chickens.

Grandma Moses

☙

"We write our own destiny. We become what we do." With that statement, Madame Chiang Kai-shek nicely sums up what CHOICE is all about. That also sums up very well one of the most human of characteristics—the ability to choose.

Choice is conscious behavior. Other species act on instinct or conditioned behavior; only humans have the innate ability to make thoughtful, reasoned choices. As human beings, we have inherited the capacity to choose between right and wrong, truth and falsehood, action and inaction. Life, and everything in it, is a series of such choices; some are large, some are small. We are confronted with literally hundreds, if not thousands, of options every day, most of which we act on in some conscious way.

You know this reality and most of your listeners do, too. Your responsibility as a speaker is to lead your audiences toward making *wise* choices. You want to help your listeners make decisions that will improve something—either themselves as individuals, their organization, their community, or something even greater than these. A speaker can play the role of an *enabler*.

It is up to you to explain the results of making the right choices and to describe the consequences of making the wrong ones. It is also important that people understand that doing nothing is also a choice, and that the option to do nothing (to choose not to choose) is in itself a choice, albeit, a limiting one.

Along with the responsibility of helping audiences confront their choice-making abilities comes the challenge of helping them realize that choices aren't limitless. No person, no organization, can do everything.

One way to illustrate the importance of choice is to help an audience understand the nature of personal, character-building choices and the relationship between those kinds of choices and the organizational choices that they may be confronting.

For example, happiness is a choice; so is fear, envy, hope, courage, despair, anger—every other emotion of which human beings are capable. These are internal choices, but they are reflected in outward options and actions. People often fail to recognize that these internal choices, and their attitude about these choices, influence their external organizational, business, and professional choices as well.

It is amazing that some people are unaware that their future is controlled in large part by this sum of choices—internal and external—and, furthermore, by the degree of control that they exercise over those choices.

The skilled speaker will try to motivate her audience to choose desired goals in order to shape outcomes in a positive way. Cause and effect is still a mystery to some. People must be empowered to understand the degree to which they are in control of their choices and to realize that these choices can cause the individual and the organization to fail, to remain stagnant, or to triumph.

So, when leading audiences to, and through, decisions, it is important to focus on the reality of what those decisions mean, both individually and organizationally. It is important that people understand their own capacities to make choices that will lead to positive outcomes.

Quotations that help illuminate or clarify the decision-making process are central to this effort. And central to selecting quotes is an understanding of your audience. A quotation about choice from a source with which your audience is unfamiliar may be wasted; a quotation from a source whose position or reputation is contrary to that of your audience will be counterproductive.

It is also important for the speaker to understand another choice—the choice of her audience to listen actively or to "tune her out" just as actively. Part of the speaker's responsibility is to prepare a presentation that will cause her audience to choose to listen. It is an act of persuasion on two levels: first, to persuade the audience to choose to "tune in" the presentation and, second, to "tune in" the content.

Choice is also closely aligned with freedom—for choice, surely, is the essence of freedom.

❧

I've always felt that a person's intelligence is directly reflected by the number of conflicting points of view he can entertain simultaneously on the same topic.

Lisa Alther

Some people regard discipline as a chore. For me, it is a kind of order that sets me free to fly.

Julie Andrews

The sad truth is that most evil is done by people who never make up their minds to be either good or evil.

Hannah Arendt

You don't get to choose how you're going to die. Or when. You can decide how you're going to live now.

Joan Baez

There is as much difference between the stage and the film as between a piano and a violin. Normally you can't become a virtuoso in both.

Ethel Barrymore

You never saw a fish on the wall with its mouth shut.

Sally Berger

I suppose I could have stayed home, baked cookies and had teas. The work that I have done . . . has been aimed . . . to assure that women can make the choices . . . whether it's full-time career, full-time motherhood or some combination.

Hillary Rodham Clinton

We are free up to the point of choice, then the choice controls the chooser.

Mary Crowley

Love is as strict as acting. If you want to love somebody, stand there and do it. If you don't, don't. There are no other choices.

Tyne Daly

The voice of conscience is so delicate that it is easy to stifle it; but it is also so clear that it is impossible to mistake it.

Mme. de Staël

Heed the still, small voice that so seldom leads us wrong, and never into folly.
Mme. du Deffand

The strongest principle of growth lies in human choice.
George Eliot

To swallow and follow, whether old doctrine or new propaganda, is a weakness still dominating the human mind.
Charlotte Perkins Gilman

After being caught for a stagecoach robbery, and asked if she would do it again: "Damn right, pardner!"
Pearl Hart

I cannot and will not cut my conscience to fit this year's fashions.
Lillian Hellman

If you play it safe in life you've decided that you don't want to grow anymore.
Shirley Hufstedler

What a sense of superiority it gives one to escape reading a book which everyone else is reading.
Alice James

Advice is what we ask for when we already know the answer but wish we didn't.
Erica Jong

The million little things that drop into your hands
The small opportunities each day brings
He leaves us free to use or abuse
And goes unchanging along His silent way.

Helen Keller

I believe that we are solely responsible for our choices, and we have to accept the consequences of every deed, word, and thought throughout our lifetime.
Elisabeth Kübler-Ross

There is no pleasure in having nothing to do; the fun is having lots to do and not doing it.
Mary Wilson Little

Make it a rule of life never to regret and never look back. We all live in suspense, from day to day, from hour to hour; in other words, we are the hero of our own story.

Mary McCarthy

There's one thing to be said for inviting trouble: it generally accepts.

May Maloo

Regret is an appalling waste of energy; you can't build on it; it is good only for wallowing in.

Katherine Mansfield

My will shall shape my future. Whether I fail or succeed shall be no man's doing but my own. I am the force; I can clear any obstacle before me or I can be lost in the maze. My choice; my responsibility; win or lose, only I hold the key to my destiny.

Elaine Maxwell

It is human nature to stand in the middle of a thing.

Mariane Moore

A BMW can't take you as far as a diploma.

Joyce A. Myers

One day I found myself saying to myself, "I can't live where I want to. I can't even say what I want to! I decided I was a very stupid fool not to at least paint as I wanted to."

Georgia O'Keeffe

Supposing you have tried and failed again and again. You may have a fresh start any moment you choose, for this thing that we call "failure" is not the falling down, but the staying down.

Mary Pickford

It depends on education to open the gates which lead to virtue or to vice, to happiness or to misery.

Jane Porter

I've always been independent, and I don't see how it conflicts with femininity.

Sylvia Porter

As a woman I can't go to war, and I refuse to send anyone else.

Jeannette Rankin

Woman must have her freedom—the fundamental freedom of choosing whether or not she shall be a mother and how many children she will have. Regardless of what man's attitude may be, that problem is hers—and before it can be his, it is hers alone. She goes through the vale of death alone, each time a babe is born. As it is the right neither of man nor the state to coerce her into this ordeal, so it is her right to decide whether she will endure it.

Margaret Sanger

We're swallowed up only when we are willing for it to happen.

Nathalie Sarraute

If I had to live my life over again, I'd dare to make more mistakes next time.

Nadine Stair

The heart has always the pardoning power.

Anne Sophie Swetchine

We are now in the hands of events. (describing the Falkland Islands situation)

Margaret Thatcher

If you don't want to get tackled, don't carry the ball.

Ann McKay Thompson

Reality is a crutch for people who can't cope with drugs.

Lily Tomlin

I've been rich and I've been poor; rich is better.

Sophie Tucker

How one lives is, after all, one of the rights left to the individual—when and if he has opportunity to choose.

Alice Walker

I believe it's possible to have a great marriage and a great career, or to have a great marriage and great children, or to have great children and a great career, but it's awfully tough to have all three at the same time.

Barbara Walters

Whenever I have to choose between two evils, I always like to try the one I haven't tried before.

Mae West

Like the winds of the sea are the ways of fate;
As the voyage along thru life;
'Tis the will of the soul
That decides its goal,
And not the calm or the strife.

Ella Wheeler Wilcox

My business took over my life—by choice.

Riva Yares

If you refuse to accept anything but the best, you very often get it.

Anon.

Chapter 9

COMMUNICATION

Many argue; not many converse.

Louisa May Alcott

❧

The importance of the art of COMMUNICATION is so well known as to almost be a cliché. But expressions *become* clichés because they are true! And it is simple truth that practically nothing can be accomplished or achieved in this life without the ability to communicate.

Quotations about communication are empowering, both for speakers and listeners. The speaker empowers her audience through her communications skills, and the audience empowers the speaker by *listening*. Active listening is a vital, but often overlooked, communication skill. Effective quotations will strengthen both ends of the communications equation.

The skilled speaker will use quotations from this chapter and from her own collection as a teaching tool. You want your audience to accept and understand the principle that they must be able to communicate—their ideas, their plans, their goals, their dreams, whatever the priority might be—before they can succeed. The use of quotations from sources meaningful to the audience will illustrate the weight that others place on being able to "pass the word."

This ability to teach about the significance of successful communication is critical if the audience is composed of people in a highly specialized profession or an occupation with its own terminology. The more specialized or complicated the profession and its language, the more likely it is that their jargon will be relatively unintelligible to outsiders or lay people. The group knows what it is talking about, but it is unlikely that anybody else will. Thus, there will be plenty of dialogue, but not much communication.

You have to help groups like these understand that to communicate means to speak in the language the listener understands. A good way to do this is to use quotations, many of them humorous, that illustrate the point about speaking English, not "professionalese."

The other communications challenge for the speaker is your own: you have to be able to communicate about communication. You have to realize that everything you do on the platform communicates something. Even the way you dress communicates a message. As long as you are visible (whether or not you are audible), you are communicating with your audience. Every word, gesture, stance, look, communicates with your audience. Your words and body language may be positive, they may be negative, but communication is going on all the time, and the effectiveness of your presentation is being judged by your listeners.

You and your audience have entered into a compact: They have agreed to allow you to communicate with them—and you must do so. They wish to communicate their thoughts and agenda with others—and you must help show them how.

☙

Listen carefully to what country people call mother wit. In those homely sayings are couched the collective wisdom of generations.

Maya Angelou

If I but knew, if I but knew
What you think inside of you.

I try, but seldom ever know
Who is false and who is true.
Who tells lies, who tells truth.

If I but knew, if I but knew
What you think inside of you.
If I but knew, if I but knew.

Leah Arendt

The silent upbraiding of the eye is the very poetry of reproach; it speaks at once to the imagination.

Clara L. Balfour

It's not whether you really cry. It's whether the audience thinks you are crying.
Ingrid Bergman

I'm going to call my Dad to tell him I love him—and listen to him say, "This call is costing you a fortune" and hang up.

Erma Bombeck

Listening, not imitation, may be the sincerest form of flattery.
Dr. Joyce Brothers

Self-expression must pass into communication for its fulfillment.
Pearl S. Buck

What a lot we lost when we stopped writing letters! You can't reread a phone call.
Liz Carpenter

Few high school students look upon the language which they speak and write as an art. Yet it is, or ought to be, the noblest of all the arts, looked upon with respect, even with reverence, and used always with care, courtesy, and the deepest respect.
Mary Ellen Chase

Search for the truth is the noblest occupation of man; its publication is a duty.

Mme. de Staël

They gave me the "V" sign. Some forgot a finger, but . . .

Liz Dreyfus

To speak ill of others is a dishonest way of praising ourselves.

Ariel and Will Durant

Oh, the comfort, the inexpressible comfort of feeling safe with a person; having neither to weigh thoughts nor to measure words but to pour them all out, just as it is, chaff and grain together, knowing that a faithful hand will take and sift them, keeping what is worth keeping, and then, with the breath of kindness, blow the rest away.

George Eliot

Language is a wonderful thing. It can be used to express thoughts, to conceal thoughts, but, more often, to replace thinking.

Kelly Fordyce

I'll not listen to reason. Reason always means what someone else has got to say.

Elizabeth Gaskell

The freedom of the press works in such a way that there is not much freedom from it.

Princess Grace of Monaco

Loneliness is never more cruel than when it is felt in close propinquity with someone who has ceased to communicate.

Germaine Greer

One has to grow up with good talk in order to form the habit of it.

Helen Hayes

Cynicism is an unpleasant way of saying the truth.

Lillian Hellman

I don't care what is written about me so long as it isn't true.

Katharine Hepburn

I resent the idea that people would blame the messenger for the message, rather than looking at the content of the message itself.

Anita Hill

Nobody's interested in sweetness and light.

Hedda Hopper

I've always been fascinated by the beauty of sign language. It's a visual language that doesn't allow for innuendo—it cuts right to the chase. With deaf people you always know where you stand.

Dawn Jeffory-Nelson

Information voids will be filled by rumors and speculation unless they are preempted by open, credible and trustworthy communication. Pull no punches. When you know an answer, give it. When you don't, say so. When you're guessing, admit it. But don't stop communication.

Jean B. Keffeler

The real menace in dealing with a five-year-old is that in no time at all you begin to sound like a five-year-old.

Jean Kerr

Television has proved that people will look at anything rather than each other.

Ann Landers

The way a question is asked limits and disposes the ways in which any answer to it—right or wrong—may be given.

Susanne K. Langer

The opposite of talking isn't listening. The opposite of talking is waiting.

Fran Leibowitz

Good communication is as stimulating as black coffee, and just as hard to sleep after.

Anne Morrow Lindbergh

Evil report, like the Italian stiletto, is an assassin's weapon.

Françoise d'Aubigné Maintenon

Satire should, like a polished razor keen,
Wound with a touch that's scarcely felt or seen.

Lady Mary Wortley Montague

The real art of conversation is not only to say the right thing in the right place but to leave unsaid the wrong thing at the tempting moment.

Lady Dorothy Nevill

Our learned persons and possessors of special information should not, when they are writing for the general public, presume to improve the accepted vocabulary. . . . They should be at pains to translate technical terms into English. And when they do forget this duty, we others who are unlearned, and naturally speak not in technical terms but in English, should refuse to be either cowed by the fear of seeming ignorant, or tempted by the hope of passing for specialists, into following their bad example.

Margaret Nicholson

How can we communicate love? I think three things are involved: We must reach out to a person, make contact. We must listen with the heart, be sensitive to the other's needs. We must respond in a language that the person can understand. Many of us do all the talking. We must learn to listen and to keep on listening.

Princess Pale Moon

Misfortune, and recited misfortune especially, may be prolonged to that point where it ceases to excite pity and arouses only irritation.

Dorothy Parker

Ideal conversation must be an exchange of thought, and not, as many of those who worry most about their shortcomings believe, an eloquent exhibition of wit or oratory.

Emily Post

Before a marriage, a man will lie awake all night thinking about something you said; after marriage, he'll fall asleep before you finish saying it.

Helen Rowland

Communication is a measurable asset.

Susan Sampsell

They went at it hammer and tongues.

Mary Schaefer

I think if women would indulge more freely in vituperation, they would enjoy ten times the health they do. It seems to me they are suffering from repression.

Elizabeth Cady Stanton

Half the misery in the world comes of want of courage to speak and to hear the truth plainly, and in a spirit of love.

Harriet Beecher Stowe

The truth is not wonderful enough to suit the newspapers; so they enlarge upon it and invent ridiculous embellishments.

Annie Sullivan

Nagging is the repetition of unpalatable truths.

Baroness Edith Summerskill

If you face a delicate situation, don't go into it wearing your spurs or you'll rip it apart. Instead, dress for the occasion. Cloak yourself in diplomacy. Vest yourself with wisdom, and wear a smile.

Ann McKay Thompson

War is the unfolding of miscalculations.

Barbara Tuchman

I personally think we developed language because of our deep inner need to complain.

Jane Wagner

When you go to school, you're supposed to learn how to listen.

Annie Dodge Wauneka

Literature is strewn with the wreckage of men who have minded beyond reason the opinion of others.

Virginia Woolf

Chapter **10**

COURAGE

The bravest thing you can do when you are not brave is to profess courage and act accordingly.

Corra May White Harris

❦

COURAGE is more than simply a physical action. It is a state of mind as much as it is a state of body—and it's in this context that I have included it.

Ordinarily a book of quotations might include a chapter on Fear. After all fear is one of the great motivators in life. However, I do not choose to dwell on the negative or on negative motivators. Thus, I have chosen to include a chapter on its opposite—on COURAGE—perhaps the better to illuminate the enervating, the negative, the illness-inducing emotion that is fear.

Most of us understand that life is basically a risky business. We can react to risk and to life in several ways: we can shrink from it in fear or we can move toward it with confidence. Helping an audience to understand that both actions are viable options is one of the prime tasks of the speaker. Drawing a distinction between the two is often one of the most difficult, but certainly one of the most important challenges you face from the platform.

The speaker can paint in the darkest possible hues the problems that lie ahead when any given course of action is taken or not taken. You can paint in pastels the Pollyanna view of the world. Or, you can use the vivid, robust colors of realism and courage to illuminate what lies ahead. As a speaker, you have to choose which colors to employ. And most often, the colors you select will say as much about you as about the topic at hand.

Making these choices is often a special challenge for a woman speaker. Many listeners will think it unsuitable to hear a woman speaking about courage or using quotations that illustrate this attribute. Thus, it is especially important when advancing your arguments that you use the words of those whose lives or work are unquestioned portraits in courage.

In the context of women—both women speakers and women whose words are courage-inspiring—I find it interesting that so often male writers speak of courage as being the emotion of the foolhardy. Courage is linked to impetuous action, to risking all. These rather noisy emotions are a fascinating contrast to the way so many women write about courage—in tones of calm, deliberate, thoughtful reality.

At the risk of seeming even more sexist, I have wondered if this is because women have been so conditioned through the years to quietly go about the everyday hurdles of homemaking, the physical dangers of childbearing, and the challenges of raising children.

I will not pursue such an obviously heated subject in what is certainly not intended to be either an inflammatory topic or an inflammatory book. I will simply leave it with you to wonder about.

I would suggest, however, that you confine your musings on this subject to your private *think* time, and concentrate your public utterances on helping your listeners find ways to convert their own concerns, doubts, and fears into positive responses.

The words about courage contained in this chapter reveal both sides of the coin—fear and the absence, or at least the control, of fear. They are intended to provide a convertibility factor for the feelings that you may have as a speaker (that most fearsome of challenges) and that your audiences may hold.

When you *encourage* (isn't that a great word!) someone—that is, when you provide courage to them—you are doing something very basic. In fact, I often find it helpful to substitute the word *encourage* for *courage*. The former sounds so human, so do-able, that it's easy to envision achieving it for an audience. Try it and I think you'll find it equally as helpful.

Encouraging, by whatever means, is one of the most wonderful things you can do for an audience. Seldom will you find the ability to build courage so readily achievable.

❦

Fear is an emotion indispensable for survival.

Hannah Arendt

There's not a cliff too awesome
    nor a stream too swift or deep,
Nor a haunted hill too eerie,
    nor a mountain trail too steep
For the questing heart to venture
    or the eager breath to dare.

Lorraine Usher Babbitt

The brave man is not he who feels no fear,
For that were stupid and irrational;
But he, whose noble soul its fear subdues,
And bravely dares the danger nature shrinks from.

Joanna Baillie

I may be compelled to face danger, but never fear it, and while our soldiers can
stand and fight, I can stand and feed and nurse them.

Clara Barton

I have no regrets. I wouldn't have lived my life the way I did if I was going to
worry about what people were going to say.

Ingrid Bergman

Courage is fear that has said its prayers.

Dorothy Bernard

Heaven sends us misfortunes as a moral tonic.

Lady Marguerite Blessington

No coward soul is mine,
No trembler in the world's storm-troubled sphere:
I see Heaven's glory shine,
And faith shines equal, arming me from fear.

Emily Brontë

I do not ask to walk smooth paths
    nor bear an easy load.
I pray for strength and fortitude
    to climb the rock strewn road.

Give me such courage and I can scale
   the hardest peaks alone,
And transform every stumbling block
   into a stepping stone.

Gail Brook Burket

Courageous risks are life giving, they help you grow, make you brave and better than you think you are.

Joan L. Curcio

Nothing in life is to be feared. It is only to be understood.

Marie Curie

To gain that which is worth having, it may be necessary to lose everything.

Bernadette Devlin

The distance is nothing; it's only the first step that is difficult.

Mme. du Deffand

Courage is the price that life exacts for granting peace. The soul that knows it not, knows no release from little things; knows not the livid loneliness of fear.

Amelia Earhart

We are not apt to fear for the fearless, when we are companions in their danger.

George Eliot

Fear is a basic emotion, part of our native equipment, and like all normal emotions has a positive function to perform. Comforting formulas for getting rid of anxiety may be just the wrong thing. Books about "peace of mind" can be bad medicine. To be afraid when one should be afraid is good sense.

Dorothy Fosdick

In order that she may be able to give her hand with dignity, she must be able to stand alone.

Margaret Fuller

There is no impossibility to him who stands prepared to conquer every hazard. The fearful are the failing.

Sarah J. Hale

It is better to die on your feet than to live on your knees.

Delores Ibarruri

In morals, what begins in fear usually ends in wickedness; in religion, what begins in fear usually ends in fanaticism. Fear, either as a principle or a motive, is the beginning of all evil.

Anna Jameson

I've learned of life this bitter truth:
Hope not between the crumbling walls
Of mankind's gratitude to find repose,
But rather,
Build within thy own soul
Fortresses!

Georgia Douglas Johnson

Avoiding danger is no safer in the long run than outright exposure. The fearful are caught as often as the bold.

Helen Keller

It's better to be a lion for a day than a sheep all your life.

Sister Elizabeth Kenny

We speak of hope; but is not hope only a more gentle name for fear?

Letitia E. Landon

By not coming forward [about rape], you make yourself a victim forever.

Kelly McGillis

Even cowards can endure hardship; only the brave can endure suspense.

Mignon McLaughlin

You can't be brave if you've only had wonderful things happen to you.

Mary Tyler Moore

Imagination frames events unknown,
In wild, fantastic shapes of hideous ruin,
And what it fears creates.

Hannah More

Life shrinks or expands in proportion to one's courage.

Anaïs Nin

My only concern was to get home after a hard day's work.

Rosa Parks

Life is a warfare; and he who easily desponds deserts a double duty: he betrays the noblest property of man, which is dauntless resolution; and he rejects the providence of that all gracious Being who guides and rules the universe.

Jane Porter

All adventures, especially into new territory, are scary.

Sally Ride

You gain strength, courage and confidence by every experience in which you really stop to look fear in the face. . . . You must do the thing which you think you cannot do.

Eleanor Roosevelt

Do not follow where the path may lead. Go instead where there is no path and leave a trail.

Muriel Strode

Strength alone knows conflict; weakness is below even defeat, and is born vanquished.

Anne Sophie Swetchine

There is nothing to fear except the persistent refusal to find out the truth, the persistent refusal to analyze the causes of happenings. Fear grows in darkness; if you think there's a bogeyman around, turn on the light.

Dorothy Thompson

To laugh is to risk appearing the fool.
To weep is to risk appearing sentimental.
To reach for another is to risk involvement.
To expose your feelings is to risk exposing your true self.
To place your ideas, your dreams before a crowd is to risk their loss.
To love is to risk not being loved in return.
To live is to risk dying.
To believe is to risk despair.
To try is to risk failure.

But risks must be taken, because the greatest hazard in life is to risk nothing.
The person who risks nothing, does nothing, has nothing, is nothing.
They may avoid suffering and sorrow, but they cannot learn, feel, change,
   grow, love, live.
Chained by their attitudes they are slaves; they have forfeited their freedom.
Only a person who risks is free.

Anonymous Chicago Teacher

'Tis not the softer things of life
   Which stimulate man's will to strive;
But bleak adversity and strife
   Do most to keep man's will alive.
O'er rose-strewn paths the weaklings creep,
   But brave hearts dare to climb the steep.

Anon.

Chapter 11

EDUCATION

Imparting knowledge is only lighting other men's candles at our lamp, without depriving ourselves of any flame.

Jane Porter

Q uotations about EDUCATION are not just by, or for, educators. The topic of education is so broad that the concept, like so many other of our topics, is empowering. Every positive act requires that education in some form occur. Education is the process of moving—via facts, information, and perceptions—from ignorance to knowledge and, hopefully, to wisdom. Helping audiences move along this path is the primary responsibility of the speaker.

Educating an audience is much like educating an individual, in that no one can be *given* an education. All that one can be given is the *opportunity to learn*. All the speaker can do is offer her listeners the opportunity to learn from *her*. Being able to stimulate this opportunity is "job one" from the platform.

Encouragement is one of the most powerful educational tools. Everyone responds to encouragement. People are elevated when their worth is recognized. Thus encouraged, they will be more open to the educational message you have to offer and will be more open to carrying their message to others.

A good quotation demonstrating the importance of education is the old adage: "What you're not up on, you're down on."

There is no vacuum in real life. People are either instructed positively (caused to be "up" on something) or they are instructed negatively (caused to be "down" on something). In any communicative act, one or the other will occur. Nobody is ever *not* educated. It is the speaker's challenge to make sure that the learning experience is a positive one.

The truth of that "up-down" aphorism is double-edged: If you don't properly communicate with your audience about your purpose, you will lose them; if the members of your audience can't communicate with *their* constituencies, they, too, will fail.

An additional aspect of this topic is the fact that, in today's society and economy, the concept of lifelong learning is almost universally embraced. There is scarcely a professional, civic, business, religious, or community group that does not have some sort of continuing education component in its activities. This commitment must be reinforced by the speaker so that continuing education is seen as continuing growth—progress that will lead the group and its members toward a greater realization of success. Quotations about the importance of learning can thus range broadly across the speaker's and audience's fields of interest.

Quotations about education should in some way illustrate a point the speaker is trying to make about learning. It should also illustrate the significance of the listener educating someone else. Since education-sparked growth also implies change, quotations should be geared toward accepting and coping with changes in a positive way. Pick the quotations that work for you and for your listeners, and use them well!

ỡ

If woman is to be council to her husband, pray train her, that he may have a learned advisor.

Abigail Smith Adams

America's future will be determined by the home and the school. The child becomes largely what it is taught, hence we must watch what we teach it, and how we live before it.

Jane Addams

Real education should educate us out of self into something far finer; into a selflessness which links us with all humanity.

Lady Nancy Astor

If it's natural to kill, why do men have to go into training to learn how?

Joan Baez

Prejudices, it is well known, are most difficult to eradicate from the heart whose soil has never been loosened or fertilized by education; they grow there, firm as weeds among rocks.

Charlotte Brontë

When God would educate a man He compels him to learn bitter lessons. He sends him to school to the necessities rather than to the graces, that, by knowing all suffering, he may know also the eternal consolation.

Celia Burleigh

Learning . . . should be a joy and full of excitement. It is life's greatest adventure; it is an illustrated excursion into the mind of noble and learned men, not a conducted tour through a jail.

Taylor Caldwell

Each day I learn more than I teach;
I learn that half knowledge of another's life
Leads to false judgment;
I learn that there is a surprising kinship
In human nature;
I learn that it is a wise father who knows his son;
I learn that what we expect we get;
I learn that there's more good than evil in this world;
That age is a question of spirit;
That youth is the best of life
No matter how numerous its years;
I learn how much there is to learn.

Virginia Church

Better build schoolrooms for the boy,
Than cells and gibbets for the man.

Eliza Cook

There is a young and impressionable mind out there that is hungry for information. It has latched on to an electronic tube as its main source of nourishment.

Joan Ganz Cooney

When we escaped from Cuba, all we could carry was our education.

Alicia Coro

We teach what we learn, and the cycle goes on.

Joan L. Curcio

Retiring Teacher's Grace:
The view from the hill is broad and beckoning for indeed we are entering the land of time enough and choice. Truly we are twice blessed for we are teachers—once and future. Our world has suffered the little children to come unto us and through them we have come to know heaven.

Dorothy Druckemiller

Education is the transmission of civilization.

Ariel and Will Durant

I got all the schooling any actress needs. That is, I learned to write enough to sign contracts.

Hermione Gingold

Good teaching is one-fourth preparation and three-fourths theatre.

Gail Godwin

Why am I a teacher? Because I'm good at it! I choose it!

Ramona Greschel

But it is not hard work which is dreary; it is superficial work. That is always boring in the long run, and it has always seemed strange to me that in our endless discussions about education so little stress is ever laid on the pleasure of becoming an educated person, the enormous interest it adds to life. To be able to be caught up in the world of thought—that is to be educated.

Edith Hamilton

The role of the teacher remains the highest calling of a free people. To the teacher, America entrusts her most precious resource, her children; and asks that they be prepared, in all their glorious diversity, to face the rigors of individual participation in a democratic society.

Shirley Hufstedler

The true purpose of education is to cherish and unfold the seed of immortality already sown within us; to develop, to their fullest extent, the capacities of every kind with which the God who made us has endowed us.

Anna Jameson

Do not call for black power or green power. Call for brain power.

Barbara Jordan

Any teacher can take a child to the classroom, but not every teacher can make him learn. He will not work joyously unless he feels that liberty is his, whether he is busy or at rest; he must feel the flush of victory and the heart-sinking of disappointment before he takes with a will the tasks distasteful to him and resolves to dance his way bravely through a dull routine of textbooks.

Helen Keller

The educator must above all understand how to wait; to reckon all effects in the light of the future, not of the present.

Ellen Key

Whatever you do to your child's body, you are doing to your child's mind.

Penelope Leach

America's future walks through the doors of our schools each day.

Mary Jean LeTendre

I do not believe that sheer suffering teaches. If suffering alone taught, all the world would be wise, since everyone suffers. To suffering must be added mourning, understanding, patience, love, openness and the willingness to remain vulnerable.

Anne Morrow Lindbergh

I touch the future. I teach.

Christa McAuliffe

We are now at a point where we must educate our children in what no one knew yesterday, and prepare our schools for what no one knows yet.

Margaret Mead

Goodbye tension, hello pension!

Fay Michaud, retiring teacher

The first idea that the child must acquire, in order to be actively disciplined, is that of the difference between good and evil; and the task of the educator lies in seeing that the child does not confound good with immobility, and evil with activity. Our aim is to discipline for activity, for work, for good; not for immobility, not for passivity, not for obedience.

Maria Montessori

Teachers can change lives with just the right mix of chalk and challenges.

Joyce A. Myers

Everywhere I go, I'm asked if I think the universities stifle writers. My opinion is that they don't stifle enough of them. There's many a best seller that could have been prevented by a good teacher.

Flannery O'Connor

The more we know, the more we want to know; when we know enough, we know how much we don't know.

Carol Orlock

The time has come when education must conduct itself like the Fortune 500 company it is.

Barbara Orwig

I was a fantastic student until ten, and then my mind began to wander.

Grace Paley

Four be the things I am wiser to know:
Idleness, sorrow, a friend, and a foe.

Dorothy Parker

The greatest obstacle to those who hope to reform American education is complacency. Most people believe that schools were good enough when they were children and that they are good enough now. But the dynamic growth of our system of education has spawned serious problems of educational quality. When you succeed at keeping almost everyone in school, you must figure out ways to educate everyone you keep in school.

Diane Ravitch

Too much rigidity on the part of teachers should be followed by a brisk spirit of insubordination on the part of the taught.

Agnes Repplier

Teaching was the hardest work I had ever done, and it remains the hardest work I have done to date.

Ann Richards

Woman, bent upon her freedom and seeking to make a better world, will not permit the . . . forces of reaction to mask themselves forever behind the plea that it is necessary to keep her in ignorance to preserve her purity.

Margaret Sanger

The true order of learning should be: first, what is necessary; second, what is useful; and third, what is ornamental. To reverse this arrangement is like beginning to build at the top of the edifice.

Lydia H. Sigourney

Some days we play with clay.
Some days we don't.
I'd like to play with clay today.
But teacher says we won't.

Judy Lynn Stewart, grade 3

[There is] a social burden placed on schools by poverty, drug abuse, violence, and hopelessness. Troubled children carry the ills of their homes and neighborhoods into their classrooms every day. In too many parts of the United States, teachers must feed their students' bodies and souls before they can even begin to feed their minds.

Nan Stone

A person educated in mind and not in morals is a menace to society.

Juanita Kidd Stout

I never taught language for the purpose of teaching it; but invariably used language as a medium for the communication of thought; thus the learning of language was coincident with the acquisition of knowledge.

Annie Sullivan

I was raised in a small town called Critz [Virginia]. It was so small that our school taught Driver's Ed and Sex Ed in the same car.

Mary Sue Terry

I gaze with hope and pride and joy
Upon my graduating boy,
And know a sudden mute relief
As deep as love, as sharp as grief:
Sharing his victory today,
I graduate from PTA!

Eleanor Graham Vance

What you teach your own children is what you *really* believe in.

Cathy Warner Weatherford

The trouble about man is twofold. He cannot learn truths which are too complicated; he forgets truths which are too simple.

Dame Rebecca West

Genuine learning has ever been said to give polish to man; why then should it not bestow added charm on women?

Emma Hart Willard

Contending for the rights of women, my main argument is built on this simple principle, that if she be not prepared by education to become the companion of man, she will stop the progress of knowledge, for truth must be common to all, or it will be inefficacious with respect to its influence on general practice.

Mary Wollstonecraft

I hear and I forget. I see and I remember. I do and I understand.

Chinese proverb

To teach is to learn.

Japanese proverb

We, the willing, led by the unqualified, have been doing the unbelievable for so long with so little, we now attempt the impossible with nothing.

Teachers' Creed

Education is what you have left over after you have forgotten everything you've learned.

Anon.

Chapter *12*

ENTHUSIASM

You will do foolish things, but do them with enthusiasm.

Colette

❧

The best definition of Hell I ever heard was that it is "a place where nobody cares." A place, in other words, where there is no enthusiasm, because being enthusiastic *means* caring. A corollary to that definition is that the saddest people on earth are those who live their lives in neutral. A life that lacks enthusiasm—for something, for somebody—is truly an empty shell, a purposeless and pitiful existence.

As a speaker, perhaps the most empowering quality you can communicate to your listeners is to cause them to care. No matter what the topic or the audience, there is something to care about. It is the speaker's responsibility to stimulate and help the audience develop that act of caring.

The speaker is not charged with changing lives forever, although it would be nice if that were possible (but think of the *responsibility*!). If, however, for just fifteen or thirty minutes you can stimulate someone to generate enthusiasm, you have done something quite remarkable. What you have done is cause people to release energy. Energy is locked up inside everybody—well, almost everybody. Most of the time it is controlled, but sometimes it just sort of bursts forth. And when it does, groups and individuals are capable of doing unbelievable things.

Of course, this energy release, this enthusiasm generation, begins with you—the speaker. If you don't have it, your audience certainly won't. It is up to you to generate it for yourself and to communicate it to your listeners. If you lack it, your audience will know it and reflect it. You will be flat; your presentation will be dull; your audience will be bored. How can an audience be energized if their speaker's batteries are dead?

The Greek origin of the word *enthusiasm*—meaning *God within*—is a wonderful clue to the speaker about what it means to be enthusiastic. Without presuming to have divine qualities or to be necessarily theological about it, you may prefer to think of *God* as translating into *life*. Then it seems very natural that when someone radiates *life within* or *God within*, they are going to be able to do something and to inspire others to do something as well. And not only must you have this life-within that radiates out through your eyes, your expression, your movement, your voice, your words— you must demonstrate that you recognize this *life* in others, and that you want to elevate your listeners to your level of enthusiasm. Thus, quotations about enthusiasm are designed to help you to inspire, to arouse, to elevate, and to communicate life-within.

Various types of quotations about enthusiasm can be used to inspire action in a variety of ways. Some can stimulate *fear*: "Here's what will happen to you if you don't do something." Some are used to *negotiate* action: "Here's what can happen if you do something." Still better are the *positive motivator* quotations: "Here's what you can achieve if you do something."

Fear is obviously not a generator of true enthusiasm—action perhaps, but action done out of a fear of consequences and not as a caring act. However, quotations concerning this kind of motivation can be good attention getters and can be very useful in setting up more positive points or action.

Negotiation is somewhat more subtle. Sometimes quotations that illustrate the advantages of a certain action or way of thinking (if their author is appropriate to your audience), can be effective thought provokers that lead listeners to think about options or alternatives. These types of quotations are also helpful in the compare and contrast mode. (Here is what *X* said about this; here is what *Y* said about it.)

Positive motivation quotations from known, respected, admired persons validate your enthusiasm and motivate your listeners in ways that are most likely to pay the greatest dividends.

Enthusiasm is the antithesis of indifference. Enthusiasm reflects caring and begets action. To be caring, to be enthusiastic, to be passionate; one can't be around people with those qualities and not catch some of their spirit.

❧

You must learn day by day, year by year, to broaden your horizon. The more things you love, the more you are interested in, the more you enjoy, the more you are indignant about, the more you have left when anything happens.

Ethel Barrymore

You need to get up in the morning and say, "Boy, I'm going to—in my own stupid way—save the world today."

Carol Bellamy

The secret of getting ahead is getting started.

Sally Berger

The trouble with some women is that they get all excited about nothing—and then marry him.

Cher

Alas! How enthusiasm decreases, as our experience increases!

Louise Colet

Jump into the middle of things, get your hands dirty, fall flat on your face, and then reach for the stars.

Joan L. Curcio

It takes great passion and great energy to do anything creative, especially in the theater. You have to care so much that you can't sleep, you can't eat, you can't talk to people. It's just got to be right. You can't do it without that passion.

Agnes De Mille

The sense of this word among the Greeks affords the noblest definition of it; enthusiasm signifies "God in us."

Mme. de Staël

It seems to me we can never give up longing and wishing while we are thoroughly alive. There are certain things we feel to be beautiful and good, and we must hunger after them.

George Eliot

I think that in order to write really well and convincingly, one must be somewhat poisoned by emotion. Dislike, displeasure, resentment, faultfinding, imagination, passionate remonstrance, a sense of injustice—they all make fine fuel.

Edna Ferber

Just don't give up trying to do what you really want to do. Where there is love and inspiration, I don't think you can go wrong.

Ella Fitzgerald

I'm sick and tired of being sick and tired.

Fannie Lou Hamer

Even virtue itself, all perfect as it is, requires to be inspirited by passion; for duties are but coldly performed which are but philosophically fulfilled.

Anna Jameson

It is for us to pray not for tasks equal to our powers, but for powers equal to our tasks, to go forward with a great desire forever beating at the door of our hearts as we travel towards our distant goal.

Helen Keller

Love the moment, and the energy of that moment will spread beyond all boundaries.

Corita Kent

How disappointment tracks the steps of hope.

Letitia E. Landon

Nothing is interesting if you're not interested.

Helen MacInness

I've just been so interested in what I was doing [genetic research] that I never thought of stopping.

Barbara McClintock

Those who don't know how to weep with their whole heart, don't know how to laugh either.

Golda Meir

Everybody's mainspring is different. And I want to say this—folks whose mainsprings are busted are better dead.

Margaret Mitchell

I still want to do my work, I still want to do my livingness. And I have lived. I have been fulfilled. I recognized what I had, and I never sold it short. And I ain't through yet!

Louise Nevelson

There seems to be no physical handicap or chance of environment that can hold a real writer down, and there is no luck, no influence, no money that will keep a writer going when she is written out.

Kathleen Norris

The football season is like pain. You forget how terrible it is until it seizes you again.

Sally Quinn

If you approach each new person you meet in a spirit of adventure, you will find yourself endlessly fascinated by the new channels of thought and experience and personality that you encounter. I do not mean simply the famous people of the world, but people from every walk and condition of life.

Eleanor Roosevelt

I am not eccentric. It's just that I am more alive than most people. I am an unpopular electric eel set in a pond of goldfish.

Dame Edith Sitwell

Integrate what you believe into every single area of your life. Take your heart to work and ask the most and best of everybody else. Don't let your special character and values, the secret that you know and no one else does, the truth—don't let that get swallowed up by the great chewing complacency.

Meryl Streep

I found more joy in sorrow
Than you could find in joy.

Sara Teasdale

Every day's a kick!

Oprah Winfrey

Novels so often provide an anodyne and not an antidote, glide one into torpid slumbers instead of rousing one with a burning brand.

Virginia Woolf

Indifference never wrote great works, nor thought out striking inventions, nor reared the solemn architecture that awes the soul, nor breathed sublime music, nor painted glorious pictures, nor undertook heroic philanthropies. All these grandeurs are born of enthusiasm, and are done heartily.

Anon.

Chapter 13

EQUALITY

As long as you keep a person down, some part of you has to be down there to hold him down, so it means you cannot soar as you otherwise might.

Marian Anderson

❦

Over the last two decades, women have focused more and more, not just on the concept of EQUALITY, but on the *reality* of it as well. We have marched for it, struck for it, spoken for it; some have even incinerated underwear for it.

Through the efforts of women who have done some or all of these things, women have been able to come a great deal closer than ever before to share equally in the American Dream. Thus, through the women's movement, we are seeing a realization of something that ought to be inalienable, but which had to be worked and fought for. Gender equality probably will remain in this kind of "keep it if you can" status for some years to come. The same is true for the struggle for racial equality. Here, too, women have been in the front lines of the battle and here, too, the battle is not yet won.

As a speaker who is also a woman, it is important to always evidence both a philosophical and a practical commitment to the concept and the reality of equality, in all of its forms.

In so many circumstances, equality equates to expectations. If you believe a person to be your equal, respond to her that way, treat her that way, then you are demonstrating a set of expectations for that person. And in this, as in so many other areas of life, people will rise to our expectations of them.

Since this book is an assemblage of quotations by women, George Bernard Shaw obviously would not qualify for inclusion. However, one of his female characters, Eliza Doolittle in *Pygmalion*, expresses this concept with a beautiful economy of words.

Eliza, in describing her feelings to Colonel Pickering about expectations, said,

> *You see, really and truly, apart from the things anyone can pick up (the dressing and the proper way of speaking, and so on), the difference between a lady and a flower girl is not how she behaves, but how she's treated. I shall always be a flower girl to Professor Higgins, because he always treats me as a flower girl, and always will; but I know I can be a lady to you, because you always treat me as a lady, and always will.*

Eliza synthesized a great truth. Her observations could serve as a human relations guidepost for us all. They should also be a guidepost for every speaker about her attitude toward her audience.

When you are working before an audience, regardless of its size or composition, it is not so much *who* they are, as *how* you treat them, that will determine the impact and the outcome of your remarks.

Using quotations about equality serves to validate your ideas or the points you are working to make. They serve to offer a set of expectations of your listeners—that they, like you, will have noble expectations; that they, like you, will evidence a commitment to equality in their personal and organizational actions.

I don't consider these sorts of expectations or the use of quotations about equality to be in the nature of lecturing or preaching to an audience. (And, indeed, it is especially important that, as a speaker, you don't come across as judgmental or "holier than thou.")

Your challenge is twofold. First you must work to convey, by your own words and actions, your belief in racial and gender equality. Second, you must inspire your listeners to integrate equality into their own personal philosophies, as well as in the organizational culture in which they function. This can be just as true for a civic club or community organization as it is for a corporation or professional association. It is a matter of reality that every organization has, and reflects, a *culture*. Your responsibility is to help elevate that culture and the way it manifests itself in its attitudes and expectations.

The value of quotations about equality helps to confirm to your listeners the universality and the validity of your arguments. They help to demonstrate, through words both appropriate and timeless, that it isn't just you, the speaker, who is making this exhortation.

Quotations not only support your statements, they support you as well. Use them, build upon them by seeking out additional and contemporary citations that enliven your content. You will be a stronger speaker, and your listeners will gain from your strength.

❧

Our struggle today is not to have a female Einstein get appointed as an assistant professor. It is for a woman schlemiel to get as quickly promoted as a male schlemiel.

Bella Abzug

If particular care and attention is not paid to the ladies, we are determined to foment a rebellion, and will not hold ourselves bound by any laws in which we have no voice or representation.

Abigail Smith Adams

Men, their rights and nothing more; women, their rights and nothing less.

Susan B. Anthony

What a minority group wants is not the right to have geniuses among them, but the right to have fools and scoundrels without being condemned as a group.

Agnes Elizabeth Benedict

I leave you love. I leave you hope. I leave you the challenge of developing confidence in one another. I leave you respect for the use of power. I leave you faith. I leave you racial dignity.

Mary McLeod Bethune

Justice is better than Chivalry if we cannot have both.

Alice Stone Blackwell

We've got a generation now who were born with semiequality. They don't know how it was before, so they think, this isn't too bad. We're working. We have our attaché cases and our three-piece suits. I get very disgusted with the younger generation of women. We had a torch to pass, and they are just sitting there. They don't realize it can be taken away. Things are going to have to get worse before they join in fighting the battle.

Erma Bombeck

Race prejudice is not only a shadow over the colored—it is a shadow over all of us, and the shadow is darkest over those who feel it least and allow its evil effects to go on.

Pearl S. Buck

So I offer you today a new legend: the winner of the hoop race will be the first to realize her dream, not society's dream, her own personal dream. And who knows? Somewhere out in this audience may even be someone who will one day follow my footsteps, and preside over the White House as the president's spouse. I wish him well!

Barbara Bush
(Commencement address to Wellesley College)

Sir, I beseech you for all the loves that hath been between us and for the love of
God, let me have justice and right, take of me some pity and compassion, for I
am a poor woman and a stranger, born out of your dominion. (to Henry VIII at
divorce trial)

Catherine of Aragon

When you belong to a minority, you have to be *better* in order to have the right
to be *equal*.

Christiane Collange

There is more difference within the sexes than between them.

Dame Ivy Compton-Burnett

Prejudice squints when it looks, and lies when it talks.

Duchess de Abrantes

When an individual is kept in a situation of inferiority, the fact is that he does
become inferior.

Simone de Beauvoir

The coming of equal rights for women is the inevitable result of progress and
enlightenment.

Emma Smith Devoe

Ordinary life widens the horizon for men. Women are walled-in behind social
conventions.

Dame Emilia Dilke

It is all right for the lion and the lamb to lie down together if they are both asleep,
but if one of them begins to get active it is dangerous.

Crystal Eastman

Today, no one questions whether women are equal to men in ability and intelligence.

Julie Nixon Eisenhower

I'm not denyin' that women are foolish: God Almighty made 'em to match men.

George Eliot

Parliamentary institutions, with their free speech and respects for the rights of
minorities, and the inspiration of a broad tolerance in thought and its expression—
all this we conceive to be a precious part of our way of life and outlook. . . . I ask
you now to cherish them and to practice them, too.

Queen Elizabeth II

I think that implicit in the women's movement is the idea that women will share in the economic burden, and men will share more equally in the home and the family.

Betty Friedan

The women who do the most work get the least money, and the women who have the most money do the least work.

Charlotte Perkins Gilman

Years ago, during a wave of crimes against women in Israel, a council of men asked Golda Meir to put a nighttime curfew on females. Meir said no. If men were the problem, she answered, let the council enforce a curfew against men.

Ellen Goodman

I ask no favors for my sex. I surrender not our claim to equality. All I ask of our brethren is that they will take their feet from off our necks, and permit us to stand upright on the ground which God has designed us to occupy.

Sarah Grimké

Move from the quicksand of injustice to the solid rock of human dignity.

Dorothy Haight

The generality of the male sex cannot yet tolerate the idea of living with an equal.

Gertrude Himmelfarb

I've never felt that I was held back because I was a woman. That doesn't mean that everyone has had this experience—in some ways I simply lucked out.

Brig. Gen. Jeanne M. Holm

God would not give us the same talents if what were right for men were wrong for women.

Sarah Orne Jewett

I became a feminist as an alternative to becoming a masochist.

Sally Kempton

Segregation was wrong when it was forced by white people, and I believe it is still wrong when it is requested by black people.

Coretta Scott King

I do believe that there still may be some special sort of resentment of women in high politics in this country. I think that some of the attacks on me have been motivated not only by politics, but also by that special resentment of women.

Jeane Kirkpatrick

Excellence in education need not mean elitism, and equity need not mean mediocrity.

Mary Jean LeTendre

Whether women are better than men I cannot say—but I can say they are certainly no worse.

Golda Meir

When men are oppressed, it's tragedy. When women are oppressed, it's tradition.

Bernadette Mosala

Man cannot fulfill his destiny alone, he cannot redeem his race unaided . . . The world has never yet seen a truly great and virtuous nation, because in the degradation of woman the very fountains of life are poisoned at their source.

Lucretia Mott

Education levels the playing field, allowing everyone to compete.

Joyce A. Myers

Let us challenge one another to govern with passion, to govern with zeal, and to govern with a sense of righteousness—but always mindful that we must govern with respect and reverence for our differences.

Dawn Clark Netsch

The miracle is, in fact, that given the overwhelming odds against women, or blacks, that so many of both have managed to achieve so much sheer excellence, in those bailiwicks of white masculine prerogatives like science, politics or the arts.

Linda Nochlin

No man should be judged by the irrational criteria of race, religion, or national origin. And I assure you I use the word "man" in the generic sense, for the principle of nondiscrimination must be a reality for women as well.

Eleanor Holmes Norton

An attorney addressing the Supreme Court: "I would like to remind you gentlemen of a legal point." Justice O'Connor: "Would you like to remind me, too?"

Sandra Day O'Connor

When Harvard men say they have graduated from Radcliffe, then we've made it.

Jacqueline Kennedy Onassis

All races need to learn to communicate with each other and a good way to start is with a smile and a blessing. It is important to understand each other's customs so that neither are blamed mistakenly.

Princess Pale Moon

As long as women consent to be unjustly governed, they will be; but directly women say: "We withhold our consent," we will not be governed any longer as long as government is unjust. Not by the forces of civil war can you govern the very weakest woman. You can kill that woman, but she escapes you then; you cannot govern her.

Emmeline Pankhurst

I will feel equality has arrived when we can elect to office women who are as incompetent as some of the men who are already there.

Maureen Reagan

What is enough? Enough is when somebody says, "Get me the best people you can find" and nobody notices when half of them turn out to be women.

Louise Renne

I believe we will have better government when men and women discuss public issues together and make their decisions on the basis of their differing areas of concern for the welfare of their families and their world. Too often the great decisions are originated and given form in bodies made up wholly of men or so completely dominated by them that whatever of special value women have to offer is shunted aside without expression.

Eleanor Roosevelt

It occurred to me when I was thirteen and wearing white gloves and Mary Janes and going to dancing school, that no one should have to dance backward all their lives.

Jill Ruckelshaus

Believe in no other God than the one who insists on justice and equality among men.

George Sand

The cry of the ghetto is being heard by a nation with its fingers in its ears.
Barbara Sizemore

The queens in history compare favorably with the kings.
Elizabeth Cady Stanton

Your little child is your only true democrat.
Harriet Beecher Stowe

One of the things about equality is not just that you be treated equally to a man, but that you treat yourself equally to the way you treat a man.
Marlo Thomas

Strong prejudices in an ill-formed mind are hazardous to government, and when combined with a position of power even more so.
Barbara Tuchman

As long as one black American survives, the struggle for equality with other Americans must also survive. This is a debt we owe to those blameless hostages we leave to the future, our children.
Alice Walker

Remember, Ginger Rogers did everything Fred Astaire did, but she did it backwards and in high heels.
Faith Whittlesey

I do not wish women to have power over men; but over themselves.
Mary Wollstonecraft

Men are taught to apologize for their weaknesses, women for their strengths.
Lois Wyse

Chapter 14

EXAMPLE

There is a transcendent power in example. We reform others unconsciously, when we walk uprightly.

Anne Sophie Swetchine

❧

Quotations on the subject of EXAMPLE are, like quotations on ATTITUDE or ACTION, what I call *empowering* quotations. They are a challenge to the speaker because whenever you stand up to speak—regardless of time, place, audience, or subject—you are an example of something to somebody.

Thoughts about example can be challenging for an audience, as well, because if you as the speaker are doing your job, you will cause your listeners to realize that they also serve as examples.

The challenge of being an example is doubled for the woman speaker. Whenever a woman stands up and opens her mouth, she is compared, analyzed, evaluated—often harshly. In similar circumstances, men are allowed to stumble, stammer, and generally be less than sterling, yet that individual man is not looked upon as being representative of the entire sex—as women are. The empowerment of women has not yet reached that stage of maturity.

Why is this? I attribute a great deal of it to the fact that women have arrived more recently to the platform, and even more recently to the boardroom or the committee chair, particularly in terms of meaningful numbers. Therefore, we women presenters are still somewhat of a curiosity, and perhaps judged on a higher level of expectation. A minority or handicapped woman who speaks has to jump through two hoops.

So the reality of being an example, inherent in every speaker, is multiplied for the woman speaker. It follows, then, that the woman presenter who is out front on the dais or platform must be an even better example than her male counterpart. (Does this sound familiar?) And she must understand and accept her role, willingly or not, as an example not just to, but *of*, other women.

During presentations, I frequently tell those in the audience what they often find difficult to understand—that they are, for whatever combination of reasons, examples; that somebody is going to copy them, emulate them, follow them. It may be because of who they are or what they have done, or even how they look or who they know. But everybody is somebody's ideal, role model, symbol, example—or counter-example.

Therefore, as presenters, we must recognize that from the moment we stand up, we become examples, good or bad, and we must help our listeners understand that the same thing is true of them.

It is incumbent upon the speaker to realize that she must serve as a *good* example. This is not always the case. Whether from lack of preparation, failure to properly understand the mission or the audience, or all around bad timing, a speaker sometimes serves as a *bad* example. Rest assured, you will be either one or the other. Make sure that you don't demonstrate the truth of my grandmother's old saying, "Everybody has a purpose in life, even if it is to serve as a bad example."

One of your tasks is to help your listeners understand that the choice to be a good example or a bad example is theirs alone. In working to meet this responsibility, a speaker can exhort, demand, encourage, wheedle, threaten, or beg her audience to be that good example.

In this endeavor, nothing is as effective as a salient quotation demonstrating the value and power of example. As individuals, our words and actions serve as examples. As a speaker, choose those words so that you are both the ideal and the instrument, the thought and the deed, that inspires your listeners.

No matter what the subject, for your various arguments to penetrate you must use examples. Illustrations work well, as do brief stories. A well-chosen quotation will fasten your point upon the listener's mind. And after the content has been long forgotten, your story and *you* will be remembered.

❧

EXAMPLE 105

Aerodynamically the bumblebee shouldn't be able to fly, but the bumblebee doesn't know it so it goes on flying anyway.

Mary Kay Ash

I will not go to bed just because my husband is sleepy and has to get up early the next morning.

Erma Bombeck

If we had no winter, the spring would not be so pleasant; if we did not sometimes taste of adversity, prosperity would not be so welcome.

Anne Bradstreet

To be one woman, truly, wholly, is to be all women. Tend one garden and you will birth worlds.

Kate Braverman

It's not what you do once in awhile,
It's what you do day in and day out
That makes the difference.

Jenny Craig

It's frightening to think that you mark your children merely by being yourself. It seems unfair. You can't assume the responsibility for everything you do—or don't do.

Simone de Beauvoir

I want to do it because I want to do it. Women must try to do things as men have tried. When they fail, their failure must be but a challenge to others.

Amelia Earhart

"One soweth and another reapeth" is a verity that applies to evil as well as good.

George Eliot

Telling lies and showing off to get attention are the mistakes I made that I don't want my kids to make.

Jane Fonda

If you have knowledge, let others light their candles at it.

Margaret Fuller

The subjective actress thinks of clothes only as they apply to her; the objective actress thinks of them only as they affect others, as a tool for the job.

Edith Head

My father was often angry when I was most like him.

Lillian Hellman

With increased opportunity comes increased stress. The stress comes from multiple conflicting demands and very little in the way of role models.

Madeleine Hemmings

Lord, who am I to teach the way
To little children day by day,
So prone myself to go astray?

Leslie Pinckney Hill

One of the surest signs of the Philistine is his reverence for the superior tastes of those who put him down.

Pauline Kael

Lawmakers-to-come will find that their predecessors were never as bad or wholly as good as their mixed notices. But if they want to profit from what has gone before, the record will be here for the listening.

Edna Kelly

Thriftiness is a famous Yankee virtue and I suppose I would have acquired it, to some extent, just from living in the Boston-Concord region, but my mother's example was probably decisive. This was a principle I tried to instill in my own children.

Rose Fitzgerald Kennedy

We have to preach what winners practice.

Mary Jean LeTendre

I feel we are all islands—in a common sea.

Anne Morrow Lindberg

My candle burns at both ends;
It will not last the night;
But ah, my foes, and oh, my friends—
It gives a lovely light!

Edna St. Vincent Millay

I have never quite understood this sex symbol business, but if I'm going to be a symbol of something, I'd rather have it sex than some of the other things they've got symbols for.

Marilyn Monroe

EXAMPLE   107

To love one that is great is almost to be great one's self.

Susanne Curchod Necker

When I was little a friend had a dog, a mutt, who was pregnant and due to have her puppies in a week or so. The dog was playing out in the yard one day and got in the way of the lawn mower and her two hind legs got cut off. She was rushed to the vet who sewed her up, and in a short time the dog learned to walk again. She didn't spend any time worrying, she just learned to walk by taking two steps in the front and flipping up her backside and taking two steps and flipping up her backside again. Soon she gave birth to six little puppies, all in perfect health. She nursed them and then weaned them. And when they learned to walk, they all walked just like her.

Gilda Radner

Instead of taking sides with one group of nations against another, the United States, by its example, should help men and women in every country to abolish war and build democracy.

Jeannette Rankin

When you talk to young girls these days about their role models, very few mention a chemist like Madame Curie, or an astrophysicist and astronaut like Sally Ride, or a zoologist like Jane Goodall. Instead, they look to someone like Madonna, whose inspiring achievement in life is to parade around in her underwear while proclaiming herself to be a "material girl." *And people wonder why the country's in trouble.*

Wynetka Ann Reynolds

It is always disagreeable to take stands. It is always easier to compromise, always easier to let things go. To many women, and I am one of them, it is extraordinarily difficult to care about anything enough to cause disagreement or unpleasant feelings, but I have come to the conclusion that this must be done for a time until we can prove our strength and demand respect for our wishes. We cannot even be of real service in this country and speak as a united body of women unless we have the respect of the men and show that when we express a wish, we are willing to stand by it.

Eleanor Roosevelt

Mankind has advanced in the footsteps of men and women of unshakable faith. Many of the great ones . . . have set stars in the heavens to light others through the night.

Olga Rosmanith

Woman is the peg on which the wit hangs his jest, the preacher his text, the cynic his grouch, and the sinner his justification.

Helen Rowland

Whatever you would have your children become, strive to exhibit in your own lives and conversation.

Lydia H. Sigourney

My career has expended me enormously intellectually. I've become more generous with myself and my time because I appreciate people who are generous with me. I find myself for the first time acting as a role model for people, a mentor.

Carole Sinclair

People who fight fire with fire usually end up with ashes.

Abigail Van Buren

I've always believed that one woman's success can only help another woman's success.

Gloria Vanderbilt

There are two ways of spreading light—to be the candle or the mirror that reflects it.

Edith Wharton

It is easy to sit in the sunshine
   And talk to the man in the shade;
It is easy to float on a well-trimmed boat,
   And point out the places to wade.

Ella Wheeler Wilcox

Once conform, once do what other people do because they do it, and a lethargy steals over all the finer nerves and faculties of the soul. She becomes all outer show and inward emptiness; dull, callous, and indifferent.

Virginia Woolf

Live with wolves, and you learn to howl.

Spanish proverb

Children may close their ears to advice, but open their eyes to example.

Anon.

Chapter **15**

FAITH

Faith and doubt both are needed—not as antagonists, but working side by side—to take us around the unknown curve.

Lillian Smith

❦

One of my favorite authors begins a best-selling book with the words, "Life is difficult." And we all know that speaking in public is difficult. But making a speech is like living a life—you have to have FAITH in order to get through them both. And, conversely, if you are consumed by fear, both can be terrifying.

Faith has been described as beginning with a leap into the unknown. I believe this is true. I also believe that the antithesis of faith—fear—is like a leap into a terrible, anticipated _known_.

As a speaker, if you are afraid of failure you will most likely fail because you are not making a leap into an unknown, but assumed, place of success. Rather, you are making a knee-trembling leap into an expected condition of failure.

I am convinced that the difference between the ultimate outcome of those two leaps is the degree to which you can generate a feeling of faith—in yourself, in your principles, in your message.

My personal faith and my inner sense of empowerment come from a belief that there is a higher power that validates who I am and confirms my worth as a human being. This is my affirmation, and it _enables_ me. It allows me to accept the difficulties of life as simply being a series of overcomable hazards, as challenges to be met and cleared—and not as impenetrable barriers.

You, the speaker, must have your own reservoir of faith that can be reflected and communicated to your listeners. That is why you use quotations about faith—to validate your conviction in your own abilities and to confirm the audience's belief in their abilities.

When we think of faith and when we express it in our remarks, we must remember that our listeners are a diverse group with a common purpose—even if that common purpose is no more elevated than deciding upon how to raise money for a Fourth of July pageant. It is the speaker's job to help that group develop, maintain, and communicate their faith that they will accomplish their task. Just as faith enables you, the speaker, you must help your listeners generate their own enabling power.

The power of words to motivate others is almost miraculous. As a speaker, you must strive to be the bearer of the motivating power of faith. You can give your listeners no greater gift.

As a speaker you must feel from the beginning that you are fully capable of delivering a message. Someone else was certain of it or they would not have invited you. A strong belief that you can and will succeed is a speaker's best insurance policy, and the affirmation of faith without which no person can succeed.

❦

I don't think that the events of my life are preordained, but they're definitely guided. I *hope* they're guided because I'd have a [heck] of a time trying to figure it out all by myself!

Joan Baez

Superstition is but the fear of belief; religion is the confidence.

Lady Marguerite Blessington

I feel no need for any other faith than my faith in human beings.

Pearl S. Buck

There is no unbelief;
Whoever plants a seed beneath the sod
And waits to see it push away the clod,
He trusts in God.

Elizabeth York Case

Yes, my voices were of God; my voices have not deceived me.

Jeanne d'Arc

You prove but too clearly, that seeking to know is too frequently learning to doubt.

Antoinette Deshoulières

Faith is a fine invention
When gentlemen can see,
But microscopes are prudent
In an emergency.

Emily Dickinson

One step ahead is all I now can see,
But He who notes the sparrow's fall, He leadeth me.
Not only by the waters still my feet may tread,
But with my hand in His, I know that I am led.
And for the lonely, rocky way, whate'er the length,
He hath shod my feet with patience and with strength.
So, though the pathway smooth or rough may be,
Oh, joyful thought, my Father leadeth me!

Ella B. Doxsee

The prayer that reforms the sinner and heals the sick is an absolute faith that all things are possible to God.

Mary Baker Eddy

No, I don't understand my husband's theory of relativity, but I know my husband and I know he can be trusted.

Elsa Einstein

No soul is desolate as long as there is a human being for whom it can feel trust and reverence.

George Eliot

Spirituality is a kind of virgin wisdom, a knowing that comes prior to experience.

Marilyn Ferguson

Doubt is hell in the human soul.

Comtesse Catherine de Gasparin

And I said to the man who stood at the gate of the year, "Give me a light that I may tread safely into the unknown." And he replied, "Go out into the darkness and put your hand into the hand of God. That shall be to you better than light and safer than a known way."

Louise Haskins

Yes, I have doubted. I have wandered off the path. I have been lost. But I always returned. It is beyond the logic I seek. It is intuitive—an intrinsic, built-in sense of direction. I seem to find my way home. My faith has wavered but has saved me.

Helen Hayes

I pray hard, work hard and leave the rest to God.

Florence Griffith Joyner

Better trust all and be deceived,
And weep that trust, and that deceiving,
Nonviolence is a spiritual weapon that can do what guns and armies only pretend to do—it can truly defend us.

Petra K. Kelly

Than doubt one heart that, if believed,
Had blessed one's life with true believing.

Fanny Kemble

I share Einstein's affirmation that anyone who is not lost on the rapturous awe at the power and glory of the mind behind the universe "is as good as a burnt out candle."

Madeleine L'Engle

Getting ahead in a difficult profession requires avid faith in yourself. That is why some people with mediocre talent, but with great inner drive, go much further than people with vastly superior talent.

Sophia Loren

Not Truth, but Faith it is that keeps the world alive.

Edna St. Vincent Millay

If faith produce no works, I see
That faith is not a living tree.
Thus faith and works together grow;
No separate life they o'er can know;
They're soul and body, hand and heart:
What God hath joined, let no man part.

Hannah More

The only way to meet affliction is to pass through it solemnly, slowly, with humility and faith, as the Israelites passed through the sea. Then its very waves of misery will divide, and become to us a wall, on the right side and on the left, until the gulf narrows before our eyes, and we land safe on the opposite shore.

Dinah Maria Mulock

No one can go it alone. Somewhere along the way is the person who gives you that job, who has faith that you can make it. And everyone has something to work with, if only he will look for it.

Grace Gil Olivarez

Trust in God: She will provide.

Emmeline Pankhurst

The only known cure for fear is faith.

Lena Kellogg Sadler

Let nothing disturb you. Let nothing frighten you. Everything passes away except God.

St. Theresa of Jesus

Faith is an excitement and an enthusiasm; it is a condition of intellectual magnificence to which we must cling as to a treasure and not squander in . . . priggish argument.

George Sand

We are not human beings trying to be spiritual. We are spiritual beings trying to be human.

Jacquelyn Small

Faith is the subtle chain
  Which binds us to the infinite; the voice
Of deep life within, that will remain
  Until we crowd it thence.

Elizabeth Oakes Smith

This I do believe above all, especially in my times of greater discouragement, that I must believe—that I must believe in my fellow men—that I must believe in myself—and I must believe in God—if life is to have any meaning.

Margaret Chase Smith

I would not attack the faith of a heathen without being sure I had a better one to put in its place.

Harriet Beecher Stowe

One by one, like leaves from a tree,
All my faiths have forsaken me.

Sara Teasdale

Fear is faith that it won't work out.

Sister Mary Tricky

Nature has created us with the capacity to know God, to experience God.

Alice Walker

The world has a thousand creeds, and never a one have I;
Nor a church of my own, though a thousand spires are
  pointing the way on high.
But I float on the bosom of faith, that bears me along like
  a river;
And the lamp of my soul is alight with love for life,
  and the world, and the Giver.

Ella Wheeler Wilcox

Chapter 16

FAMILY

No matter how many communes anybody invents, the family always creeps back.

Margaret Mead

❦

No compilation of quotations is complete without quotations about FAMILY. What to some might seem a rather restricted, or restrictive, category is, to me, one of the most expansive.

I suppose it depends upon how you define *family*. I see it, and use it in this chapter, in its most encompassing sense: the family of man, the family of nations, the family of belief, the family of occupations, the family of friends and loved ones, and, of course, the family that comprises our unique roots and heritage.

I see all the various families as transmitting a sense of identity, of belonging, of kinship. Family celebrates diversity as well as commonality. Family implies a support base as well as a multifaceted prism of identities.

For some given period of time, an audience is a family of sorts. At least during the time you are before them, they are gathered together for a common purpose of interest. They are focused not just on you as their speaker, but on the umbrella organization or intent for which they have assembled.

Your responsibility as a speaker is to help this disparate group of individuals fulfill some set of goals or desires. You can help them think as a family and work together to achieve these goals.

One of the greatest causes of organizational failure today is that sense of un-connectedness, of detachment, of aloneness, of anonymity. Some define it as alienation, but however you characterize it, it is symptomatic of widespread societal needs.

What is remarkable is that often a speaker, regardless of her experience or gifts of persuasion, can utter a set of words or thoughts that may cause a group of unconnected people to gain the sense of belonging or encouragement that will turn indifference into action.

Thus, as unlikely as it may seem, I consider quotations about family to be, in their own way, as *empowering* as quotations about ACTION, or CHANGE, or CHOICE.

A shared concept of family, if only for a single project or activity, can be a powerful motivator for restoration of individual spirits. The reality of a common family of beliefs can weld together a group that has little else in common.

When a speaker helps a group of people see themselves as a family, she puts into action the principle that the whole is greater than its parts. She strengthens the individuals who hear her; she empowers them to do something perhaps over and above their individual abilities to do *anything*.

Some of the quotations in this chapter are intended to elaborate upon this holistic concept of family. I encourage the reader to seek out and develop her own collection of quotations that will enable her to communicate her own concepts and sense of family. They will be as empowering to her as their transmission will be to the audience.

Do not put such unlimited power into the hands of the husbands. Remember, all men would be tyrants if they could.

Abigail Smith Adams

My 10-year daughter is my #1 power source.

Hanan Mikhail Ashrawi

For it is impossible for a man to put forward fair and honest views about our affairs if he has not, like everyone else, children whose lives may be at stake.

Asphasia
(from speech given by Pericles, written by Asphasia)

You see much more of your children once they leave home.

Lucille Ball

The most effective form of birth control I know is spending the day with my kids.

Jill Bensley

Don't turn a small problem into a big problem—say yes to your mother.

Sally Berger

I'm going to stop punishing my children by saying, "Never mind! I'll do it myself."

Erma Bombeck

I love people. I love my family, my children . . . but inside myself is a place where I live all alone and that's where you renew your springs that never dry up.

Pearl S. Buck

It is not a bad thing that children should occasionally, and politely, put parents in their place.

Colette

The secret of having a personal life is not answering too many questions about it.

Joan Collins

The pedigree of honey
Does not concern the bee;
A clover, any time, to him
Is aristocracy.

Emily Dickinson

Cleaning your house while your kids are still growing is like shoveling the walk before it stops snowing.

Phyllis Diller

The family is the nucleus of civilization.

Ariel and Will Durant

To most men their early home is no more than a memory of their early years. The image is never marred. There's no disappointment in memory, and one's exaggerations are always on the good side.

George Eliot

A mother is not a person to lean on but a person to make leaning unnecessary.

Dorothy Canfield Fisher

It's always been my feeling that God lends you your children until they're about eighteen years old. If you haven't made your points with them by then, it's too late.

Betty Ford

A woman can do *anything*, but not *everything*. Consequently, the wise woman shares the tasks and the credit, if any, with family, friends, and colleagues.

June E. Gabler

Hard indeed, in a world which has come to feel that it is more important to have an automobile to get away from the home with, than to have a home which you might like to stay in.

Katherine Fullerton Gerould

[There is a] peculiar American utopianism that refuses to see the need for family authority, for the realistic socialization of children, and for the deliberate passing down of value systems from generation to generation.

Georgie Ann Geyer

My father dealt in stocks and shares and my mother also had a lot of time on her hands.

Hermione Gingold

There wouldn't be half as much fun in the world if it weren't for children and men, and there ain't a mite of difference between them under the skins.

Ellen Glasgow

We need not power or splendor,
Wide hall or lordly dome;
The good, the true, the tender,
These form the wealth of home.

Sarah J. Hale

Make a memory with your children,
Spend some time to show you care;
Toys and trinkets can't replace those
Precious moments that you share.

Elaine Hardt

Before you were conceived I wanted you
Before you were born I loved you
Before you were here an hour I would die for you
This is the miracle of life.

Maureen Hawkins

Babies don't need fathers, but mothers do. Someone who is taking care of a baby
needs to be taken care of.

Amy Heckerling

Mama seemed to do only what my father wanted, and yet we lived the way my
mother wanted us to live.

Lillian Hellman

There is in all this cold and hollow world
No fount of deep, strong, deathless love;
Save that within a mother's heart.

Felicia Hemans

God sent children for another purpose than merely to keep up the race—to
enlarge our hearts; and to make us unselfish and full of kindly sympathies and
affections; to give our souls higher aims; to call out all our faculties to extended
enterprise and exertion; and to bring round our firesides bright faces, happy
smiles, and loving, tender hearts.

Mary Botham Howitt

There would have to be something wrong with someone who could throw out
a child's first Valentine card saying, "I love you, Mommy."

Ginger Hutton

A mother is a person who seeing there are only four pieces of pie for five people, promptly announces she never did care for pie.

Tenneva Jordan

For any normal woman in normal circumstances there is bound to be a special excitement and joy and gratitude to God when she holds her first baby in her arms.

Rose Fitzgerald Kennedy

There is this to be said about little children: they keep you feeling old.

Jean Kerr

The only thing that seems eternal and natural in motherhood is ambivalence.

Jane Lazarre

Likely as not, the child you can do least with will do the most to make you proud.

Mignon McLaughlin

No matter how old a mother is she watches her middle-aged children for signs of improvement.

Florida Scott Maxwell

At work, you think of the children you have left at home. At home, you think of the work you've left unfinished. Such a struggle is unleashed within yourself. Your heart is rent.

Golda Meir

Some have predicted that by the year 2000, all the poor will be women and children. There is a sizable list of reasons for this, which include lack of child support payments, teenage pregnancy, the divorce rate, and the impact of a growing acceptance of single motherhood.

Nancy M. Neuman

If a child lives with criticism,
He learns to condemn.
If a child lives with hostility,
He learns to fight.
If a child lives with ridicule,
He learns to be shy.
If a child lives with shame,
He learns to feel guilty.
If a child lives with tolerance,

He learns to be patient.
If a child lives with encouragement,
He learns confidence.
If a child lives with praise,
He learns to appreciate.
If a child lives with fairness,
He learns justice.
If a child lives with security,
He learns to have faith.
If a child lives with approval,
He learns to like himself.
If a child lives with acceptance and friendship,
He learns to find love in the world.

Dorothy L. Nolte

Of all the joys that lighten suffering earth, what joy is welcomed like a new-born child?

Caroline Norton

Having family responsibilities and concerns just has to make you a more understanding person.

Sandra Day O'Connor

If you bungle raising your children, I don't think whatever else you do well matters very much.

Jacqueline Kennedy Onassis

The best way to keep children home is to make the home atmosphere pleasant— and let the air out of the tires.

Dorothy Parker

In the career of female fame, there are few prizes to be attained which can vie with the obscure state of a beloved wife, or a happy mother.

Jane Porter

That's the thing the kids don't understand [about marriage] . . . It's not just a man. It's your house, your kids, your family, your time, everything. Everything in your life is who you marry.

Anna Quindlen

Oh, to be only half as wonderful as my child thought I was when he was small, and only half as stupid as my teen-ager now thinks I am.

Rebecca Richards

I said to my mother-in-law, "My house is your house."
She said, "Get the hell off my property!"

Joan Rivers

For there is no friend like a sister
In calm or stormy weather;
To cheer one on the tedious way,
To fetch one if one goes astray,
To lift one if one totters down,
To strengthen whilst one stands.

Christina Rossetti

We want better reasons for having children than not knowing how to prevent them.

Dora Russell

Intreat me not to leave thee, or to return from following after thee; for whither thou goest, I will go; and where thou lodgest, I will lodge: thy people shall be my people, and thy God my God: Where thou diest, will I die, and there will I be buried: the Lord do so to me, and more also, if ought but death part thee and me.

The Bible, Ruth 1:16,17

The strength of a nation, especially of a republican nation, is in the intelligent and well-ordered homes of the people.

Lydia H. Sigourney

Miserable people cannot afford to dislike each other. Cruel blows of fate call for extreme kindness in the family circle.

Dodie Smith

Children require guidance and sympathy far more than instruction.

Annie Sullivan

We didn't have much, but we sure had plenty.

Sherry Thomas

Even my mother didn't like me all the time, but she let me come home anyway.

Ann McKay Thompson and Marcia Mitchell

No man is responsible for his father, that is entirely his mother's affair.

Margaret Turnbull

And so our mothers and grandmothers have, more often than not anonymously, handed on the creative spark, the seed of the flower they themselves never hoped to see—or like a sealed letter they could not plainly read.

Alice Walker

A man in the house is worth two in the street.

Mae West

Every child born into the world is a new thought of God, an ever fresh and radiant possibility.

Kate Douglas Wiggin

We flatter those we scarcely know,
We please the fleeting guest,
And deal full many a thoughtless blow
To those who love us best.

Ella Wheeler Wilcox

The absurd duty, too often inculcated, of obeying a parent only on account of his being a parent, shackles the mind and prepares it for a slavish submission to any power but reason.

Mary Wollstonecraft

God could not be everywhere and therefore he made mothers.

Jewish proverb

No one can say of his house, "There is no Trouble here."

Oriental proverb

The Universal Declaration of Human Rights describes the family as the natural and fundamental unit of society. It follows that any choice and decision with regard to the size of the family must irrevocably rest with the family itself and cannot be made by anyone else.

United Nations

Chapter 17

FREEDOM

When the freedom they wished for most was freedom from responsibility, then Athens ceased to be free and was never free again.

Edith Hamilton

❧

To be a captive, without control over one's life, decisions, or future surely must be the most dehumanizing and demoralizing of conditions.

One can be a captive in the figurative as well as the literal sense. And it is the primary responsibility of the skilled speaker to provide words, examples, ideas, and concepts, that are at least figuratively liberating.

The unpleasant fact in so many peoples' lives is that they are captives of their own concepts. They think themselves limited, or un-able, and so they are. They find themselves unable to organize, to plan, to strategize, to anticipate, and thus become captives to the intentions or actions of others. They *re-act* rather than *act*.

Because so many people find themselves in this condition, the speaker has a great opportunity to serve as a freedom-bearing force. She can help people conceptualize thinking, working, and living in an atmosphere of true freedom.

When you help your audience face up to and think through the freedom-denying circumstances in their lives and work, you may be in a better freedom-delivering position even than someone they live or work with every day. The speaker has, for that moment, the power of the platform, and from it, can help people come to realizations they might never have come to on their own. What a wonderful opportunity this is for you.

A related opportunity that comes from being a speaker is that once you are on that platform you are absolutely free to say almost anything! This kind of freedom carries with it, of course, attendant responsibility because this freedom costs a dear price to acquire and retain. Therefore, as a speaker, you must approach your presentation with the certain knowledge that you will use your freedom of speech wisely.

Don't ever forget that the freedom to speak is the license to destroy. You are free to diminish, to demean, to depress. You are equally free to uplift, to teach, to encourage. The choices are yours, but it is your audience that inherits the results.

Because you have this power, this *empowerment*, you must internalize this sense of responsibility both for yourself and for your listeners. You must use it to convey a sense of respect for those listeners, a sense that you are both aware and appreciative of the power inherent in you as a speaker and in your audience, and in that bond of power between you.

Those women who authored quotations about freedom in all of its manifestations are women who realize the power of that prize. Many of these words are from women who had to pay a great price to obtain freedom; some are from women who never obtained it, but who understood its value nevertheless.

When you use quotations by women about freedom, realize that these are powerful validators for the points you wish to make. Therefore, use them wisely and well.

ॐ

It was we, the people; not we, the white male citizens; nor yet we, the male citizens; but we, the whole people, who formed the Union.

Susan B. Anthony

What can be heavier in wealth than freedom?

Sylvia Ashton-Warner

Free men freely work: whoever fears God, fears to sit at ease.

Elizabeth Barrett Browning

We are unalterably opposed to the presentation of the female body being stripped, bound, raped, tortured, mutilated, and murdered in the name of commercial entertainment and free speech.

Susan Brownmiller

None who have always been free can understand the terrible fascinating power of the hope of freedom to those who are not free.

Pearl S. Buck

There is nothing more liberating than age.

Liz Carpenter

There are days when solitude is a heady wine that intoxicates you with freedom, others when it is a bitter tonic, and still others when it is a poison that makes you beat your head against the wall.

Colette

Liberty! It is for noble minds, who despise death, and who know how upon occasion to give it to themselves. It is not for those weak beings who enter in composition with guilt, who cover their selfishness with the name of prudence. . . . It is for wise people who delight in humanity, praise justice, despise their flatterers, and respect the truth. As long as you are not such a people, O my fellow citizens, you will talk in vain of liberty.
O liberty, how many crimes are committed in thy name!
O liberty! How they have played with you. (last words before the guillotine)

Mme. de la Platiere

We lost the American Colonies because we lacked that statesmanship "to know the right time, and the manner of yielding what is impossible to keep."
Queen Elizabeth II

It is difficult for power to avoid despotism. The possessors of rude health—the characters never strained by a doubt—the minds that no questions disturb and no aspirations put out of breath—there, the strong, are also the tyrants.
Comtesse Catherine de Gasparin

The world is full of lonely people, all isolated in a private, secret dungeon.
Loretta Girzartis

The strongest bulwark of authority is uniformity; the least divergence from it is the greatest crime.
Emma Goldman

I will not get into anything where it will not be possible for me to be a free agent.
Edith Starrett Green

It is easy to be independent when you've got money. But to be independent when you haven't got a thing—that's the Lord's test.
Mahalia Jackson

All government and exercise of power, no matter in what form, which is not based on love, and directed by knowledge, is tyranny.
Anna Jameson

No nation is wise enough to rule another.
Helen Keller

Power over must be replaced by *shared power*, by the power to do things, by the discovery of our own strength as opposed to a passive receiving of power exercised by others, often in our name.
Petra K. Kelly

Free choice is the greatest gift God gives to his children.
Elisabeth Kübler-Ross

We are, each of us, our own prisoner. We are locked up in our own story.
Maxine Kumin

To move freely you must be deeply rooted.

Bella Lewitzky

But total freedom is never what one imagines and, in fact, hardly exists. It comes as a shock in life to learn that we usually only exchange one set of restrictions for another. The second set, however, is self-chosen, and therefore easier to accept.

Anne Morrow Lindbergh

Censorship, like charity, should begin at home; but, unlike charity, it should end there.

Clare Boothe Luce

Freedom for supporters of the government only, for the members of one party only—no matter how big its membership may be—is no freedom at all. Freedom means there is freedom for the man who thinks differently.

Rosa Luxemburg

The human animal needs a freedom seldom mentioned; freedom from intrusion. He needs a little privacy.

Phyllis McGinley

Men who use terrorism as a means to power, rule by terror once they are in power.

Helen MacInnes

What are people for? What is living for? If the answer is a life of dignity, decency, and opportunity, then every increase in population means a decrease in all three. The crowd is a threat to every single being. . . . People minus space equals poverty.

Marya Mannes

Let us forget such words, and all they mean, as Hatred, Bitterness and Rancor, Greed, Intolerance, Bigotry.
Let us renew our faith and pledge to Man,
his right to be Himself, and free.

Edna St. Vincent Millay

Until you've lost your reputation, you never realize what a burden it was or what freedom really is.

Margaret Mitchell

The song of the warbler, joyful at his release, has drawn forth the cry of many birds.

Nomura Motoni

Lower voter participation is a silent threat to our democracy. . . . It underrepresents young people, the poor, the disabled, those with little education, minorities and you and me.

Nancy M. Neuman

Indira [Gandhi] and I belong by upbringing and education on the same side, that of human rights, the need to work for freedom from oppressions that continue to crush humanity in so many parts of the world.

Vijaya Lakshmi Pandit

We are here to claim our right as women, not only to be free, but to fight for freedom. It is our privilege, as well as our pride and our joy, to take some part in this militant movement, which, as we believe, means the regeneration of all humanity.

Christabel Pankhurst

A democratic form of government, a democratic way of life, presupposes free public education over a long period; it presupposes also an education for personal responsibility that too often is neglected.

Eleanor Roosevelt

The basic freedom of the world is woman's freedom. A free race cannot be born of slave mothers. A woman enchained cannot choose but give a measure of that bondage to her sons and daughters. No women can call herself free until she can choose consciously whether she will or will not be a mother.

Margaret Sanger

Knowledge and goodness—these make degrees in heaven, and they must be the graduating scale of a true democracy.

Catherine M. Sedgwick

The strongest reason why we ask for a woman to have a voice in the government under which she lives . . . is because of her birthright to self-sovereignty; because as an individual she must rely on herself.

Elizabeth Cady Stanton

F—is for freedom—let's hear it ring.
R—is for rights—a most treasured thing.
E—is for equality—all men the same.
E—is for elections—our leaders we name.
D—is for dream—for which our forefathers fought.
O—is for opportunity—our great nation has brought.
M—is for mankind—let us have peace among men.

Kristi Staubus, grade 6

The literature of a people must so ring from the sense of its nationality; and nationality is impossible without self-respect, and self-respect is impossible without liberty.

Harriet Beecher Stowe

There can be no liberty unless there is economic liberty.

Margaret Thatcher

I started with this idea in my head, "There's two things I've got a right to, death or liberty."

Harriet Tubman

Every successful revolution puts on in time the robe of the tyrant it has deposed.
Barbara Tuchman

I'm no prude, but I find it nothing short of obscene that women are forced to expose ourselves to politicians—forced to submit our private matters, our private decisions . . . to public debate! Men's reproduction isn't regulated by the state—and it shouldn't be. Neither should women's.

Faye Wattleton

The arts are the rain forests of society. They produce the oxygen of freedom, and they are the early warning system when freedom is in danger.

June Wayne

Taught from infancy that beauty is woman's sceptre, the mind shapes itself to the body, and roaming around its gilt cage, only seeks to adorn its prison.

Mary Wollstonecraft

To enjoy freedom we have to control ourselves.

Virginia Woolf

The morning comes, the morning goes,
And still my desk just overflows.

I'm never bored, I'm never sad.
But can it be I'm going mad?

Next week this time I fly away
To take a swift two weeks with pay.

I'll laugh, I'll sing,
I'll drink and snack.
I may not bother coming back!

Not true: I will. I love to roam.
Yet half the fun is coming home.

Anon.

Chapter 18

FRIENDSHIP

Alone we can so do little; together we can do so much.

Helen Keller

❦

The topic of FRIENDSHIP is approached in its broadest sense. As used here, friendship is not limited to an amicable feeling between two people. Rather, friendship is used in the sense of the congeniality and commonality individuals and groups must experience in order to attain a shared purpose or goal. And in this sense, the speaker can be right on target with appropriate quotations that will help build these feelings in her listeners.

One of the primary tasks of the speaker is to help individual listeners recognize that they have a common bond or purpose, and that working *as a team* they can accomplish extraordinary things. Thus it is appropriate to use quotations that can help illustrate and promote good feelings and good will. This sort of activity is often referred to as *consensus building,* and it is among the speaker's greatest challenges.

Usually the group to which you are speaking knows that they have a common interest or purpose. But some groups may think the only thing they have in common is that they are gathered in one spot to hear a presentation; they may not be particularly aware of any common interests beyond that of the moment. However, if you can cause them to feel some greater sense of purpose, to realize some heightened awareness of what they have in common, you can accomplish any number of significant things.

As a speaker, you are perhaps in a better position than anyone else to do this. At least in theory you have a broader perspective because you have some distance from the members of the audience as individuals. You see them as a group and thus are able to visualize—and help them visualize—what they might accomplish as a group. You are not burdened with any particular knowledge of the individual weaknesses of your listeners so you can focus on the big picture and help your listeners rise to that level as well.

There is another important gift that you have as a speaker. By helping people to expand their human contact and consciousness you have the power to enrich lives. Through your words you can cause individuals to recognize their commonality—and in today's alienated society that is a splendid gift indeed.

Sociologists tell us that individual wellness is rarely possible without association with other people. By the selective use of the right thought or quotation, perhaps you will be able to cause some small amount of interaction to take place. In turn, this interaction might motivate individuals to think and act and work as a team. Thus, not only can you uplift and inform your listeners, you can inspire them to see that *united* they have the power to make a difference.

Will one little quotation about friendship change the world? No, but it could help change one attitude. It could help build a bridge between otherwise unconnected people. And if enough attitudes are changed and enough human bridges are built, who knows where it could lead.

❦

"Stay" is a charming word in a friend's vocabulary.

Louisa May Alcott

The easiest kind of relationship for me is with ten thousand people. The hardest is with one.

Joan Baez

Writers seldom choose as friends those self-contained characters who are never in trouble, never unhappy or ill, never make mistakes, and always count their change when it is handed to them.

Catherine Drinker Bowen

Intimacies between women often go backwards, beginning in revelations and ending up in small talk without loss of esteem.

Elizabeth Bowen

Celebrate the happiness that friends are always giving,
make every day a holiday and celebrate just living!

Amanda Bradley

Give truth, and your gift will be paid in kind,
And honor will honor meet;
And the smile which is sweet will surely find
A smile that is just as sweet.

Madeline S. Bridges

If we would build on a sure foundation in friendship, we must love friends for their sake rather than for our own.

Charlotte Brontë

People's lives change. To keep all your old friends is like keeping all your old clothes—pretty soon your closet is so jammed and everything so crushed you can't find anything to wear. Help these friends when they need you; bless the years and happy times when you meant a lot to each other, but try *not* to have the guilts if new people mean more to you now.

Helen Gurley Brown

The person who tries to live alone will not succeed as a human being. His heart withers if it does not answer another heart. His mind shrinks away if he hears only the echoes of his own thoughts and finds no other inspiration.

Pearl S. Buck

The nice thing about teamwork is that you always have others on your side.

Margaret Carty

Loneliness is the universal problem of rich people.

Joan Collins

Amid all the easily loved darlings of Charlie Brown's circle, obstreperous Lucy holds a special place in my heart. She fusses and fumes and she carps and complains. That's because Lucy cares. And its the caring that counts. When we, as youngsters, would accuse our mother of picking on us her wise reply was, "All you'll get from strangers is surface pleasantry or indifference. Only someone who loves you will criticize you."

Judith Crist

To have a good enemy, choose a friend; he knows where to strike.

Diane de Pointiers

Friends and flowers are charming while they are fresh.

Mme. de Sartory

It is the friends that you can call at 4 a.m. that matter.

Marlene Dietrich

To me, the sea is like a person—like a child that I've known a long time. It sounds crazy, I know, but when I swim in the sea I talk to it. I never feel alone when I'm out there.

Gertrude Ederle

Animals are such agreeable friends, they ask no questions, they pass no criticisms.

George Eliot

If I'm such a legend, why am I so lonely?

Judy Garland

To be alone is to be different; to be different is to be alone.

Suzanne Gordon

If I don't have friends, then I ain't got nothin'.

Billie Holiday

It is my melancholy fate to like so many people I profoundly disagree with and often heartily dislike people who agree with me.

Mary Kingsley

Platonic friendship: the interval between the introduction and the first kiss.

Sophie Irene Loeb

The more I traveled the more I realized that fear makes strangers of people who should be friends.

Shirley MacLaine

There is an important difference between love and friendship. While the former delights in extremes and opposites, the latter demands equality.

Françoise d'Aubigné Maintenon

I always felt that the great high privilege, relief, and comfort of friendship was that one had to explain nothing.

Katherine Mansfield

The richer your friends, the more they will cost you.

Elizabeth Marbury

Sometimes you have to get to know someone really well to realize you're really strangers.

Mary Tyler Moore

God gives us our relatives; thank God we can choose our friends!

Ethel Watts Mumford

In my friend, I find a second self.

Isabel Norton

There isn't much that I can do,
But I can sit an hour with you,
And I can share a joke with you,
And sometime share reverses, too . . .
   As on our way we go.

Maude V. Preston

I am a big believer that you have to nourish any relationship. I am still very much a part of my friends' lives and they are very much a part of my life. A First Lady who does not have this source of strength and comfort can lose perspective and become isolated.

Nancy Reagan

Friendship with oneself is all important, because without it one cannot be friends with anyone else in the world.

Eleanor Roosevelt

When they are alone they want to be with others, and when they are with others they want to be alone. After all, human beings are like that.

Gertrude Stein

Loneliness is the most terrible poverty.

Mother Teresa

No person is your friend who demands your silence, or denies your right to grow.
Alice Walker

A friend is one who knows all about you and likes you anyway.

Christi Mary Warner

He's the kind of man who picks his friends—to pieces.

Mae West

I have lost friends, some by death—others through sheer inability to cross the street.
Virginia Woolf

To attract good fortune, spend a new penny on an old friend, share an old pleasure with a new friend and lift up the heart of a true friend by writing his name on the wings of a dragon.

Chinese proverb

In time of prosperity friends will be plenty; in time of adversity not one in twenty.
English proverb

On the road between the homes of friends, grass does not grow.

Norwegian proverb

It takes two to make a quarrel, but only one to end it.

Spanish proverb

Shared joy is double joy, and shared sorrow is half-sorrow.

Swedish proverb

Chapter 19

GIVING

The human contribution is the essential ingredient. It is only in the giving of oneself to others that we truly live.

Ethel Percy Andrus

❧

Speaking is a gift. But I am not referring to one's gifts or abilities as a public speaker. The gift, in this case, is a mutual one: The audience gives the speaker the gift of their time, the speaker gives the audience the gift of her talent and knowledge.

As a speaker, this imposes a responsibility that shouldn't be taken lightly. When making a presentation you have a unique opportunity to give more than just information. Properly prepared and properly motivated, you are giving ideas, knowledge, hope, encouragement.

You are also giving of yourself by sharing who you are, what you believe, what you know, and how you feel. A speaker communicates her *self* in many ways. Obviously, she reveals through her words, but often even more obviously, through her presence, dress, and posture, her *attitude*.

Every day we leave something of ourselves behind. Whether positive or negative, we make an imprint on something or somebody. In this regard, speaking is a microcosm of life. No speaker has ever left the podium without feeling that she has left something of herself behind.

When we consider the mutuality of sharing or giving between listener and speaker, it is important to remember that your efforts must be genuine. You can share without giving, but you cannot give without sharing. You must ask yourself if you are willing to do both. If not, you will never truly communicate with your listeners.

The spirit of mutuality that constitutes genuine communication reminds me of what might be called the *law of reciprocity* that is at work in nature. Human beings breathe in oxygen and breathe out carbon dioxide; plants breathe in carbon dioxide and breathe out oxygen. (Perhaps the admonition to "stop and smell the roses" is more of a biological imperative than a recipe for relaxation.)

This same law is at work on the platform. As a presenter, you give to your listeners. They likewise give to you—not only their time, but their attention, encouragement, commitment, even to following your advice or acting upon your words. The completion of this cycle of reciprocity should be the goal of any speaker's efforts.

Many of the quotations in this chapter have to do with the sharing of gifts of one kind or another. While it is true that there are some things in life that we earn, most things we receive are gifts. Thus, when you speak, it is important that you help your listeners understand the centrality of giving. You can help them accept the principle of reciprocity in their own lives and actions—that they must give and share things like time, effort, talent, commitment.

It is sad to observe the fear that many people have of giving; they are afraid to *risk* giving. Perhaps they are afraid that they or their gift will be rejected. One of your greatest gifts to your audience is to help them overcome this fear, and to understand that whether as individuals or as organizations, they actually risk very little—and stand to gain a great deal—when they open up their own unique talent banks and give of themselves. Help them realize that this is a bank that can never be overdrawn. Conversely, if the balance is not withdrawn and shared, it begins to shrink and the remaining capital gradually disappears.

❧

Giving thanks is one course from which we never graduate.

Valerie Anders

The human contribution is the essential ingredient. It is only in the giving of oneself to others that we truly live.

Ethel Percy Andrus

He that will not give some portion of his ease, his blood, his wealth, for others' good, is a poor, frozen churl.

Joanna Baillie

Life begets life. Energy creates energy. It is by spending oneself that one becomes rich.

Sarah Bernhardt

In a time lacking in truth and certainty and filled with anguish and despair, no woman should be shamefaced in attempting to give back to the world, through her work, a portion of its lost heart.

Louise Bogan

Guilt is the gift that keeps on giving.

Erma Bombeck

For happiness brings happiness,
and loving ways bring love,
And giving is the treasure
that contentment is made of.

Amanda Bradley

For Life is the mirror of king and slave.
Tis just what you are and do;
Then give to the world the best you have,
And the best will come back to you.

Madeline S. Bridges

A child's kiss set on thy singing lips shall make thee glad:
A poor child served by thee shall make thee rich;
A sick child helped by thee shall make thee strong;
Thou shalt be served thyself by every sense of service which thou renderest.

Elizabeth Barrett Browning

Some people give time, some money, some their skills and connections, some literally give their life's blood . . . but everyone has something to give.

Barbara Bush

Little deeds of kindness,
Little words of love,
Help to make earth happy
Like the heaven above.

Julia Fletcher Carney

If we can't turn the world around we can at least bolster the victims.

Liz Carpenter

If I had influence with the good fairy who is supposed to preside over the christening of all children, I should ask that her gift to each child in the world be a sense of wonder so indestructible that it would last throughout life.

Rachel Carson

An effort made for the happiness of others lifts above ourselves.

Lydia M. Child

Sow good services; sweet remembrances will grow from them.

Mme. de Staël

Why are we so blind? That which we improve, we have; that which we hoard, is not for ourselves.

Dorothée DeLuzy

If I can stop one heart from breaking,
I shall not live in vain:
If I can ease one life the aching,
Or cool one pain,
Or help one fainting robin
Unto his nest again,
I shall not live in vain.

Emily Dickinson

Service is what life is all about.

Marian Wright Edelman

What do we live for, if it is not to make life less difficult for each other?

George Eliot

I never hated a man enough to give him his diamonds back.

Zsa Zsa Gabor

If someone listens, or stretches out a hand, or whispers a kind word of encouragement, or attempts to understand a lonely person, extraordinary things begin to happen.

Loretta Girzartis

If every American donated five hours a week, it would equal the labor of 20 million full-time volunteers.

Whoopi Goldberg

Money is never to be squandered or spent ostentatiously. Some of the greatest people in history have lived lives of the greatest simplicity. Remember it's the you inside that counts. Money doesn't give you any license to relax. It gives an opportunity to use all your abilities, free of financial worries, to go forward, and to use your superior advantages and talents to help others.

Rose Fitzgerald Kennedy

Like many other virtues, hospitality is practiced, in its perfection, by the poor. If the rich did their share, how the woes of this world would be lightened!

Mrs. C. M. Kirkland

If you find that life is flat,
Full of this, with none of that,
  Try giving!
Introspection makes it flatter;
A few more years—what will it matter?
  Try giving!
If the world is dark and bitter;
Things all tend to make a quitter—
  Try giving!
Forget yourself in helping others;
Know that all men are your brothers,
You will see then life is sweeter
Than you thought, and far completer—
  When you give!

Margaret Gordon Kuhlman

He who plants a tree, he plants love,
Tents of coolness spreading out above
Wayfarers he may not live to see.
Gifts that grow are best.

Lucy Larcom

One can never pay in gratitude; one can only pay "in kind" somewhere else in
life.

Anne Morrow Lindbergh

Woman softens her own troubles by generously solacing those of others.

Françoise d'Aubigné Maintenon

Compassion is the little light
Whose gleam goes dancing through the night,
And only the cold and hungry men
Know how it quickens hope again.

Aline Michaelis

I sometimes give myself admirable advice, but I am incapable of taking it.

Lady Mary Wortley Montague

Love never reasons, but profusely gives; gives like a thoughtless prodigal, its all,
and trembles then lest it has done too little.

Hannah More

When faith and hope fail, as they do sometimes, we must try charity, which is
love in action. We must speculate no more on our duty, but simply do it. When
we have done it, however blindly, perhaps Heaven will show us why.

Dinah Maria Mulock

I have sacrificed everything in my life that I consider precious in order to
advance the political career of my husband.

Pat Nixon

Your luck is how you treat people.

Bridget O'Donnell

Almsgiving tends to perpetuate poverty; aid does away with it once and for all. Almsgiving leaves a man just where he was before. Aid restores him to society as an individual worthy of all respect and not as a man with a grievance. Almsgiving is the generosity of the rich; social aid levels up social inequalities. Charity separates the rich from the poor; aid raises the needy and sets him on the same level with the rich.

Eva Perón

There isn't much that I can do,
But I can share my flowers with you,
And I can share my books with you,
And sometimes share your burdens, too . . .
  As on our way we go.

Maude V. Preston

I like to give my energy to activities that affirm the oneness of humankind.

Claire Randall

When you cease to make a contribution you begin to die.

Eleanor Roosevelt

In olden times sacrifices were made at the altar—a custom which is still continued.

Helen Rowland

When your schedule leaves you brain-drained and stressed to exhaustion, it's time to give up something. Delegate. Say no. Be brutal. It's like cleaning out a closet—after a while, it gets easier to get rid of things. You discover that you really didn't need them anyway.

Marilyn Ruman

Giving whether it be of time, labor, affection, advice, gifts, or whatever, is one of life's greatest pleasures.

Rebecca Russell

Through charity to God we conceive virtues, and through charity toward our neighbors, they are brought to the birth.

St. Catherine of Siena

I had found a kind of serenity, a new maturity. . . . I didn't feel better or stronger than anyone else but it seemed no longer important whether everyone loved me or not—more important now was for me to love them. Feeling that way turns your whole life around; living becomes the act of giving. When I do a perform-ance now, I still need and like the adulation of an audience, of course, but my *real* satisfaction comes from what I have given of myself, from the joyful act of singing itself.

Beverly Sills

You have not lived a perfect day, even though you have earned your money, unless you have done something for someone who will never be able to repay you.

Ruth Smeltzer

In all ranks of life the human heart yearns for the beautiful; and the beautiful things that God makes are his gift to all alike.

Harriet Beecher Stowe

We deceive ourselves when we fancy that only weakness needs support. Strength needs it more. A straw or a feather sustains itself long in the air.

Anne Sophie Swetchine

To keep a lamp burning we have to keep putting oil in it.

Mother Teresa

No one would remember the Good Samaritan if he'd only had good intentions—he had money, too.

Margaret Thatcher

Once the word charity meant fellow-love;
Restore its meaning, you more fortunate;
Give us not your gold, give us yourselves instead,
   Your thought, your time, your service for our need.

Princess Amelie Rives Troubetzkoy

God first, other people second, I'm third.

Nellie Hershey Tullis

The more independent you want to be, the more generous you must be with yourself as a woman.

Diane Von Furstenberg

After the verb 'To Love,' 'To Help' is the most beautiful verb in the world.

Bertha Von Suttner

You do not have to be right to be generous. If he has the spirit of true generosity, a pauper can give like a prince.

Corrine V. Wells

With every deed you are sowing a seed, though the harvest you may not see.

Ella Wheeler Wilcox

Four goals for a meaningful life:
—seek out a need of the world
—work
—forget self
—trust God

Jennie Fowler Willing

If we cannot climb to the mountaintop
With those whom the world calls great,
If we cannot join in their lofty work
Nor share in their high estate,
  We can sing a song as we pass along
Through the toiling crowds below,
And its notes may fall on some listening ear
With a balm that little know.

Fannie Herron Wingate

You can stand tall without standing *on* someone. You can be a victor without having victims.

Harriet Woods

Thank the Lord that you can give, instead of depending on others to give to you.

Anon.

Her little girl was late arriving home from school so the mother began to scold her daughter, but stopped and asked, "Why are you so late?"
"I had to help another girl. She was in trouble," replied the daughter.
"What did you do to help her?"
"Oh, I sat down and helped her cry."

Anon.

Chapter **20**

HAPPINESS

The greater part of our happiness or misery depends on our dispositions and not our circumstances.

Martha Washington

❦

HAPPINESS, like so many feelings or emotions or conditions, is a matter of choice. It is also a state of mind that can be created, can be generated, can be sustained—often in the absence of any empirical evidence as to why it should be so.

It might be going a bit far to call happiness an illusion, but it is certainly a matter of attitude more than a matter of *matter*. Understanding the physics of happiness is one of the speaker's greatest challenges.

I have been before audiences who were there because they had to be, and who were sitting there counting the threads in the carpet until they could be released from bondage. People in that frame of mind are one of the most difficult hurdles a speaker must clear. What is fascinating is that their frame of mind can be as much *your* choice as theirs.

Happiness can be generated. Emotions, we are learning, are contagious. Negativism begets negativism. Positive attitudes and outlooks can break down feelings to the contrary, if the message is both skillfully and appropriately framed. Thus, the speaker must prepare both herself and her message to create in her audience a frame of mind that will be receptive. She must work to convert an attitude of unhappiness or ennui (for whatever combination of reasons) into, at least, an attitude of receptivity. If that doesn't happen, no positive messages are going to be received.

One of the emotional components of happiness is the willingness to extend oneself to others. Happiness, self-contained and hoarded, quickly gives way either to egotism or it simply dissipates and is gone. Happiness, in order to be maintained, must be shared. The speaker works to share her happiness with her audience, and she works to generate that same happiness in those who are hearing her. In this context, I equate happiness to any number of positive, productive emotions or outcomes. Happiness doesn't have to mean gaiety or frivolity—although neither condition is to be avoided if the time and the place are appropriate.

One of the prime reasons speakers should utilize quotations about happiness is that they are, if well chosen, great medicine against pessimism. Happiness, in whatever manifestation, implies a positive *state of mind.* It is, therefore, the state of mind which must be achieved before a positive *attitude* can be generated, and before a positive *outcome* can be gained. Thus, helping an audience generate positive feelings leads directly toward the generation of productivity—whether personal, organizational, or institutional.

Using quotations about happiness helps the speaker lead her audiences toward *outward* thinking. When one looks outward, one can conceive of positive change or productive action. You can't look down and plan ahead; you can't *think down* and be productive.

Never confuse the state of mind that we are defining here as happiness with being light or insubstantial. It isn't. The upward-looking emotion of happiness is a mental framework of strength and substance that allows good things to get thought and positive thoughts to get done. Use these quotations to stimulate upward thinking.

❦

We learn the inner secret of happiness when we learn to direct our inner drives, our interest and our attention to something outside ourselves.

Ethel Percy Andrus

Happiness is good health and a bad memory.

Ingrid Bergman

Those who are formed to win general admiration are seldom calculated to bestow individual happiness.

Lady Marguerite Blessington

Never fear spoiling children by making them too happy. Happiness is the atmosphere in which all good affections grow—the wholesome warmth necessary to make the heart-blood circulate healthily and freely; unhappiness—the chilling pressure which produces here an inflammation, there an excrescence, and, worst of all, "the mind's green and yellow sickness"—ill temper.

Ann Eliza Bray

To have meaningful work is a tremendous happiness.

Rita Mae Brown

The Greeks said grandly in their tragic phrase, "Let no one be called happy till his death"; to which I would add, "Let no one till his death, be called unhappy."

Elizabeth Barrett Browning

Service to a just cause rewards the worker with more real happiness and satisfaction than any other venture of life.

Carrie Chapman Catt

Gratitude is the memory of the heart; therefore forget not to say often, I have all I ever enjoyed.

Lydia M. Child

The true way to render ourselves happy is to love our duty and find in it our pleasure.

Françoise de Motteville

Our happiness in this world depends upon the affections we are enabled to inspire.

Duchesse de Praslin

There is in all of us an impediment to perfect happiness, namely, weariness of what we possess, and a desire for what we have not.

Virginia des Rieux

Whether happiness may come or not, one should try and prepare one's self to do without it.

George Eliot

Instant gratification takes too long.

Carrie Fisher

Unexpected joy is always so keen that . . . it seems to hold enough to reconcile one to the inevitable.

Jessie B. Fremont

I wouldn't be satisfied with a life lived solely on the barricades. I reserve my right to be frivolous.

Betty Friedan

Melancholy attends the best joys of an ideal life.

Margaret Fuller

Take my word for it, the saddest thing under the sky is a soul incapable of sadness.

Comtesse Catherine de Gasparin

To attain happiness in another world we need only to believe something, while to secure it in this world we must needs do something.

Charlotte Perkins Gilman

To love what you do and feel that it matters—how could anything be more fun?
Katherine Graham

Those who would enjoyment gain must find it in the purpose they pursue.
Sarah J. Hale

The little things
That make life sweet
Are worth their weight in gold;
They can't be bought
At any price
And neither are they sold.

Estelle Waite Hoover

Normal day, let me be aware of the treasure you are. Let me learn from you, love you, bless you before you depart. Let me not pass you by in quest of some rare and perfect tomorrow. Let me hold you while I may, for it may not always be so. One day I shall dig my nails into the earth, or bury my face in the pillow, or stretch myself taut, or raise my hands to the sky and want, more than all the world, your return.

Mary Jean Iron

Not for the mighty world, O Lord, tonight,
nations and kingdoms in their fearful might—
Let me be glad the kettle gently sings,
let me be glad for little things.

Edna Jaques

It is the people who can do nothing who find nothing to do, and the secret of happiness in this world is not only to be useful, but to be forever elevating one's uses.

Sarah Orne Jewett

Many persons have a wrong idea of what constitutes true happiness. It is not attained through self-gratification but through fidelity to a worthy purpose.

Helen Keller

No thoroughly occupied man was ever yet very miserable.

Letitia E. Landon

Happiness is like a crystal,
Fair and exquisite and clear,
Broken in a million pieces,
Shattered, scattered, far and near.
Now and then along life's pathway,
Lo! some shining fragments fall;
But there are so many pieces
No one ever finds them all.

You may find a bit of beauty,
Or an honest share of wealth,
While another just beside you
Gathers honor, love, or health.
Vain to choose or grasp unduly,
Broken is the perfect ball;
And there are so many pieces
No one ever finds them all.

Yet the wise, as on they journey,
Treasure every fragment clear,
Fit them as they may together,
Imagining the shattered sphere,
Learning ever to be thankful,
though their share of it is small;
For it has so many pieces
No one ever finds them all.

Priscilla Leonard

Happiness, to some elation, is to others, mere stagnation.

Amy Lowell

Women endowed with remarkable sensibilities enjoy much, but they also suffer much. The greater the light the stronger will be the shadow.

Anna Cora Mowatt

Too many wish to be happy before becoming wise.

Susanne Curchod Necker

Just the knowledge that a good book is waiting one at the end of a long day makes that day happier.

Kathleen Norris

Sorrow is tranquility remembered in emotion.

Dorothy Parker

Happiness must be cultivated. It is like character. It is not a thing to be safely let alone for a moment, or it will run to weeds.

Elizabeth Stuart Phelps

The habit of dissipating every serious thought by a succession of agreeable sensations is as fatal to happiness as to virtue; for when amusement is uniformly substituted for objects of moral and mental interest, we lose all that elevates our enjoyments above the scale of childish pleasures.

Anna Maria Porter

Happiness is a sunbeam which may pass through a thousand bosoms without losing a particle of its original ray; nay, when it strikes on a kindred heart, like the converged light on a mirror, it reflects itself with redoubled brightness. It is not perfected till it is shared.

Jane Porter

You're as happy as you allow yourself to be—so why be unhappy?

Marilyn Quayle

The life that has grown up and developed without laughter, and without the sunny brightness which youth justly claims as its right, lacks buoyancy and elasticity, and becomes heavy and unsympathetic, if not harsh and morose.

Mrs. G. S. Reany

Happiness is caring.
And liking one another.

Camille Reed, age 10

Glad that I live am I;
That the sky is blue;
Glad for the country lanes,
And the fall of dew.

Lizette W. Reese

It is not easy to find happiness in ourselves, and it is not possible to find it elsewhere.

Agnes Repplier

Happiness is not a goal, it is a by-product.

Eleanor Roosevelt

Happiness is not a state to arrive at—but a manner of traveling.

Margaret Lee Runbeck

"Keep aloof from sadness," says an Icelandic writer, "for sadness is a sickness of the soul." The gloomy soul aggravates misfortune, while a cheerful smile often dispels those mists that portend a storm.

Lydia H. Sigourney

The best advice on the art of being happy is about as easy to follow as advice to be well when one is sick.

Anne Sophie Swetchine

If you really want to be happy, nobody can stop you.

Sister Mary Tricky

My satisfaction comes from my commitment to advancing a better world.

Faye Wattleton

Too much of a good thing can be wonderful.

Mae West

If only we'd stop trying to be happy, we could have a pretty good time.

Edith Wharton

Laugh and the world laughs with you,
Weep and you weep alone;
For the sad old earth must borrow its mirth,
But has trouble enough of its own.

Sing and the hills will answer,
Sigh and it's lost on the air;
For the echoes bound to a joyful sound,
But shrink from voicing a care.

Ella Wheeler Wilcox

Every now and then, when you're on stage, you hear the best sound a player can hear. It's a sound you can't get in movies or in television. It is the sound of a wonderful, deep silence that means you've hit them where they live.

Shelley Winters

May your every wish be granted.

Ancient Chinese curse

Chapter **21**

HERITAGE

There is no king who has not had a slave among his ancestors, and no slave who has not had a king among his.

Helen Keller

❦

Where we come from, and from whom we come, are always matters of interest, because those two aspects of our being tend to determine so many facets of our character.

For a skilled presenter, these aspects have dual importance: first, because they allow the audience to gain at least a glimpse of insight into our perspective as a speaker; second, because they allow the speaker to gain some valuable insights into her audience.

In the first instance, I find that letting my audiences know something about me, in the sense of my HERITAGE, has a very humanizing effect. (In this context, when speaking of *who I am*, I am referring to things much more distinctive than my ethnicity, ancestry, or nationality.)

Through the introduction which I have provided the program chairman or through comments I may make during my presentation (or both), audiences learn: that I was raised in Oklahoma, that my husband and I farmed in Illinois after we were married, that we have lived in Arizona since the early 50's, that my grandparents were Oklahoma "dry land" farmers, that my father taught school in Indian Territory, and/or that my mother was a school teacher. There is very probably *something* in my background that most everyone in the audience can relate to. I am no longer just *the speaker* to those listeners; I am a person just like they are, a person with whom they have something in common.

Many speakers feel that it is important to build a persona or a mystique that sets them apart from the audience and, in this way, maintain the assumed credibility that comes from being the expert from afar. And some believe that it's important to maintain a level of demeanor and image that enhances one's standing in an audience's eyes. However, I am convinced that allowing an audience a glimpse of the speaker's humanity, rather than serving as an image diminisher, can serve as an image—and message—enhancer. Audiences are much more likely to find credible a speaker with whom they can relate person to person, or about whose background or heritage they have some understanding.

On the other side of the coin, any presentation—no matter how well planned or carefully thought out—will be less than a smashing success if the speaker fails to take the audience's own heritage into consideration.

This does not mean that you have to take some sort of cultural inventory before addressing a group. Generally, that is neither practical nor relevant. However, if you know enough about your audience to know that they come from all across the nation or from a particular region/state/city or from specific occupations, then you already know enough to be able to draw some heritage-related conclusions.

Again, I am not referring to racial or ethnic-related remarks. I am referring to the perspective-setting commonalities which can allow the group to understand that the speaker has done her homework and cares enough about their group to have incorporated something about them into her remarks. This, in itself, can be an important starting point for motivating your listeners to want to relate to you and to accept what you have to say.

Are they all from the Southwest, or the East Coast, or the Pacific Northwest? If they are, then there are certain items of regional or local heritage that they will generally have in common. The better you can relate these commonalities to what you have to say, the more likely it is that your listeners will resonate to your points. You can use such opportunities to contrast, if appropriate, those commonalities with something in your own background that will allow the audience to feel comfortable both with you and with themselves.

One obvious heritage-related contrast that speakers can use very effectively, especially if it differs from their listeners, is accent. I personally am a bit sorry to see the rise of what some commentators have called "Johnny Carson English"—that essentially nonaccented speech that makes it impossible to guess a person's regional heritage. To me, part of the richness of this nation is our diversity, and hearing a person from New England, the Deep South, or some other part of the country with characteristic patterns of speech is a genuine delight. Regional accents remind us that, although we are one nation, we are a nation of individuals and of distinguishable regions.

One of the first pieces of advice I would give to any aspiring speaker is: If you have an accent, keep it. As long as you speak clearly and correctly and people can understand you, be proud of how you sound and why you came to sound that way.

In a broader context, it can often be valuable for a speaker to use quotations about our common heritage as American citizens. Regardless of the differences in our ancestry, ethnicity, or backgrounds, you can draw unifying conclusions and make points that transcend any other differences.

The use of quotations about heritage show that a speaker knows her audience. That knowledge allows you to validate your remarks with the sort of familiarity that sets you apart from another speaker. "Show your roots" may not be good practice for people who color their hair, but it is sound advice to speakers who want to add individuality, friendliness, or even a homespun flavor to their presentations.

❦

I speak to the black experience, but I am always talking about the human condition—about what we can endure, dream, fail at, and still survive.

Maya Angelou

With the loss of tradition we have lost the thread which safely guided us through the vast realms of the past, but this thread was also the chain fettering each successive generation to a predetermined aspect of the past. It could be that only now will the past open up to us with unexpected freshness and tell us things that no one as yet had ears to hear.

Hannah Arendt

Women have got to make the world safe for men since men have made it so darned unsafe for women.

Lady Nancy Astor

You must know the story of your culture and be proud of your ancestors.

Romana Banuelos

America, America! God shed His grace on thee
And crown thy good with brotherhood from sea to shining sea!

Katherine Lee Bates

No individual can arrive even at the threshold of his potentialities without a culture in which he participates. Conversely, no civilization has in it any element which in the last analysis is not the contribution of an individual.

Ruth Benedict

My father died after a long illness. My mother entrusted me with the knowledge of business. I knew about the property. I knew about money she had in the bank account. I knew about all her insurance. She wanted me to be knowledgeable in case something ever happened to her. She wanted me to know that there was enough money there for me to go to college. And she would be counting on me to help my brother who was four years younger. She was giving me information so there would never be anyone who could tell me there wasn't the money to do certain things. We would review the monthly bank statements and the bank accounts. Most children don't have the vaguest idea of how much money their family makes, how much money they have or where the money is. But she thought it was important that I know that. So I guess I was lucky.

Hortense Canady

There's a magical tie to the land of our home, which the heart cannot break, though the footsteps may roam.

Eliza Cook

That past which is so presumptuously brought forward as a precedent for the present, was itself founded on some past that went before it.

Mme. de Staël

America is not a melting pot but a Mosaic.

Pat M. Derian

A great civilization is not conquered from without until it has destroyed itself from within.

Ariel and Will Durant

True patriotism doesn't exclude an understanding of the patriotism of others.

Queen Elizabeth II

You don't have to have fought in a war to love peace.

Geraldine Ferraro

We grew up founding our dreams on the infinite promise of American advertising.

Zelda Fitzgerald

Oh, wondrous power! how little understood, entrusted to the mother's mind alone, to fashion genius, form the soul for good, inspire a West, or train a Washington.

Sarah J. Hale

There is not enough loving-kindness afloat in the continental United States to see a crippled old lady across an Indian trail.

Margaret Halsey

What Rome was capable of, the achievement of her empire shows. The Roman character had great qualities, great potential strength. If the people had held together, realizing their interdependence and working for a common good, their problems, completely strange and enormously difficult though they were, would not have proved too much for them. But they were split into sharpest oppositions, extremes that ever grew more extreme and so more irresponsible. A narrow selfishness kept men blind when their own self-preservation demanded a world-wide outlook.

Edith Hamilton

I empathize with those who yearn for a simpler world, for some bygone golden age of domestic and international tranquility. Perhaps for a few people at some time in history there was such an age. But for the mass of humanity it is an age that never was.

Shirley Hufstedler

Every creative act draws on the past whether it pretends to or not. It draws on what it knows. There is no such thing, really, as a creative act in a vacuum.

Ada Louise Huxtable

I see so many of these new folks nowadays, that seem to have neither past nor future. Conversation's got to have some root in the past, or else you've got to explain every remark, an' it wears a person out.

Sarah Orne Jewett

Science and time and necessity have propelled us, the United States, to be the general store for the world, dealers in everything. Most of all, merchants for a better way of life.

Lady Bird Johnson

The world is grand, beautiful, thrilling. But I love New York.

Dorothy Kilgallen

There is a spirit and a need and a man at the beginning of every great human advance. Each of these must be right for that particular moment of history, or nothing happens.

Coretta Scott King

Give me your tired, your poor,
   Your huddled masses yearning to breathe free,
The wretched refuse of your teaming shore.
   Send these, the homeless, tempest-tossed to me.
I lift my lamp beside the golden door!

Emma Lazarus

If you don't remember history accurately, how can you learn?

Maya Lin

And the forest calls and I soon shall go
Where the last of my kindred tread;
For I'd rather die with a dying race
Than live where the light has fled.

Lillith Lorraine

Yes, we have a good many poor tired people here already, but we have plenty of mountains, rivers, woods, sunshine and air, for tired people to rest in. We have Kansas wheat and Iowa corn and Wisconsin cheese for them to eat, Texas cotton for them to wear. So give us as many as come—we can take it, and take care of them.

Mary Margaret McBride

Every society honors its live conformists and its dead troublemakers.

Mignon McLaughlin

Knowledge of [another] culture should sharpen our ability to scrutinize more steadily, to appreciate more lovingly, our own.

Margaret Mead

Our generation reclaimed the land, our children fought the war, and our grand-children should enjoy the peace.

Golda Meir

When you travel through the wheat fields of Kansas for a day and a night and see endless herds grazing on the pastureland, when you have spent weeks visiting factory after factory in city after city producing at top speed, when you have seen the tireless effort, the intelligent application of management and labor and their ever-increasing cooperation, you realize that there are enough resources, actual and potential, enough brains and good will in this country to turn the whole world into a paradise.

Agnes Meyer

Americans relate all effort, all work, and all of life itself to the dollar. Their talk is of nothing but dollars. The English seldom sit happily chatting for hours on end about pounds. In England, public business is its own reward, nobody would go into Parliament in order to become rich, neither do riches bring public appointments.

Nancy Mitford

Democracy just doesn't happen. It didn't "just happen" [216] years ago and doesn't "just happen" now. Like our Founders we have to study about it, learn about it, teach our children about it, protect it, fight for it when necessary, nurture it, and live by the rules.

Betty Southard Murphy

Students of all cultures are supposed to come together on campus to learn from each other and about each other . . . This trend toward ethnic identification has often come at the expense of the unity represented by the symbol of the melting pot.

Sandra Day O'Connor

Truly there is nothing in the world so blessed or so sweet as the heritage of children.

Carolina Oliphant

It doesn't matter who my father was; it matters who I remember he was.

Anne Sexton

It is one proof of a good education, and of a true refinement of feeling, to respect antiquity.

Lydia H. Sigourney

Slavery, it is true, was to some extent introduced into New England, but it never suited the genius of the people, never struck deep root, or spread so as to choke the good seed of self-helpfulness . . . . People, having once felt the thorough neatness and beauty of execution which came of free, educated, and thoughtful labor, could not tolerate the clumsiness of slavery.

Harriet Beecher Stowe

What is a city? A city is more than buildings and roads. A city is families to feed and to house; children to educate; men and women to employ and to transport. A city is businesses to build; profits to be made; culture and recreation to be enjoyed; opportunities to be realized. But, more important than anything, a city is people. A city is *all of us*.

Annette Strauss

The United States is not a nation of people which in the long run allows itself to be pushed around.

Dorothy Thompson

Traditions are group efforts to keep the unexpected from happening.

Barbara Tober

Ceremony is really a protection in times of emotional involvement, particularly at death. If we have a social formula to guide us and do not have to extemporize, we feel better able to handle life. If we ignore ceremony entirely, we are not normal, warm human beings. Conversely, if we never relax it, if we "stand on ceremony" in all things, we are rigid. We must learn which ceremonies may be breached occasionally at our convenience and which ones may never be if we are to live pleasantly with our fellow man.

Amy Vanderbilt

I am an American.
I am a Bald eagle standing proud silhouetting my breast feathers against the
   Northern blowing winds.
I am an American.
I am a patriot standing tall and brave against the afterthought of a battle.
I am an American.
I am a free bounding deer prancing across the meadows letting the sun bounce
   off my tawny hide.
I am an American.
I am a hard working pioneer plowing my land to make meals for my family who
   traveled far across the Atlantic Ocean to gain their freedom.
I am an American.

Linda Whiting, grade 7

Masterpieces are not single and solitary births; they are the outcome of many years of thinking in common, of thinking by the body of the people, so that the experience of the mass is behind the single voice.

Virginia Woolf

Birth, ancestry, and that which you yourself have not achieved can hardly be called your own.

Greek proverb

Though a tree grow ever so high, the falling leaves return to the ground.

Malay proverb

Chapter 22

HUMOR

Laughter can be more satisfying than honor; more precious than money; more heart-cleansing than prayer.

Harriet Rochlin

❧

I don't want to be in an audience or hear a speaker who doesn't have a sense of humor! Whether it is a eulogy or a report to the stockholders, the speaker with a sense of humor will be more effective than the speaker without one. In fact, I am convinced that the more serious or profound the subject, the more it's strengthened by moments of lightness.

I personally subscribe to the theory that laughing is genuinely, physiologically therapeutic. When you occasionally lighten up during your remarks and allow your listeners to laugh, you're bringing them together. You are also helping them increase the flow of oxygen to their brains, heightening their ability to focus and concentrate on what you are saying! How's that for getting a lot from one little laugh?

It is important to clarify the difference between the use of humor and the telling of jokes, or the speaker attempting to categorize herself as a humorist. Using humor is not telling a joke. It is not using gags or gimmicks to force a laugh. It is allowing your listeners to laugh or smile, to recognize irony, to better understand, to empathize.

The use of humor can take many forms. For me, the most effective is self-deprecating humor. Any speaker who can gently make fun of herself is almost guaranteed to have a successful presentation. Why? First of all, because humor punctures pomposity. It proves that you are not overly impressed with yourself and expect your listeners to feel the same way. Second, by humanizing yourself, you open up the acceptance level of your audience.

People want their speaker to have a level of expertise that makes her worthy of being listened to. But they also *don't* want to think that you are perfect or infallible. Giving the impression that you are far above your audience may give your listeners license to decide that they probably won't understand anything you say; or if they do understand it, they probably aren't talented enough to do anything about it. That is *not* the recipe for success on the platform.

The speaker who gives the impression of aloofness is practically inviting her audience to sit back, mentally fold their arms, and radiate an attitude of "Prove it!"

But the speaker who reveals something of herself through self-deprecating humor can deliver the same message and persuade the same group of listeners to be *with* her, to be willing to not just listen passively, but to be willing to *help* her deliver her message.

It is also important to use humor as "audience relaxers" sprinkled throughout your speech—and not just in the introductory warm-up time. These breathers allow your audience, in the midst of content, to relax a little bit. They also provide a moment to let an important point sink in.

Among the most effective ways to work these breathers into your remarks are through the use of quotations that illustrate the humor, the incongruity, or the humanity of a situation.

Obviously, the quotations must be appropriate to your audience. They may poke fun at the trade jargon of a profession and help the audience laugh at themselves—but they must *never* be deprecating or ridiculing. They may provoke shared laughter at the foibles of the group, but *never* (unless you're doing a "roast") should they be directed at the individual.

You must also know your audience well enough to know what they *won't* laugh at so that you won't offend their sensibilities. Never assume that simply because you find something amusing, your audience will.

One absolute rule is to never, *ever* use humor that demeans a group, a race, a sect, a religion, or a nation. We must concentrate on bringing the world together, not on fragmenting it. We should ennoble and honor people, especially those who are strangers or are different. The old saw about "the one who sees the light must carry the torch" applies to you as the presenter. Lift up; don't put down.

However, a humorous story or quotation that is nonoffensive and that you obviously enjoy, if the enjoyment is sincere, will evoke contagious laughter from the audience simply at seeing your own enjoyment in telling it.

Remember, people like to laugh. They will laugh with you, they will laugh (it is hoped because you have humanized yourself through self-deprecation) at you. And they will remember that they liked you long after they've forgotten every serious point you made.

What better way to be remembered than for having made someone laugh?

❧

My husband will never chase another woman. He's too fine, too decent, too old.

Gracie Allen

Man forgives woman anything save the wit to outwit him.

Minna Antrim

I believe in the total depravity of inanimate things . . . the elusiveness of soap, the knottiness of strings, the transitory nature of buttons, the inclination of suspenders to twist and of hooks to forsake their lawful eyes and cleave only unto the hairs of their hapless owner's head.

Katherine Ashley

I married beneath me—all women do.

Lady Nancy Astor

You grow up the day you have your first real laugh, at yourself.

Ethel Barrymore

I'm going to clean this dump—just as soon as the kids are grown.

Erma Bombeck

When someone who is known for being comedic does something straight, it's always "a big breakthrough" or a "radical departure." Why is it no one ever says that if a straight actor does comedy? Are they presuming comedy is easier?

Carol Burnett

Don't get your knickers in a knot. Nothing is solved and it just makes you walk funny.

Kathryn Carpenter

Back where I was raised, the collection was taken in a tin pie pan passed from person to person. The preacher always reminded, "Pennies sound pretty, but they don't fold good!"

Liz Carpenter

Sometimes when I look at my children I say to myself, "Lillian, you should have stayed a virgin."

Lillian Carter

Very stupid to kill the servants. Now we don't even know where to find the marmalade.

Agatha Christie

I have never married because I have three pets at home that answer the same purpose as a husband. I have a dog that growls every morning, a parrot that swears all afternoon, and a cat that comes home late at night.

Marie Corelli

Errol Flynn died on a 70-foot boat with a 17-year-old girl. Walter has always wanted to go that way, but he's going to settle for a 17-footer with a 70-year-old.

Betsy Cronkite

Never go to bed mad. Stay up and fight.

Phyllis Diller

If love means never having to say you're sorry, then marriage means always having to say everything twice.

Estelle Getty

If women can sleep their way to the top, how come they aren't there? . . . There must be an epidemic of insomnia out there.

Ellen Goodman

Chaplin's genius was in comedy. He had no sense of humour.

Lita Grey (Charlie Chaplin's former wife)

The average Hollywood film star's ambition is to be admired by an American, courted by an Italian, married to an Englishman, and have a French boy friend.

Katharine Hepburn

The important thing in acting is to be able to laugh and cry. If I have to cry, I think of my sex life. If I have to laugh, I think of my sex life.

Glenda Jackson

I asked a man in prison once how he happened to be there and he said he had stolen a pair of shoes. I told him if he had stolen a railroad he would be a United States Senator.

"Mother" Mary Jones

The average, healthy, well-adjusted adult gets up at 7:30 in the morning feeling just plain awful.

Jean Kerr

No good deed goes unpunished.

Clare Boothe Luce

I had been a humor writer all my life, but when I was writing this novel, I said, "Ah ha, because this is important, it can't be funny." A great fallacy!

Judith Martin

Moses dragged us for 40 years through the desert to bring us to the one place in the Middle East where there was no oil.

Golda Meir

When our knowledge coalesces with our humanity and our humor, it can add up to wisdom.

Carol Orlock

People are more fun than anybody.

Dorothy Parker

Behind every great man there is a surprised woman.

Maryon Pearson

I hate housework! You make the beds, you do the dishes—and six months later you have to start all over again.

Joan Rivers

When you know to laugh and when to look upon things as too absurd to take seriously, the other person is ashamed to carry through even if he was serious about it.

Eleanor Roosevelt

Love, the quest; marriage, the conquest; divorce, the inquest.

Helen Rowland

There is so little difference between husbands you might as well keep the first.

Adele Rogers St. Johns

You can live without music
You can live without books
But civilized man cannot live without cooks!

Inice Simpson

A woman without a man is like a fish without a bicycle.

Gloria Steinem

When he's late for dinner, I know he's either having an affair or is lying dead in the street. I always hope it's the street. (on husband Hume Cronyn)

Jessica Tandy

(After her husband's speech to a convention of farmers, when someone asked, "Why on earth can't you get Harry to use a more genteel word?")
"Good Lord, it's taken me years to get him to use the word *manure*!"

Bess Truman

If you are looking for a kindly, well-to-do older gentleman who is no longer interested in sex, take out an ad in *The Wall Street Journal*.

Abigail Van Buren

That is the best—to laugh with someone because you both think the same things are funny.

Gloria Vanderbilt

Humor is such a strong weapon, such a strong answer. Women have to make jokes about themselves, laugh about themselves, because they have nothing to lose.

Agnes Varda

We are not amused.

Queen Victoria

If evolution was worth its salt, by now it should've evolved something better then survival of the fittest. Yeah, I told 'em I think a better idea would be survival of the wittiest.

Jane Wagner

It's hard to be funny when you have to be clean.

Mae West

Fear not a jest. If one throws salt at thee thou wilt receive no harm unless thou hast sore places.

Latin proverb

A sense of humor is what makes you laugh at something which would make you mad if it happened to you.

Anon.

Give me a sense of humor, Lord,
Give me the grace to see a joke,
To get some pleasure out of life
And pass it on to other folk.

Anon.

Laughing stirs up the blood, expands the chest, electrifies the nerves, clears away the cobwebs from the brain, and gives the whole system a cleansing rehabilitation.

Anon.

Bumper sticker: Auntie Em: Hate you,
                Hate Kansas, Taking dog.
                Dorothy

Anon.

Little boy to his dad, "You remember I asked you the other night how much is a million dollars?"
"Yes," answered the dad.
"Well, Dad, 'a hell of a lot of money' isn't the real answer."

Anon.

Two women in Houston out for a walk came upon a frog who said, "Pick me up and kiss me and I'll turn back into a Houston Oil Man."
The first woman picked him up and put him in her purse.
The second asked, "Why not kiss him?"
The first answered, "Oil men are a dime a dozen—but a talking frog—now, that's something!"

Anon.

A self-righteous preacher reprimanded a farmer because he cussed and drank, "I'm over 60 years old and I've never cussed or drunk."
Farmer: "Yeah, and you've never farmed either."

Anon.

A man saw his neighbor's car rolling slowly out the driveway with no one at the wheel. He jumped in and put on the emergency brake. "I stopped it!" he shouted triumphantly.

"I know," said his disgusted neighbor walking from behind the vehicle. "I was pushing it."

Anon.

Chapter **23**

LEADERSHIP

What I wanted to be when I grew up was—in charge.

Brigadier General Wilma Vaught

❦

Almost by definition a speaker is a leader. You are asked to speak or present because someone thinks you have something to say worth listening to. Because of your position, your background, your training, your experience, or some combination of these factors, you are looked up to (often literally) on the platform. This imposes some challenges on you. It also provides you with wonderful opportunities to challenge your listeners. Both of you will gain in the process.

Because you are a speaker/leader, you must be able to organize your own vision and purpose in such a way that you will inspire your listeners toward the same end. You must be able to seize the leadership opportunity inherent in every presentation to motivate your listeners to action. Because every presentation has a purpose, and every group of listeners has some sort of common goal, it is your task to define those objectives so that they are meaningful to the audience.

There is another word very closely associated with leadership. That word is *learning*. The Japanese word for teacher is *sensei*, which means honored leader. In addition to inspiring, motivating, and leading when you speak, you receive an extra dividend—you also learn! You *always* learn when you instruct others. And, if you have prepared your presentation well and then executed it properly, your listeners learn—and may be inspired to lead as well.

You do not have to have a lifetime of presentation experience to accept this challenge. You simply begin by realizing that, while leadership may be an inexact science and difficult to quantify in many respects, it is not an inert science. And like speaking, leadership is also not a theoretical science. They are applied sciences because both speaking and leading require planning, organization, commitment, and action.

Although the qualities inherent in leading through speaking are an art and a science, they are not qualities that are genetic. The abilities to speak and to lead are qualities that can, and must, be learned.

Quotations about leadership are intended to help you define and refine those qualities in yourself that will help you lead yourself (in the sense of accepting the challenges before you) and will help you lead others (which you do every time you stand up and make a presentation). They are intended to be a reference point from which you can draw inspiration, insight, and strength from significant people who have something substantial to say on the subject. They can stimulate your own thinking and validate your ideas.

Sadly, finding quotations by women on the subject of leadership has been somewhat difficult. Do women lead? Absolutely! Do they write or speak about it? Not as much as one would hope.

If speaking were simply a matter of standing up, opening your mouth, and waiting to see what came out, there would be no need for a book like this or for preparation of any kind. It would all just sort of be "doin' what comes natur'lly." Since nothing in life of any consequence works out that way, the conscientious speaker will take every opportunity to prepare to speak, prepare to lead, and prepare to learn. With these three preparations in hand, your words will inspire others and your work will enrich your own being.

❦

You can't have a Congress that responds to the needs of the workingman when there are practically no people here who represent him. And you're not going to have a society that understands its humanity if you don't have more women in government.

Bella Abzug

I could not run away from the situation. I had become, whether I liked it or not, a symbol, representing my people. I had to appear. (referring to singing at the Lincoln Memorial after having had a concert canceled because of her race)

Marian Anderson

Power is strength and the ability to see yourself through your own eyes and not through the eyes of another. It is being able to place a circle of power at your own feet and not take power from someone else's circle.

Lynn V. Andrews

The biggest need in politics and government today is for people of integrity and courage, who will do what they believe is right and not worry about the political consequences to themselves.

Reva Beck Bosone

I shall be an autocrat; that's my trade. And the good Lord will forgive me; that's His.

Catherine the Great

What you always do before you make a decision is consult. The best public policy is made when you are listening to people who are going to be impacted. Then, once policy is determined, you call on them to help you sell it.

Elizabeth Dole

If [women] understood and exercised their power they could remake the world.
Emily Taft Douglas

I realized that public affairs were also *my* affairs. I became active in politics because I saw the possibility, if we all sat back and did nothing, of a world in which there would no longer be any stages for actors to act on.

Helen Gahagan Douglas

I will make you shorter by a head.

Queen Elizabeth I

We are told that "the hand which rocks the cradle rules the world." I have lived in this world for over fifty years, but find no evidence of rulership in the act of cradle-rocking. If it had been recorded that "the hand which rocks the cradle" bears the burdens of the world, the connection between truth and poetry would have been self-evident.

Rebecca Latimer Felton

Off-the-rack solutions, like bargain basement dresses, never fit anyone.

Françoise Giroud

I see something that has to be done and I organize it.

Elinor Guggenheimer

You don't manage people; you manage things. You lead people.

Admiral Grace Hooper

There are two kinds of directors in the theater. Those who think they are God and those who are certain of it.

Rhetta Hughes

Failing to plan is a plan to fail.

Effie Jones

Too many people let others stand in their way and don't go back for one more try.

Rosabeth Moss Kanter

Unfortunately, history is not on our side. No society in history has ever made the successful transition from leader of one economic era to leader of a new economic era. They've usually failed because they've jumped too late.

Christine D. Keen

One can never consent to creep when one feels an impulse to soar.

Helen Keller

Women need to see ourselves as individuals capable of creating change. That is what political and economic power is all about: having a voice, being able to shape the future. Women's absence from decision-making positions has deprived the country of a necessary perspective.

Madeleine Kunin

Power is your ability to be a leader and get people to follow.

Sandra Kurtzig

Today the real test of power is not capacity to make war but capacity to prevent it.

Anne O'Hare McCormick

To lead means to direct and to exact; and no man dare do either. He might be unpopular.

Marya Mannes

The Glass Ceiling hinders not only individuals but society as a whole. It effectively cuts our pool of potential corporate leaders by half. It deprives our economy of new leaders, new sources of creativity—the "would be" pioneers of the business world.

Lynn Martin

A leader who doesn't hesitate before he sends his nation into battle is not fit to be a leader.

Golda Meir

I'm no lady; I'm a member of Congress, and I'll proceed on that basis.

Mary Norton

Most of man's problems upon this planet, in the long history of the race, have been met and solved either partially or as a whole by experiment based on common sense and carried out with courage.

Frances Perkins

A women's organization was the catalyst to trigger a flip-flop in my mind that I wasn't a follower, I was a leader. And in spite of my first reaction, that of fear, and a feeling I couldn't do it, I took the risk. Don't listen to other people's negativity; they filter through their own experiences. Learn to trust your own feelings. If you feel in your gut you have a winner, you have to do it no matter what.

Ginger Purdy

You take people as far as they will go, not as far as you would like them to go.

Jeannette Rankin

I'm really glad that your young people missed the Depression and missed the big war. But I do regret that they missed the leaders that I knew, leaders who told us when things were tough and that we'd have to sacrifice, and that these difficulties might last awhile. . . . They brought us together and they gave us a sense of national purpose.

Ann Richards

Women's place is in the House—and in the Senate.

Gloria Schaffer

Many women have more power than they recognize, and they're very hesitant to use it, for they fear they won't be loved.

Patricia Schroeder

Leadership is not manifested by coercion, even against the resented. Greatness is not manifested by unlimited pragmatism, which places such a high premium on the end justifying any means and any methods.

Margaret Chase Smith

I'll stay until I'm tired of it. So long as Britain needs me, I shall never be tired of it.
Margaret Thatcher

If the first woman God ever made was strong enough to turn the world upside down all alone, these women together ought to be able to turn it back, and get it right side up again! And now they is asking to do it, the men better let them.
Sojourner Truth

The only safe ship in a storm is leader*ship*.

Faye Wattleton

Being consistent meant not departing from convictions already formulated; being a leader meant making other persons accept these convictions. It was a narrow track, and one-way, but a person might travel a considerable distance on it. A number of dictators have.

Jessamyn West

The extent to which you are able to transform your "self-concern" into "other-concern" will determine your effectiveness in getting others to follow along.
Anon.

There's nothing so unequal as the equal treatment of unequals. Individualize your leadership.

Anon.

Chapter 24

LIFE

Don't be afraid your life will end; be afraid that it will never begin.

Grace Hansen

❧

We rarely stop and actually consider *LIFE*. It is something that, after all, we have, use, live. The business, the *busy-ness*, of life is so all-consuming that we almost never stop to examine the package that the gift is in. Unless threatened, life is rarely considered.

Like a child ripping away at a hammered-goldleaf-wrapped package to get at the plastic toy inside, we generally look at things, and not the substance of the thing, life itself.

As a speaker, you are dealing in life and the stuff of life. You are talking about leadership, vision, management, time, sales, goals, ideas, personal and organizational survival. As you work from the platform you are generally educating, encouraging, challenging, exhorting your listeners to action. But when you do, do you frame the issue in the urgency of the *now* of it, as well as the *how* of it?

Why the *now* of it? Because life is an extremely temporary condition. We have some number of years allotted to us (none of us knows how many) and that's *all* we have! Since this is a given, what is important is that we focus not on *how many?* over which we have no control, but on making the most of what we do have.

As a speaker, you have the wonderful opportunity to help people focus on the joy of living in the now and doing something of significance—now. Now is the surety; tomorrow is only a possibility. You need to help your listeners get a fix on life—both the *now* and the *how*—and understand that doing something is almost always better than thinking about doing something.

Your job is also to help your audience realize the reciprocal nature of these principles, and of life itself. Life is a continuum. We are indebted to someone else for it, we didn't create our own. But we can make a payment on it by caring, sharing, doing with and for others. From the platform, you try with your gifts and skills to elicit those same responses from others.

But, a lone speaker on a lonely platform can always use some help when it comes to helping people deal with the *how* and the *now* of life.

Few of us are so gifted or exalted that we can teach these lessons with neither support nor reference. Thus, the wisdom of others is a very valuable ally in this effort.

This chapter contains the thoughts of a wide variety of women on life. Some are philosophers, some are teachers, some are optimists, some are cynics. But all have expressed themselves about the importance of living life and making it a life of consequence.

To me these questions have been a jolt of reality or an inspiration. These are words that I use to try to challenge or motivate my listeners. As I am helped, I try to help others. I try to convey a sense of purpose, of the value of life as a reciprocal gift, of the need to do what needs to be done while there is still the opportunity to do it. If my audience gains half as much from hearing these words as I get from repeating them, then we have both profited from the encounter.

❧

You do not know what life means when all the difficulties are removed! I am simply smothered and sickened with advantages. It is like eating a sweet dessert the first thing in the morning.

Jane Addams

Behold, we live through all things,—famine, thirst,
Bereavement, pain; all grief and misery,
All woe and sorrow; life inflicts its worst
On soul and body,—but we cannot die,
Though we be sick, and tired, and tired, and faint, and worn,
Lo, all things can be borne!

Elizabeth Akers Allen

The very commonplaces of life are components of its eternal mystery.

Gertrude Atherton

Life! we've been long together
Through pleasant and through cloudy weather;
'Tis hard to part when friends are dear,—
Perhaps 'twill cost a sigh, a tear;
Then steal away, give little warning,
Choose thine own time;
Say not "Good night," but in some brighter clime
Bid me "Good morning."

Anna Letitia Barbauld

Life would be as insupportable without the prospect of death, as it would be without sleep.

Lady Marguerite Blessington

Experience isn't interesting 'till it begins to repeat itself—in fact, 'till it does that, it hardly *is* experience.

Elizabeth Bowen

I finally figured out the only reason to be alive is to enjoy it.

Rita Mae Brown

I am so absorbed in the wonder of earth and the life upon it that I cannot think of heaven and the angels. I have enough for this life.

Pearl S. Buck

Instead of looking at life as a narrowing funnel, we can see it ever widening to choose the things we want to do, to take the wisdoms we've learned and create something.

Liz Carpenter

Life itself is the proper binge.

Julia Child

I like living. I have sometimes been wildly, despairingly, acutely miserable, racked with sorrow, but through it all I still know quite certainly that just to be alive is a grand thing.

Agatha Christie

The pleasures of the world are deceitful; they promise more than they give. They trouble us in seeking them, they do not satisfy us when possessing them, and they make us despair in losing them.

Mme. de Lambert

Living is a form of not being sure, not knowing what's next or how. The moment you know how, you begin to die a little.

Agnes De Mille

Life appears like a long shipwreck of which the debris are friendship, glory, and love. The shores of existence are strewn with them.

Mme. de Staël

To live is so startling it leaves little time for anything else.

Emily Dickinson

The strongest desire known to human life is to continue living. The next strongest is to use the instruments by which life is generated for its own rewards, not for the sake of generation. The third potent desire is to excel and be acknowledged.

Dorothy Dudley

Most human beings today waste some twenty-five to thirty years of their lives before they break through the actual and conventional lies which surround them.

Isadora Duncan

Whenever tragedy strikes and people ask, "Why did this have to happen to me?" I always want to say to them, "Why not you? Are you so much different from the rest of the human race?"

Geraldine Emmett

Alone I walked the ocean strand,
  A pearly shell was in my hand;
I stooped and wrote upon the sand
  My name—the year—the day.

As onward from the spot I passed,
  One lingering look behind I cast,
A wave came rolling high and fast,
  And washed my lines away.

Hannah Flagg Gould

There is no such thing as security. There never has been.

Germaine Greer

I gave my life to learning how to live. Now that I have organized it all . . . it's just about over.

Sandra Hochman

The bread of life is love, the salt of life is work, the sweetness of life is poesy, and the water of life is faith.

Anna Jameson

We have not sat at the feet of older women and learned from them. There's been no time. We're too busy building our professions, attending club meetings, decorating our new homes, running children from one enrichment program to another, buying more and more things, keeping fit at the health club and trying to be the super ladies of the '80s and '90s.

Barbara Jenkins

It's gonna be a long hard drag, but we'll make it.

Janis Joplin

Life is either a daring adventure or nothing at all. Security is mostly a superstition. It does not exist in nature.

Helen Keller

A sacred burden is this life ye bear; look on it; lift it; bear it solemnly; fail not for sorrow; falter not for sin; but onward, upward, till the goal ye win.

Fanny Kemble

Life isn't a matter of milestones but of moments.

Rose Fitzgerald Kennedy

If a problem can be solved with money, then you don't have a problem.

Katherine Keough

Life can only be understood backwards but it must be lived forward.

Susan Kierbegaard

This life isn't bad for a first draft.

Joan Konner

Growing up is, after all, only the understanding that one unique and incredible experience is what everyone shares.

Doris Lessing

The most exhausting thing in life is being insincere.

Anne Morrow Lindbergh

Mistakes are part of the dues one pays for a full life.

Sophia Loren

I've always felt that I would develop into a really fine actress because I care more about life beyond the camera than the life in front of it.

Shirley MacLaine

Who would venture upon the journey of life, if compelled to begin it at the end?
Françoise d'Aubigné Maintenon

I want to meet my God awake.

Empress Maria Theresa

Why are we so fond of life which begins with a cry and ends with a groan?
Mary, Countess of Warwick

Life in the twentieth century is like a parachute jump: you have to get it right the first time.

Margaret Mead

It is not true that life is one damn thing after another. It's the same damn thing over and over again.

Edna St. Vincent Millay

Reality is something you rise above.

Liza Minnelli

Life's under no obligation to give us what we expect.

Margaret Mitchell

How short is human life! The very breath
Which frames my words accelerates my death.

Hannah More

Life is what we make it, always has been, always will be.

Grandma Moses

What a death in life it must be—an existence whose sole aim is good eating and drinking, splendid houses and elegant clothes! Not that these things are bad in moderation—and with something higher beyond. But with nothing beyond?

Dinah Maria Mulock

In the midst of life we are in debt.

Ethel Watts Mumford

What we call reality is an agreement that people have arrived at to make life more livable.

Louise Nevelson

People living deeply have no fear of death.

Anaïs Nin

Life is easier to take than you'd think; all that is necessary is to accept the impossible, do without the indispensable, and bear the intolerable.

Kathleen Norris

You might as well live.

Dorothy Parker

Turning away from the rest of the world, and turning inward—is death.

Connie Warner Pepple

I wanted a perfect ending. . . . Now I've learned, the hard way, that some poems don't rhyme, and some stories don't have a clear beginning, middle and end. Life is about not knowing, having to change, taking the moment and making the best of it, without knowing what's going to happen next. Delicious ambiguity.

Gilda Radner

A little work, a little sleep, a little love and it's all over.

Mary Roberts Rinehart

I could not, at any age, be content to take my place in a corner by the fireside and simply look on. Life was meant to be lived. Curiosity must be kept alive. The fatal thing is the rejection. One must never, for whatever reason, turn his back on life.

Eleanor Roosevelt

Live virtuously, my lord, and you cannot die too soon, nor live too long.

Lady Rachel Russell

In great moments life seems neither right nor wrong, but something greater, it seems inevitable.

Margaret Sherwood

One learns in life to keep silent and draw one's own confusions.

Cornelia Otis Skinner

No matter how big or soft or warm your bed is, you still have to get out of it.

Grace Slick

You know, your career is just your career. Your life is your *life*!

Sissy Spacek

Life is meant to be lived. The miser who hoards it only cheats himself.

Geri Trotta

Motherhood is neither a duty nor a privilege, but simply the way that humanity can satisfy the desire for physical immortality and triumph over the fear of death.

Dame Rebecca West

Life is the only real counselor; wisdom unfiltered through personal experience does not become a part of the moral tissue.

Edith Wharton

I think of death as some delightful journey
That I shall take when all my tasks are done.

Ella Wheeler Wilcox

Biography is to give a man some kind of shape after his death.

Virginia Woolf

Life is what happened to you while you were making other plans.

Anon.

Chapter **25**

LITERATURE

The role of a writer is not to say what we all can say, but what we are unable to say.

Anaïs Nin

❦

Why should LITERATURE be a chapter in a book of quotations whose primary focus is a reference for the speaker? The answer lies in the nature, in the very definition of the word. The dictionary defines *literature* as "writing that is adjudged to be of excellence or worth, writing capable of evoking an emotional response from a reader" (or in our case, a listener).

Thus quotations drawn from the great writings of the past carry with them their own validation. The *sifting* has been done by time, and the words and thoughts that remain demonstrate a universality and transcendence that gives the statement the weight of both age and merit.

This is certainly not to suggest that all literature had to have been written sometime in the past. There is much contemporary writing that meets all the tests needed to qualify—except age. Contemporary works of all kinds can be a great source of quotations, often in a language to which your listeners' ears are more attuned.

I would also mention that by literature I don't just mean the so-called classics of Western (European) writing. Writers who think well and write well come from all literary traditions and from all continents and are (need it be said?) of both sexes. Salient, well-constructed thoughts transcend their source. The universality of the truths they communicate causes them to be effective for the speaker even if the audience doesn't have the slightest idea of their source. (I once read that fully half of the quotations that people believe to be biblical are actually from Shakespeare!)

Some beginning speakers feel that the use of so-called literary quotations will cause them to sound pompous—or worse, stodgy or old-fashioned. Actually just the opposite is true. Using the words of a great thinker or a great author to support your point has a validating effect that could be the difference between an audience thinking, "Who does she think she is?" and "She knows what she's talking about!"

When trying to determine the most appropriate quotations to use, it is important to remember that there is a difference between a strong, timely quotation and a cliché. "The only thing we have to fear is fear itself" is a powerful statement, but it has been so overworked and used in so many ways to prove so many different points that it lacks in context much of the power of the words themselves. But the speaker can keep from falling into the cliché trap by saying, for instance, "To paraphrase Roosevelt's famous statement about fear, 'The only thing *we* have to fear' is not being prepared for what we know we must do."

Many people also shrink from using quotations from literature because they think, "Everybody knows those words; I need something different." Remember that nothing is truly learned forever. Wisdom must be learned over and over again by each generation. An older audience may know that Gertrude Stein or George Eliot said something, but a younger group may not be familiar with either the quotation or the author. What you, the presenter, take for granted may be a new gem of truth for your listeners. And for those who are familiar with the source and context of the quotation, you have created a common bond through a point of reference known and appreciated by both speaker and listener.

Using literary references doesn't mean you are trying to impress. It means you care about your audience, care about your topic, and think enough of both to research while preparing your speech. It means giving your remarks a richness and flavor that makes your presentation one of consequence. And in some small way, it means you are doing your individual part to elevate our world just a little bit above the ordinary.

❦

It is rarely that you see an American writer who is not hopelessly sane.

Margaret Anderson

The answers you get from literature depend upon the questions you pose.

Margaret Atwood

In short, [a novel is] only some work in which the most thorough knowledge of human nature, the happiest delineation of its varieties, the liveliest effusions of wit and humour are conveyed to the world in the best chosen language.

Jane Austen

Writing, I think, is not apart from living. Writing is a kind of double living. The writer experiences everything twice. Once in reality and once in that mirror which waits always before or behind.

Catherine Drinker Bowen

In Communist countries, you execute your poets. In the free world, the poets execute themselves.

Kate Braverman

I was gravely warned by some of my female acquaintances that no woman could expect to be regarded as a lady after she had written a book.

Lydia M. Child

I've always believed in writing without a collaborator, because where two people are writing the same book, each believes he gets all the worry and only half the royalties.

Agatha Christie

Sit down and put down everything that comes into your head and then you're a writer. But an author is one who can judge his own stuff's worth, without pity, and destroy most of it.

Colette

There is no frigate like a book to take us lands away
Nor any courses like a page of prancing poetry
This traverse may the poorest take without oppress of toil
How frugal is the chariot that bears the human soul!

Emily Dickinson

It is a joy to find thoughts one might have, beautifully expressed ... by someone ... wiser than oneself.

Marlene Dietrich

It has taken me years of struggle, hard work and research to learn to make one simple gesture, and I know enough about the art of writing to realize that it would take as many years of concentrated effort to write one simple, beautiful sentence.

Isadora Duncan

Only a fool would try to compress a hundred centuries into a hundred pages of hazardous conclusions. We proceed.

Ariel and Will Durant

No story is the same to us after a lapse of time; or rather we who read it are no longer the same interpreters.

George Eliot

Literature must be seen in terms of the contemporary concern for survival.

Louise Erdrich

Life can't ever really defeat a writer who is in love with writing, for life itself is a writer's lover until death—fascinating, cruel, lavish, warm, cold, treacherous, constant.

Edna Ferber

Very young writers often do not revise at all. Like a hen looking at a chalk line, they are hypnotized by what they have written. "How can it be altered?" they think. It has to be altered. You have to learn how.

Dorothy Canfield Fisher

If I read a book that impresses me, I have to take myself firmly in hand before I mix with other people; otherwise they would think my mind rather queer.

Anne Frank

If I couldn't read, I couldn't live.

Thelma Green

Only the poet can look beyond the detail and see the whole picture.

Helen Hayes

Nothing you write, if you hope to be any good, will ever come out as you first hoped.

Lillian Hellman

I like density, not volume. I like to leave something to the imagination. The reader must fit the pieces together, with the author's discreet help.

Maureen Howard

Writing is one of the few professions left where you take all the responsibility for what you do. It's really dangerous and ultimately destroys you as a writer if you start thinking about responses to your work or what your audience needs.

Erica Jong

Literature is my Utopia. Here I am not disfranchised. No barrier of the senses shuts me out from the sweet, gracious discourse of my book friends. They talk to me without embarrassment or awkwardness.

Helen Keller

The one thing a writer has to have is a pencil and some paper. That's enough, so long as she knows that she and she alone is in charge of that pencil, and responsible, she and she alone, for what it writes on that paper.

Ursula K. Le Guin

What release to write so that one forgets oneself, forgets one's companion, forgets where one is or what one is going to do next—to be drenched in sleep or in the sea. Pencils and pads are curling blue sheets alive with letters heaped upon the desk.

Anne Morrow Lindbergh

All books are either dreams or swords. You can cut or you can drug with words.

Amy Lowell

All autobiographies are alibi-ographies.

Clare Boothe Luce

It was a book to kill time for those who like it better dead.

Rose Macauley

The writer by nature of his profession is a dreamer and a conscious dreamer. How, without love and the intuition that comes from love, can a human being place himself in the situation of another human being? He must imagine, and imagination takes humility, love, and great courage. How can you create a character without love and the struggle that goes with love?

Carson McCullers

Looking back, I imagine I was always writing. Twaddle it was too. But far better to write twaddle or anything, anything, than nothing at all.

Katherine Mansfield

If I'm a lousy writer, then a lot of people have got lousy taste.

Grace Metalious

A person who publishes a book appears willfully in public with his pants down.

Edna St. Vincent Millay

No entertainment is as cheap as reading, nor any pleasure so lasting.

Lady Mary Wortley Montague

The role of a writer is not to say what we all can say, but what we are unable to say.

Anaïs Nin

There seems to be no physical handicap or chance of environment that can hold a real writer down, and there is no luck, no influence, no money that will keep a writer going when she is written out.

Kathleen Norris

It's difficult to beat making your living thinking and writing about subjects that matter to you.

Eleanor Holmes Norton

Man is a problem-solving animal and the organizing of vast subjects must give pleasure, evidently; nothing seems to me to involve more intellectual effort than the organizing of a big novel, and I cannot imagine anything more rewarding.

Joyce Carol Oates

This is not a novel to be tossed aside lightly. It should be thrown with great force.

Dorothy Parker

Never use the word *gossip* in a pejorative sense. It's the stuff of biography and has to be woven in.

Joan Peyser

Nothing stinks like a pile of unpublished writing.

Sylvia Plath

To take for granted as truth all that is alleged against the fame of others, is a species of credulity that men would blush at on any other subject.

Jane Porter

Most people don't realize that writing is a craft. You have to take your apprenticeship in it like everything else.

Katherine Anne Porter

The reason that fiction is more interesting than any other form of literature to those of us who really like to study people, is that in fiction the author can really tell the truth without hurting anyone and without humiliating himself too much.

Eleanor Roosevelt

When creative juices flow
Catch them with a pen
Cause if you don't
You may find you can't
Recapture them again.

June Shanahan

Poetry ennobles the heart and the eyes, and unveils the meaning of all things upon which the heart and the eyes dwell. It discovers the secret rays of the universe, and restores to us forgotten paradise.

Dame Edith Sitwell

The difference between a story and a painting or photograph is that in a story you can write, "He's still alive." But in a painting or a photo you can't show 'still.' You can just show him being alive.

Susan Sontag

Aspiring writers have to be willing to keep at it until they drop.

Danielle Steel

The art of writing is the art of applying the seat of the pants to the seat of the chair.

Mary Heaton Vorse

Deliver me from writers who say the way they live doesn't matter. I'm not sure a bad person can write a good book. If art doesn't make us better, then what on earth is it for?

Alice Walker

What discoveries I've made in the course of writing stories, all begin with the particular, never the general.

Eudora Welty

Writing is so difficult that I often feel that writers, having had their hell on earth, will escape punishment hereafter.

Jessamyn West

Journalism is the ability to meet the challenge of filling space.

Dame Rebecca West

To write weekly, to write daily, to write shortly, to write for busy people catching trains in the morning or for tired people coming home in the evening, is a heartbreaking task for men who know good writing from bad.

Virginia Woolf

The more sins you confess, the more books you will sell.

Anon.

Writing a book is like scrubbing an elephant: there's no good place to begin or end, and it's hard to keep track of what you've already covered.

Anon.

Chapter 26

LOVE

Nobody has ever measured, not even poets, how much the heart can hold.

Zelda Fitzgerald

❦

So many songs, poems, letters, and books have been written about LOVE, so many thoughts and words have been devoted to it, that the subject has almost become trite in its consideration.

The same is true when considering quotations about love, and how and when to use them. One can easily employ these quotations to fall into a sort of philosophical vacuousness that robs one's topic of whatever substance might have been in it originally.

Quotations about love derive their validity from the little line in the *Sound of Music* that says, "Love isn't love 'till you give it away." This is the essence of love from the speaker's perspective: the giving—actually, the sharing—of something that brings the topic into focus.

It is seldom the speaker's responsibility—unless her forum happens to be the pulpit—to speak *on* love. But in helping your listeners understand the beauty of caring, of sharing, of a devotion to something—be it a cause or a creature—quotations concerning love are both appropriate and useful.

When using quotations from this category, it is important to note that love in this context is not a weak or vapid sentiment. It is a robust reality that empowers the speaker or the listener. And it is in this context of energy that the speaker should employ these quotations.

When we use quotations about love, we should use them to reveal the substance of a strongly held feeling or emotion. And we should use them to help our listeners grasp that substance and employ it in their own lives or work.

We must help an audience understand and, hopefully, be willing to demonstrate the substance of giving, of sharing, of expressing a belief or a commit-ment with the heart, as well as the mind. This being said, though, it is always the speaker's task to remember that her responsibility is to promote and encour-age *action* in her audiences, not merely contemplation.

That is why these quotations are expressions of the actions of many differ-ent sorts of women who cared enough to give, to share, to put the force of their life into something that would outlive them. For some of these authors, it was, literally, their life that was the tool by which their love was pronounced. For others, it was a cause or an organization to which the substance of their love was dedicated. For still others, it was the very living of their lives that has brought forth the lesson and the example. Regardless of how it was manifested, love—and its example—is the commonality that ties these quotations together.

When we speak about a concept that is larger than life—such as love—it is essential that we not only validate that concept, but our own qualifications to speak about it, through the words and thoughts of those whose example is qualification enough. Thus, these quotations are designed to help empower the speaker as much as they are intended to help the speaker empower and inspire her listeners.

Inspiration by example is one of the speaker's greatest tools. Use these and your own collection of quotations about love to inspire and thus to motivate and lead. You will find that, more often than not, you will always be among the motivated.

Love is the only thing that we can carry with us when we go, and it makes the end so easy.

Louisa May Alcott

Unremembered and afar
I watched you as I watched a star,
Through darkness struggling into view,
And loved you better than you knew.

Elizabeth Akers Allen

A lady's imagination is very rapid; it jumps from admiration to love, from love to matrimony in a moment.

Jane Austen

A woman's head is always influenced by heart; but a man's heart by his head.

Lady Marguerite Blessington

The prerequisite for making love is to like someone enormously.

Helen Gurley Brown

How do I love thee? Let me count the ways.
I love thee to the depth and breadth and height
My soul can reach, when feeling out of sight
For the ends of Being and ideal Grace.
I love thee to the level of everyday's
Most quiet need, by sun and candlelight.
I love thee freely, as men strive for Right;
I love thee purely, as they turn from Praise.
I love thee with the passion put to use
In my old griefs, and with my childhood's faith.
I love thee with a love I seemed to lose
With my lost saints—I love thee with the breath,
Smiles, tears, of all my life!—and, if God choose,
I shall but love thee better after death.

Elizabeth Barrett Browning

You can give without loving, but you cannot love without giving.

Amy Carmichael

Where there is great love there are always miracles.

Willa Cather

Standing, as I do, in the view of God and eternity I realize patriotism is not enough. I must have no hatred or bitterness toward anyone.

Edith Cavell

The cure for all the ills and wrongs, the cares, the sorrows, and the crimes of humanity, all lie in the one word "love." It is the divine vitality that everywhere produces and restores life. To each and every one of us, it gives the power of working miracles.

Lydia M. Child

Love is not enough. It must be the foundation, the cornerstone—but not the complete structure. It is much too pliable, too yielding.

Bette Davis

Almost all married people fight, although many are ashamed to admit it. Actually a marriage in which no quarreling at all takes place may well be one that is dead or dying from emotional undernourishment. If you care, you probably fight.

Flora Davis

To love one who loves you, to admire one who admires you, in a word, to be the idol of one's idol, is exceeding the limit of human joy; it is stealing fire from heaven.

Delphine de Girardin

When loving hearts are separated, not the one which is exhaled to heaven, but the survivor, it is which tastes the sting of death.

Duchesse de Praslin

However old a conjugal union, it still garners some sweetness. Winter has some cloudless days, and under the snow a few flowers still bloom.

Mme. de Staël

Tears may be dried up, but the heart—never.

Marguerite de Valois

Gold does not satisfy love; it must be paid in its own coin.

Dorothée DeLuzy

Tennis is like marrying for money. Love has nothing to do with it.

Phyllis Diller

In love there are no vacations. No such thing. Love has to be lived fully with its boredom and all that.

Marguerite Duras

In the man whose childhood has known caresses and kindness, there is always a fibre of memory that can be touched to gentle issues.

George Eliot

The wonder of a little child!
He stirs the fonts of love;
Hard hearts grow kind at the sight of him;
He bears men's thoughts above.
There is no trouble in the bliss
That lingers in a baby's kiss.

Marianne Farningham

It seems that it is madder never to abandon one's self than often to be infatuated; better to be wounded, a captive and a slave, than always to walk in armor.

Margaret Fuller

Husbands are like fires. They go out if unattended.

Zsa Zsa Gabor

The people people have for friends
Your common sense appall,
But the people people marry
Are the queerest folk of all.

Charlotte Perkins Gilman

The story of love is not important. What is important is that one is capable of love. It is perhaps the only glimpse we are permitted of eternity.

Helen Hayes

My mother was dead for five years before I knew that I loved her very much.

Lillian Hellman

Love has nothing to do with what you are expecting to get—only what you are expecting to give—which is everything. What you will receive in return varies. But it really has no connection with what you give. You give because you love and cannot help giving. If you are very lucky, you may be loved back. That is delicious but it does not necessarily happen.

Katharine Hepburn

If we can still love those who made us suffer, we can love them all the more.
Anna Jameson

Love is like a beautiful flower which I may not touch, but whose fragrance makes the garden a place of delight just the same.
Helen Keller

I've had an exciting life; I married for love and got a little money along with it.
Rose Fitzgerald Kennedy

If we make our goal to live a life of compassion and unconditional love, then the world will indeed become a garden where all kinds of flowers can bloom and grow.
Elisabeth Kübler-Ross

Love doesn't just sit there like a stone; it has to be made, like bread, remade all the time, made new.
Ursula K. Le Guin

A woman without a man cannot meet a man, any man . . . without thinking, even if it's for a half-second, perhaps this is *the* man.
Doris Lessing

Him that I love, I wish to be free—even from me.
Anne Morrow Lindbergh

A youth with his first cigar makes himself sick; a youth with his first girl makes everybody sick.
Mary Wilson Little

It's matrimonial suicide to be jealous when you have a really good reason.
Clare Boothe Luce

All great lovers are articulate, and verbal seduction is the surest road to actual seduction.
Marya Mannes

Love is a flame which burns in heaven, and whose soft reflections radiate to us. Two worlds are opened, two lives given to it. It is by love that we double our being; it is by love that we approach God.
Aimee Martin

Love, it is a flower and you its only seed.

Amanda McBroom

The hearts of small children are delicate organs. A cruel beginning in this world can twist them into curious shapes. The heart of a hurt child can shrink so that forever afterward it is hard and pitted as the seed of a peach. Or, again, the heart of such a child may fester and swell until it is misery to carry within the body, easily chafed and hurt by the most ordinary things.

Carson McCullers

One of the oldest human needs is having someone to wonder where you are when you don't come home at night.

Margaret Mead

'Tis not love's going hurts my days, but that it went in little ways.

Edna St. Vincent Millay

Absence in love is like water upon fire; a little quickens, but much extinguishes it.

Hannah More

We can only learn to love by loving.

Iris Murdock

The quarrels of lovers are like summer showers that leave the country more verdant and beautiful.

Susanne Curchod Necker

Marriage—a book in which the first chapter is written in poetry and the remaining chapters in prose.

Beverley Nichols

Holy as heaven a mother's tender love, the love of many prayers and many tears which changes not with dim, declining years.

Caroline Norton

By the time you swear you're his, shivering and sighing, and he vows his passion is infinite, undying—lady, make a note of this: one of you is lying.

Dorothy Parker

Next to the love between man and his Creator . . . the love of one man and one woman is the loftiest and the most illusive ideal that has been set before the world. A perfect marriage is like a pure heart: those who have it are fit to see God.

Elizabeth Stuart Phelps

Love must be learned, and learned again and again; there is no end to it. Hate needs no instruction, but only wants to be provoked.

Katherine Anne Porter

Great is the power of might and mind,
But only love can make us kind,
And all we are or hope to be
Is empty pride and vanity—
If love is not a part of all
The greatest man is very small.

Helen Steiner Rice

Marriage: a souvenir of love.

Helen Rowland

Whenever I date a guy, I think, is this the man I want my children to spend their weekends with?

Rita Rudner

Loving is not just caring deeply, it's, above all, understanding.

Françoise Sagan

Fond as we are of our loved ones, there comes at times during their absence an unexplained peace.

Anne Shaw

Trouble is a part of your life, and if you don't share it you don't give the person who loves you enough chance to love you enough.

Dinah Shore

Some pray to marry the man they love,
  My prayer will somewhat vary:
I humbly pray to Heaven above
  That I love the man I marry.

Rose Pastor Stokes

Love is something like the clouds that were in the sky before the sun came out. You cannot touch the clouds, you know; but you feel the rain and know how glad the flowers and the thirsty earth are to have it after a hot day. You cannot touch love either; but you feel the sweetness that it pours into everything.

Annie Sullivan

In the opinion of the world, marriage ends all, as it does in a comedy. The truth is precisely the opposite: it begins all.

Anne Sophie Swetchine

Who ran to help me when I fell,
And would some pretty story tell,
Or kiss the place to make it well?
My Mother.

Anne Taylor

No one worth possessing
Can be quite possessed.

Sara Teasdale

Love is a fruit in season at all times, and within reach of every hand.

Mother Teresa

Some people are more turned on by money than they are by love. In one respect they are alike. They're both wonderful as long as they last.

Abigail Van Buren

The modern rule is that every woman must be her own chaperone.

Amy Vanderbilt

Love lights more fires than hate extinguishes.

Ella Wheeler Wilcox

When poverty comes in at the door, love flies out the window.

Anon.

Chapter **27**

MEN

I'm fascinated by a man with a twinkle in his eye.

Jacqueline Bisset

❧

uite obviously, this is a book by a woman consisting of the words of women. It is intended for the use of women speakers. The exclusion of quotations by MEN, while done with forethought, is also done without malice. It is also done without apology. And, while those expected to use these resources are primarily female, I would not be offended in the least if it were also of value—or at least of interest—to men.

This book of quotations is intended to broaden the perspective and the range of resources available to the speaker. It is intended to allow the woman speaker to expand her thinking (beyond the already extensive catalog of the wisdom of men) to include a greater content of the wisdom of women. It is sort of an equal time offering because, while fifty-two percent of America is female, the same ratio certainly hasn't been demonstrated in most quotation books.

As a speaker and presenter of many years' experience, I have never tried to limit my quotations and illustrations simply to those of women. I hope no one who uses this book will either. For a woman speaker to use only the thoughts of women would be as self-defeating and limiting as for a man to use only the words of other men. Until recently, of course, the only problem has been that there have been so few compilations of women's quotations from which to draw.

I should also say that just because the book is devoted exclusively to quotations by women, it is certainly not intended to be an anti-male offering. For women to reflect gender-based hostility from the platform is not just self-defeating, it is stupid!

A book of women's quotations would be incomplete if it did not include a selection of choice things that women have said *about* men.

The quotations in this chapter are of all types—wise, witty, caustic, kind, funny, insightful, silly. Some do, indeed, reflect the kind of anti-male bias to which I alluded. Sometimes these can be very effective in helping a woman speaker make a point, even if useful only as a bad example.

As a presenter, I encourage you to develop your own selection of "women on men" quotations—ones that will be most appropriate to your interests, audiences, and speaking challenges and opportunities. Use these as a reader's guide to expanding your own sources.

And never forget that, as the majority sex, we have an obligation to assist our minority brethren as much as possible in seeking their own enlightenment.

❧

If a man watches three football games in a row, he should be declared legally dead.

Erma Bombeck

Positive Reinforcement is hugging your husband when he does a load of laundry. Negative Reinforcement is telling him he used too much detergent.

Dr. Joyce Brothers

A girl can wait for the right man to come along but in the meantime that still doesn't mean she can't have a wonderful time with all the wrong ones.

Cher

A man can be part of the design of your life, not necessarily the redesign of your life.

Glenn Close

Men nearly always take their first risk of soul or body for the sake of some woman.

Mrs. J. C. Croly

Most women set out to change a man, and when they have changed him they do not like him.

Marlene Dietrich

Think of me as a sex symbol for the men who don't give a damn.

Phyllis Diller

For women, divorce can be the gateway to destitution. For men, it is more likely to be a golden parachute to freedom.

Barbara Ehrenreich

In the love of a brave and faithful man there is always a strain of maternal tenderness; he gives out again those beams of protecting fondness which were shed on him as he lay on his mother's knee.

George Eliot

If men can run the world, why can't they stop wearing neckties? How intelligent is it to start the day by tying a little noose around your neck?

Linda Ellerbee

Men weren't really the enemy—they were fellow victims suffering from an outmoded masculine mystique that made them feel unnecessarily inadequate when there were no bears to kill.

Betty Friedan

Macho does not prove mucho.

Zsa Zsa Gabor

Mender of toys, leader of boys,
Changer of fuses, kisser of bruises,
Bless him, dear Lord.
Mover of couches, soother of ouches,
Pounder of nails, teller of tales,
Reward him, O Lord.
Hanger of screens, counselor of teens,
Fixer of bikes, chastiser of tykes,
Help him, O Lord.
Raker of leaves, cleaner of eaves,
Dryer of dishes, fulfiller of wishes . . .
Bless him, O Lord.

Jo Ann Heidbreder

. . . we will no longer be led only by that half of the population whose socialization, through toys, games, values and expectations, sanctions violence as the final assertion of manhood, synonymous with nationhood.

Wilma Scott Heide

Plain women know more about men than beautiful ones do.

Katharine Hepburn

Men have always detested women's gossip because they suspect the truth: their measurements are being taken and compared.

Erica Jong

Marrying a man is like buying something you've been admiring for a long time in a shop window. You may love it when you get it home, but it doesn't always go with everything else in the house.

Jean Kerr

We seem to have a great nostalgia for the good old days—"when men were men"—or so we think. I think we have greatly romanticized this picture. It was so much easier for a man to *look* masculine when women were subservient. A man didn't have to be a real man at all, and he could fool everybody, including himself. . . . He played a role, and no one ever really knew or thought about what he was or felt beneath the surface of that role.

Eda Le Shan

Getting along with men isn't what's truly important. The vital knowledge is how to get along with a man, one man.

Phyllis McGinley

Men have always been afraid that women could get along without them.

Margaret Mead

His voice was as intimate as the rustle of sheets.

Dorothy Parker

The great truth is that women actually like men, and men can never believe it.

Isabel Patterson

[Women] can go wherever they want—as long as we teach men how to do housework! The world will really change for us when they start doing their share.

Sally Jessy Raphael

Every man wants a woman to appeal to his better side, his nobler instincts and his higher nature—and another woman to help him forget them.

Helen Rowland

Why get married and make one man miserable when I can stay single and make thousands miserable.

Carrie Snow

What is most beautiful in virile men is something feminine; what is most beautiful in feminine women is something masculine.

Susan Sontag

Why does a woman work ten years to change a man's habits and then complain that he's not the man she married?

Barbra Streisand

Strephon's kiss was lost in jest,
   Robin's lost in play,
But the kiss in Colin's eyes
   Haunts me night and day.

Sara Teasdale

One of the things being in politics has taught me is that men are not a reasoned or reasonable sex.

Margaret Thatcher

The young men of today seem mostly to be interested in the manner rather than the matter.

Alice B. Toklas

It is possible that blondes also prefer gentlemen.

Mamie Van Doren

It's not the men in my life that counts, it's the life in my men.

Mae West

The only time a woman really succeeds in changing a man is when he's a baby.
Natalie Wood

Sexiness wears thin after a while and beauty fades, but to be married to a man who makes you laugh every day, ah, now that's a real treat!

Joanne Woodward

Chapter 28

OPTIMISM

The world is round and the place which may seem like the end may also be the beginning.

Ivy Baker Priest

❧

A pessimist should never be a platform speaker; it is a job for optimists only. As a communicator, it is part of your responsibility to your audience to take whatever might be the difficult realities of your topic and convert those realities into understandable, positive opportunities.

I often describe myself as a pragmatic optimist. To be an optimist is not to deny reality, but rather to understand the nature of things as they are and then to have the vision, courage, faith, and willingness to alter the existing reality in a way that will help lead to a positive outcome.

The speaker who does not at least try to communicate this pragmatic optimism is not likely to receive a second speaking invitation from a group—and shouldn't! Anybody can deliver a recitation of problems. But it takes a speaker with skill to help convert those problems into opportunities, and to leave her listeners with not only the desire to make a difference, but also with the belief that they *can* make a difference.

When you are fortunate enough to receive that blessed opportunity to present before other people, then it must be one of your articles of faith, deeply ingrained in your personal philosophy, that you will elevate your audience. This is a challenge that is much easier said than done. But, as the writer said, "Life is difficult." Understanding that is easy; doing something about it, and helping others do something about it, is the skill part.

It is important to balance the problem-definition part of your remarks with timely stories and quotations that keep your presentation from being a downer.

Conventional wisdom holds that a speech should close on an upward tilt, and I absolutely agree. However, there is nothing that says you can't have a whole series of uppers in the body of your remarks as well. As with humorous quotations, those about optimism certainly should not be used just as opening and closing material.

This collection of quotations is designed to provide you with thoughts that can both enliven your speech and inspire you as the speaker. These statements of optimism come from women whose lives are a composite of positives and negatives, yet they have left us a record of positive responses to their often negative circumstances. I hope you will draw upon these resources to help fuel your own growing store of elevating quotations and illustrations.

Remember that as a speaker you haven't done your job if you don't leave your listeners with a *can do* belief, a *can do* attitude, and a *can do* commitment.

❧

Some people are still unaware that reality contains unparalleled beauties. The fantastic and unexpected, the ever-changing and renewing is nowhere so exemplified as in real life itself.

Berenice Abbott

One of the things I learned the hard way was that it doesn't pay to get discouraged. Keeping busy and making optimism a way of life can restore your faith in yourself.

Lucille Ball

Invest in the human soul. Who knows, it might be a diamond in the rough.

Mary McLeod Bethune

Be glad today. Tomorrow may bring tears.
Be brave today. The darkest night will pass.
And golden rays will usher in the dawn.
Who conquers now shall rule the coming years.

Sarah Knowles Bolton

It has never been, and never will be easy work! But the road that is built in hope is more pleasant to the traveler than the road built in despair, even though they both lead to the same destination.

Marion Zimmer Bradley

Life without idealism is empty indeed. We just have hope or starve to death.

Pearl S. Buck

Always look out for the sunlight the Lord sends into your days.

Hope Campbell

A child's world is fresh and new and beautiful, full of wonder and excitement. It is our misfortune that for most of us that clear-eyed vision, that true instinct for what is beautiful and awe-inspiring, is dimmed and even lost before we reach adulthood.

Rachel Carson

Nothing is so good as it seems beforehand.

George Eliot

When doubts and fears are growing,
It's hard to keep on going
From day to day not knowing
Just what the end will be.
Take each day as you find it,
If things go wrong, don't mind it,
For each day leaves behind it
A chance to start anew.

Gertrude Ellgas

The inner side of every cloud
Is bright and shining;
Therefore I turn my clouds about,
And always wear them inside out,
To show the lining.

Ellen Thornycroft Fowler Felkin

I do not despair about our addiction to violence. In order to live longer, we have given up red meat, sugar, salt, tobacco, caffeine, and alcohol. Surely, we can give up violence as well.

SuEllen Fried

The English word "crisis" is translated by the Chinese with two little characters; one means "danger," the other "opportunity."

Jean Hougk

We're still not where we're going but we're still not where we were.

Natasha Josefowitz

Although the world is full of suffering, it is full also of the overcoming of it.

Helen Keller

Birds sing after a storm, why shouldn't we?

Rose Fitzgerald Kennedy

I have never wanted to be anything but a gymnast. Maybe it is dangerous—but when you start thinking of danger, you might as well give up.

Olga Korbut

Hope is love's happiness, but not its life.

Letitia E. Landon

But to look back all the time is boring. Excitement lies in tomorrow.

Natalia Makarova

If the people have no bread, let them eat cake.

Marie Antoinette

In times of unrest and fear, it is perhaps the writer's duty to celebrate, to single out some of the values we can cherish, to talk about some of the few warm things we know in a cold world.

Phyllis McGinley

After all, tomorrow is another day.

Margaret Mitchell

At dawn of Love, at dawn of Life,
At dawn of Peace that follows Strife,
At dawn of all we long for so—
The sun is rising—let us go.

Louise Chandler Moulton

Take the hope from the heart of man and you make him a beast of prey.

Ouida

It's such an act of optimism to get through a day and enjoy it and laugh and do all that without thinking about death. What spirit human beings have!

Gilda Radner

There are no problems—only opportunities to be creative.

Dorye Roettger

Only she who attempts the absurd can achieve the impossible.

Sharon Schuster

The fact that God has prohibited despair gives misfortune the right to hope all things, and leaves hope free to dare all things.

Anne Sophie Swetchine

There is nothing more demoralizing than sudden, overwhelming disillusionment.

Dorothy Thompson

220

OPTIMISM

Teaching is the greatest act of optimism.

Colleen Wilcox

Talk happiness. The world is sad enough
Without your woe. No path is wholly rough.

Ella Wheeler Wilcox

Hope tells a flattering tale,
Delusive, vain, and hollow.
Ah! Let not hope prevail,
Lest disappointment follow.

Miss Wrother

He who has health has hope. And he who has hope has everything.

Arabian proverb

Walk on a rainbow trail;
  walk on a trail of song,
  and all about you will be beauty.
There is a way out of every dark mist,
  over a rainbow trail.

Navajo song

Chapter 29

PHILOSOPHY

A healthful hunger for a great idea is the beauty and blessedness of life.

Jean Ingelow

❧

I thought a good deal about what to name this chapter—whether to label it Philosophy or Truth. I finally settled on PHILOSOPHY because this chapter is a collection of perspectives on an assortment of philosophies as perceived by diverse women in varying circumstances at different times in history. Whether or not these are truths to me, or to you, is less relevant than that they were truths to the women who spoke them.

I have included this chapter and its quotations in the hope that, by reading and reflecting upon them, they might help to clarify or crystallize your own beliefs into an operational philosophy, or else expand the philosophy under which you now live.

From my own perspective, my philosophy (of the worth of the individual, of the necessity to put back more than we take from life, and the compilation of everything else that I believe in) is the bedrock upon which my life is based and from which my decisions are made. It provides the moral and intellectual foundation for the person I know as *me*. It defines who I am to me.

Every single quotation in this chapter does not represent my personal view of truth. But, in thinking through many of these philosophies, I have been better able to form my own. I hope you will be able to use them for the same purpose, as well as to enliven your presentations and enlighten your listeners.

This latter point—enlightening an audience—is a vital task for a speaker. As a speaker, you must have a motivating philosophy. Your philosophy, your personal assemblage of truths, is your moral strength. If you have none, you are rudderless. Even worse, if you operate with the rudder of situational ethics, steering wherever the prevailing wind takes you, you are without an anchor. Perhaps some of the following quotations about philosophy will help to strengthen you and your presentations.

There are no dangerous thoughts; thinking itself is dangerous.

Hannah Arendt

Do not do what you would undo if caught.

Leah Arendt

It is worse than folly . . . not to recognize the truth, for in it lies the tinder for tomorrow.

Pearl S. Buck

It is a wholesome and necessary thing for us to turn again to the earth and in the contemplation of her beauties to know the sense of wonder and humility.

Rachel Carson

It makes all the difference in the world to your life whether you arrive at a philosophy and a religion or not. It makes the difference between living in a world which is merely a constant changing mass of phenomena and living in a significant, ordered universe.

Mary Ellen Chase

"Whosoever quarrels with his fate does not understand it," says Bettine; and among all her sayings she spoke none wiser.

Lydia M. Child

There are sadistic scientists who hasten to hunt down error instead of establishing the truth.

Marie Curie

Perseverance and audacity generally win.

Dorothée DeLuzy

It is good a philosopher should remind himself, now and then, that he is a particle pontificating on infinity.

Ariel and Will Durant

To live and let live, without clamour for distinction or recognition; to wait on divine love; to write truth first on the tablet of one's own heart—this is the sanity and perfection of living, and my human ideal.

Mary Baker Eddy

Can any man or woman choose duties? No more than they can choose their birthplace, or their father and mother.

George Eliot

A vacuum can only exist, I imagine, by the things that enclose it.

Zelda Fitzgerald

Some truths are moral illnesses.

Marilyn French

Reverence the highest, have patience with the lowest. Let this day's performance of the meanest duty be thy religion. Are the stars too distant, pick up the pebble that lies at thy feet, and from it learn the all.

Margaret Fuller

I've always argued that it is just as desirable, just as possible, to have philosopher plumbers as philosopher kings.

Edith Starrett Green

The only causes of regret are laziness, outbursts of temper, hurting others, prejudice, jealousy and envy.

Germaine Greer

A man may be as much a fool from the want of sensibility as the want of sense.

Anna Jameson

Never worry too much about the things you can replace, worry only about the things you can't replace.

Winnie Johnson

I do not want the peace which passeth understanding, I want the understanding which bringeth peace.

Helen Keller

As a girl my temper often got out of bounds. But one day when I became angry at a friend over some trivial matter, my mother said to me, "Elizabeth, anyone who angers you conquers you."

Sister Elizabeth Kenny

Learn to get in touch with silence within yourself and know that everything in this life has a purpose. There are no mistakes, no coincidences, all events are blessings given to us to learn from.

Elizabeth Kübler-Ross

The Dust Bowl overlaid on the Great Depression taught us to "use it up, wear it out, make it do, or do without."

Mary Tullis Kunde

The only thing that makes life possible is permanent, intolerable uncertainty; not knowing what comes next.

Ursula K. Le Guin

Think wrongly, if you please, but in all cases think for yourself.

Doris Lessing

I have a simple philosophy. Fill what's empty. Empty what's full. And scratch what itches.

Alice Roosevelt Longworth

Fate keeps happening.

Anita Loos

The only people with whom you should try to get even, are those who have helped you.

May Maloo

Cherokee Traditional precepts:
Have a good mind. No matter what situation you're in, find something good about it, rather than the negative things. And in dealing with other human beings, find the good in them as well.
We are all interdependent. Do things for others—tribe, family, community—rather than just for yourself.
Look forward. Turn what has been done into a better path. If you're a leader, think about the impact of your decisions on seven generations into the future.

Chief Wilma Mankiller

The truth is friendship is every bit as sacred and eternal as marriage.

Katherine Mansfield

A soul occupied with great ideas best performs small duties.

Harriet Martineau

The negative cautions of science are never popular. If the experimentalist would not commit himself, the social philosopher, the preacher, and the pedagogue try the harder to give a shortcut answer.

Margaret Mead

We cannot take anything for granted beyond the first mathematical formulae. Question everything else.

Maria Mitchell

Study as if you are going to live forever; live as if you were going to die tomorrow.

Marion Mitchell

Since trifles make the sum of human things,
and half our misery from our foibles springs;
since life's best joys consist in peace and ease,
and few can save or serve, but all may please;
let the ungentle spirit learn from thence,
a small unkindness is a great offense.

Hannah More

For every ailment under the sun,
There is a remedy, or there is none;
If there be one, try to find it;
If there be none, never mind it.

Mother Goose

Don't take the will for the deed; get the deed!

Ethel Watts Mumford

Innocence and mystery never dwell long together.

Susanne Curchod Necker

I firmly believe that mankind is so instinctively, unconsciously involved with the survival and growth of the species that when an individual attempts to live selfishly, he will either fail or fall into despair.

Joyce Carol Oates

I saw that nothing was permanent. You don't want to possess anything that is dear to you because you might lose it.

Yoko Ono

The way I see it, if you want the rainbow, you gotta put up with the rain.

Dolly Parton

Never eat more than you can lift.

Miss Piggy

The virtues, like the muses, are always seen in groups. A good principle was never found solitary in any heart.

Jane Porter

To achieve, you need thought. You have to know what you are doing and that's real power.

Ayn Rand

What one decides to do in a crisis depends on one's philosophy of life, and that philosophy cannot be changed by an incident. If one hasn't any philosophy in crises, others make the decision.

Jeannette Rankin

I have never given very deep thought to a philosophy of life though I have a few ideas that I think are useful to me:
   Do whatever comes your way to do as well as you can.
   Think as little as possible about yourself.
   Think as much as possible about other people.
   Dwell on things that are interesting.
   Since you get more joy out of giving joy to others you should put a good deal of thought into the happiness that you are able to give.

Eleanor Roosevelt

The universe is made of stories, not of atoms.

Muriel Rukeyser

Art is not a study of positive reality, it is the seeking for ideal truth.

George Sand

Sanity is a cozy lie.

Susan Sontag

Rose is a rose is a rose is a rose.

Gertrude Stein

Sublime is the dominion of the mind over the body, that for a time can make flesh and nerve impregnable, and string the sinews like steel, so that the weak become so mighty.

Harriet Beecher Stowe

We forgive too little; forget too much.

Anne Sophie Swetchine

How many never think who think they do!

Jane Taylor

I'm extraordinarily patient provided I get my own way in the end.

Margaret Thatcher

Never face facts; if you do you'll never get up in the morning.

Marlo Thomas

I can therefore I am.

Simone Weil

We need so often in this life this balancing of scales,
This seeing how much in us wins and how much in us fails;
Before you judge another—just to lay him on the shelf,
It would be a splendid plan to take a walk around yourself.

Helen Welshimer

Suffering is also one of the ways of knowing you're alive.

Jessamyn West

One cannot think well, love well, sleep well—if one has not dined well.

Virginia Woolf

If thine enemy wrong thee, buy each of his children a drum.

Chinese proverb

It is easier to pull down than to build up.

Latin proverb

A man's true ideals are those he lives by, not always those he talks about.

Anon.

If your outgo exceeds your income, your upkeep will be your downfall.

Anon.

Chapter 30

POLITICS

When good people in any country cease their vigilance and struggle, then evil men prevail.

Pearl S. Buck

ife *is* POLITICS. And it has nothing to do with holding or seeking elective office. Life is politics at its very root, literally, because the word is derived from the Greek word for citizenship. Since there can be no true citizenship in the absence of participation, politics means being a part of the world around you. This is a status that is characteristic of practically everything we do in life.

Unless we are members of a cloistered monastic order, we live, work, and function in the midst of other people. In this milieu, we spend a greater part of every waking day trying to communicate, convince, direct, manage, interact, or otherwise "politic" with people. By whatever name, it is an everyday function of every person with whom you come into contact—including yourself! So regardless of what you call yourself, you and all around you are politicians.

A speaker is certainly a politician in this encompassing context. When you are on the platform in front of that committee or chairing that meeting, you are engaged in a very real political activity. And the greater your ability to use your participation skills, the more likely you are to generate some positive participatory outcomes from your listeners.

When you work to understand who the group is, both collectively and individually; when you try to understand motivations, interests, concerns; when you attempt to read their agenda, both published (even if not on paper) and hidden; you are participating. When you do these things you are putting yourself into active participation with your listeners, and you are striving to bring them into active participation with you.

This is important for the speaker because participation also implies giving and seeking commitments—commitments of time and energy and mind, of work and accomplishment.

When you speak, you will likely never succeed to any greater degree than that which you commit to your audience. If you approach the presentation in a half-hearted or unprepared way, you will probably do poorly. If your commitment, your interactive participation isn't there, neither are you. Thus for the speaker, the better your political (participation) skills, the more successful you will be.

The same is true for your audience. The more you demonstrate participation, the more you will likely elicit participation from them. And the more participation you get from your listeners, the more participation you will be able to inspire them to give to their own (or your own) interests.

The outstanding examples of women in this field are too great to confine to one chapter. Their quotations are scattered throughout this book. But included in this chapter are the words of women that can serve as an example of practically every form of participatory citizenship—from elective office to volunteerism of every kind.

These words can serve as illustrations of the worth of participation, of investing in a cause. Some are self-deprecating and some are tongue-in-cheek. Some are distillations of truth so salient that reading the words invokes the almost instant mental response of "Yes!" Some are expressions of frustration that reveal just how difficult it is to be a participant.

Regardless of how it is done, all these words are great point-makers. All provide the woman speaker with validating reinforcement. And they will, I hope, serve to inspire you to seek out your own good examples and use them to inspire the politician-participator in yourself and your audiences.

❦

Abortion doesn't belong in the political arena. It's a private right like many other rights concerning the family.

Bella Abzug

I am more and more convinced that man is a dangerous creature; and that power, whether vested in many or a few, is ever grasping, and, like the grave, cries, "Give, give!"

Abigail Smith Adams

Revolutionaries do not make revolutions. The revolutionaries are those who know when power is lying in the street and then they can pick it up. Armed uprising by itself has never yet led to a revolution.

Hannah Arendt

People who talk about peace are very often the most quarrelsome.

Lady Nancy Astor

Dr. Kissinger was surprised that I knew where Ghana was.

Shirley Temple Black

Why does a slight tax increase cost you two hundred dollars and a substantial tax cut save you thirty cents?

Peg Bracken

People on the whole are very simpleminded, in whatever country one finds them. They are so simple as to take literally, more often than not, the things their leaders tell them.

Pearl S. Buck

The greatest danger in any argument is that real issues are often clouded by superficial ones, that momentary passions may obscure permanent realities.

Mary Ellen Chase

The challenge is to practice politics as the art of making what appears to be impossible, possible.

Hillary Rodham Clinton

The feeble tremble before opinion, the foolish defy it, the wise judge it, the skillful direct it.

Jeanne de la Platiere

We need to know what really goes on in the world so that we can think for ourselves and take an intelligent part in government.

Gertrude Dieken

The conservative who resists change is as valuable as the radical who proposes it.

Ariel and Will Durant

Mankind is not disposed to look narrowly into the conduct of great victors when their victory is on the right side.

George Eliot

Monarchs ought to put to death the authors and instigators of war, as their sworn enemies and as dangers to their states.

Queen Elizabeth I

Winning may not be everything, but losing has little to recommend it.

Dianne Feinstein

Party organization matters. When the door of a smoke-filled room is closed, there's hardly ever a woman inside.

Millicent Fenwick

A nation's strength ultimately consists in what it can do on its own, and not in what it can borrow from others.

Indira Gandhi

Advisors are generally brilliant theoreticians but wretched practioners.

Françoise Giroud

There is no hope even that women, with her right to vote, will ever purify politics.

Emma Goldman

I've been married to one Marxist and one Fascist, and neither one would take the garbage out.

Lee Grant

I'm opposed to abortion because I happen to believe that life deserves the protection of society.

Ella Grasso

There are permanent professional candidates for state and local office, and there are permanent professional political appointees as well. . . . This special estate detaches a person from his private calling so that he no longer is seen to represent some segment of society in government, but rather becomes a representative *of* government to everyone else. . . . If a politician is something other than a politician, we think that the other thing—whatever it is—must be purged. . . . Maybe that is what we want of our political life. But it is surely not what we acknowledge wanting; and it does fly in the fact of the attractive, if perhaps too romantic, concept of a government and politics composed of people who bring special talents and interests and insights from the normal, nongovernmental world.

Meg Greenfield

Beware of people carrying ideas. Beware of ideas carrying people.

Barbara Grizzuti Harrison

Intellectuals can tell themselves anything, sell themselves any bill of goods, which is why they were so often patsies for the ruling classes in 19th-century France and England, or 20th-century Russia and America.

Lillian Hellman

Liberals have learned at a fearful cost the lesson that absolute power corrupts absolutely. They have yet to learn that absolute liberality corrupts absolutely.

Gertrude Himmelfarb

It is the weakness and danger of republics, that the vices as well as the virtues of the people are represented in their legislation.

Mary H. Hunt

Social opinion is like a sharp knife. There are foolish people who regard it only with terror, and dare not touch or meddle with it; there are more foolish people, who, in rashness or defiance, seize it by the blade, and get cut and mangled for their pains; and there are wise people, who grasp it discreetly and boldly by the handle, and use it to carve out their own purposes.

Anna Jameson

Every politician should have been born an orphan and remain a bachelor.

Lady Bird Johnson

Preparedness never caused a war, unpreparedness never prevented one.

Florence Kahn

There's one sure way of telling when politicians aren't telling the truth—their lips move.

Felicity Kendal

You've got to rattle your cage door. You've got to let them know that you're in there, and that you want out. Make noise. Cause trouble. You may not win right away, but you'll sure have a lot more fun.

Florynce Kennedy

If American women would increase their voting turnout by ten percent, I think we would see an end to all of the budget cuts in programs benefiting women and children.

Coretta Scott King

You can fool all of the people some of the time, and some of the people all of the time. And that's sufficient.

Rose King

It is not lack of polling data or campaign contributions which keeps many women from ascending higher on the political ladder. It is fear and loathing for the political system itself.

Madeleine Kunin

Bureaucracy, the rule of no one, has become the modern form of despotism.

Mary McCarthy

The more I became involved in "big time" politics, the more I realized how vicious the in-fighting could get in the desire to make things better.

Shirley MacLaine

A candidate able to raise money is a candidate whose race is taken seriously.

Ruth Mandel

We need to devise a system within which peace will be more rewarding than war.

Margaret Mead

There's no difference between one's killing and making decisions that will send others to kill. It's exactly the same thing, or even worse.

Golda Meir

Politics is social work with power.

Barbara Mikulski

Knowledge is power, if you know it about the right person.

Ethel Watts Mumford

I can't think of any other time that a women's issue has so affected politics. It has suddenly become clear that someone who does not respect women is not fit to be Prime Minister of Japan.

Kii Nakamura

The [1987 U.S. League of Women Voters] debates are the last thing left that is not managed by the campaign consultants and the media professionals. If the parties sponsor the debates, we will see two canned campaign commercials that will go on for 90 minutes, and I don't think the American people will learn anything from that.

Nancy M. Neuman

The 50 states serve as laboratories for the development of new social, economic, and political ideas. . . . Citizens cannot learn the lessons of self-government if their local efforts are devoted to reviewing proposals formulated by a faraway national legislature.

Sandra Day O'Connor

This is *no* bake-off. (response to reporters who kept trying to focus the campaign on women's issues when two women were running for Governor of Nebraska)

Kay Orr

The mistake a lot of politicians make is in forgetting they've been appointed and thinking they've been anointed.

Mildred Webster Pepper

The Greek word for *idiot*, literally translated, means one who does not participate in politics. That sums up my conviction on the subject.

Gladys Pyle

We have to get it into our heads once and for all that we cannot settle disputes by eliminating human beings.

Jeannette Rankin

I don't believe in a government elite. Power is insidious. It cannot be held too long by any one person.

Dixy Lee Ray

Our children should learn the general framework of their government and then they should know where they come in contact with the government, where it touches their daily lives and where their influence is exerted on the government. It must not be a distant thing, someone else's business, but they must see how every cog in the wheel of a democracy is important and bears its share of responsibility for the smooth running of the entire machine.

Eleanor Roosevelt

My failure to get the nomination was a good thing. A politician ought to know how it feels to be licked.

Katherine St. George

The urgent need today is to develop and support leaders on every level of government who are independent of the bossism of every political machine—the big-city machine, the liberal Democrat machine, and the Republican kingmaker machine.

Phyllis Schlafly

What a sad commentary it is that a public official has to take so much time to refute lies and go into such detail to document that refutation. No wonder many fine people avoid public service.

Margaret Chase Smith

If you just set out to be liked, you would be prepared to compromise on anything at any time, and you would achieve nothing.

Margaret Thatcher

If the mind is open enough to perceive that a given policy is harming rather than serving [a nation's] self-interest, and self-confident enough to acknowledge it and wise enough to reverse it, that is a summit in the art of government.

Barbara Tuchman

Some say we are in politics from the cradle to the grave. I say—we're in politics from conception to resurrection.

Dolores Tucker

Do you want to trace your family tree? Run for public office.

Patricia H. Vance

Years ago fairy tales all began with "Once upon a time . . ."—now we know they all begin with, "If I am elected."

Carolyn Warner

What a country calls its vital interests are not things that help its people live, but things that help it make war. Petroleum is a more likely cause of international conflict than wheat.

Simone Weil

Government must be responsive to the needs and the *dreams* of its people.

Mary Ellen Withrow

The distinction between democracy and dictatorship tends to disappear during war.

Frieda Wunderlich

When an elephant is in trouble even a frog will kick him.

Hindu proverb

Chapter 31

RELIGION

There are more tears shed over answered prayers than over unanswered prayers.

St. Theresa of Jesus

❧

Unless it is the requested topic, most speakers will avoid references to sex, politics, or religion. So one might wonder why a chapter of quotations about RELIGION has been included in this book. It isn't to get you in trouble with your audience, I assure you.

These quotations on the subject of religion have a great deal to do with the sharing of universal truths. You might find that this wisdom can be appropriate for many topics or occasions or audiences. These are precepts that can be applied universally or to a particular religious practice or denomination.

Quotations from writings of or about religion can provide a sense of commonality almost regardless of the topic area. This is true because any serious (*serious* in the sense of well-prepared and thought out) presentation ought to have some uniform, universal principles as its base.

The topic may be "How to Be a Volunteer," "How to Organize a Volunteer Organization," or "How to Start an Organization Using Volunteers." In every case, there is a uniform principle that should underlie the proposition. And very often the uniform principles expressed in the great religious writings of the world provide an excellent framework for the work at hand.

It is vital that the conscientious speaker remembers never to let personal religion, that is, denominational viewpoints, color the universality of her remarks. Only when we expand our perspective beyond the parochial and into the universal can we comfortably use quotations about religion to general audiences.

During the years I was in public office, prayer in schools once again became an issue. When asked how I stood on the matter, I would reply that I had no problem with prayer in schools as long as my minister wrote the prayer. Many people took my words literally and never quite got what I meant. My point was intended to illustrate that each one of us approaches religion from our own perspective and that we act with great disregard when we attempt to impose that perspective on others.

Universal truths are just that—universal, and often common to all the world's great religions. I find it both fascinating and revealing that there is some version of the Golden Rule in the teachings of every major religion. Appropriate quotations concerning religion are not limiting, rather they are un-limiting in their philosophical underpinning.

Another good reason to use quotations from this category has to do with the richness of the writing with which these sentiments are expressed. Considering the major role that religion has played in the history of humankind, to omit quotations merely because they contain a religious reference is to limit an understanding of our heritage. There are words from the Psalms, from the Apostles, from Lao Tsu, from the Koran, from the Buddha, that communicate wisdom meaningful to almost any group.

Whether you are a seasoned speaker or a beginner, I encourage you to build your own library of universal truths—concepts that uplift and inspire through the teachings of the world's great religions. You not only will enrich your speeches in this way, you will also enrich your own thinking in the process.

ॐ

All things bright and beautiful,
All creatures great and small,
All things wise and wonderful,
The Lord God made them all.

Mrs. Alexander

God is a sure paymaster. He may not pay at the end of every week, or month, or year, but remember He pays in the end.

Anne of Austria

People see God every day, they just don't recognize Him.

Pearl Bailey

Religion converts despair which destroys, into resignation which submits.

Lady Marguerite Blessington

Men judge us by the success of our efforts. God looks at the efforts themselves.

Charlotte Brontë

God answers sharp and sudden some prayers,
And thrusts the thing we have prayed for in our face,
A gauntlet with a gift in't.

Elizabeth Barrett Browning

One sweetly solemn thought
  Comes to me o'er and o'er;
I am nearer home today
  Than I ever have been before.

Phoebe Cary

A religious life is a struggle and not a hymn.

Mme. de Staël

I never spoke with God
Nor visited in Heaven,
Yet certain am I of the spot
As if the chart were given.

Emily Dickinson

Religions are born and may die, but superstition is immortal. Only the fortunate can take life without mythology.

Ariel and Will Durant

I would no more quarrel with a man because of his religion than I would because of his art.

Mary Baker Eddy

We hand folks over to God's mercy, and show none ourselves.

George Eliot

When we have exhausted our store of endurance;
When our strength has failed ere the day is half done;
When we've reached the end of our hoarded resources;
Our Father's full giving is only begun.

Annie J. Flint

When I left home and faced the realities of the world, I put my thoughts of God in cold storage for awhile, because I couldn't reconcile what I believed, deep inside, with what was going on around me. But that early period, when God was as real as the wind that blew from the sea through the pine trees in the garden, left me with inner peace, which, as I grew older, swelled—until, perforce, I had to open my mind to God again.

Jane Goodall

Christ made no distinction, but opened the door wide to woman as to man.

Gail Hamilton

Divine love is a sacred flower, which in its early bud is happiness, and in its full bloom is heaven.

Eleanor Louisa Hervey

Mine eyes have seen the glory of the coming of the Lord:
He is trampling out the vintage where the grapes of wrath are stored;
He hath loosed the fateful lightning of his terrible swift sword.
His truth is marching on.

Julia Ward Howe

I can see, and that is why I can be so happy, in what you call the dark, but which to me is golden. I can see a God-made world, not a man-made world.

Helen Keller

I have served as spiritual leader to many people. They in turn have ministered to me. God's work is always reciprocal.

Bishop Leontine Kelly

Natives who beat drums to drive off evil spirits are objects of scorn to smart Americans who blow horns to break up traffic jams.

Mary Ellen Kelly

Randomness scares people. Religion is a way to explain randomness.

Fran Leibowitz

The wonderful thing about saints is that they were human. They lost their tempers, scolded God, were egotistical or testy or impatient in their turns, made mistakes and regretted them. Still they went on doggedly blundering toward heaven.

Phyllis McGinley

Many are saved from sin by being so inept at it.

Mignon McLaughlin

No man is a Christian who cheats his fellows, perverts the truth, or speaks of a "clean bomb," yet he will be the first to make public his faith in God.

Marya Mannes

Every formula which expresses a law of nature is a hymn of praise to God.

Maria Mitchell

Nobody can deny but religion is a comfort to the distressed, a cordial to the sick, and sometimes a restraint on the wicked; therefore, whoever would laugh or argue it out of the world, without giving some equivalent for it ought to be treated as a common enemy.

Lady Mary Wortley Montague

In agony or danger, no nature is atheist. The mind that knows not what to fly to, flies to God.

Hannah More

It is not Christianity, but priestcraft that has subjected woman as we find her.

Lucretia Mott

It makes no difference what background a person has whether Indian or non-Indian. To all who have never felt accepted, who are living a life of loneliness, who seem to be unimportant to anyone—I am thrilled to say: God is love! His love is real and He loves and yearns to touch your life. That touch is important and God makes his contact through people, passing his love right now through me to you.

Princess Pale Moon

In our constant search for security we can never gain any peace of mind until we secure our own soul.

Margaret Chase Smith

It must be Sunday, everybody is telling the truth.

Phoebe Snow

The Bible and the Church have been the greatest stumbling blocks in the way of women's emancipation.

Elizabeth Cady Stanton

No one is so thoroughly superstitious as the godless man.

Harriet Beecher Stowe

O Maker my Maker! my hope is in thee.
My Jesus, dear Savior! now set my soul free.
From this my hard prison, my spirit uprisen,
Soars upward to thee.
Thus moaning and groaning, and bending the knee,
I adore, and implore that thou liberate me.

Mary Stuart, Queen of Scots
(prayer written before her execution)

What is resignation? It is putting God between one's self and one's grief.

Anne Sophie Swetchine

I always find that statistics are hard to swallow and impossible to digest. The only one I can remember is that if all the people who go to sleep in church were laid end to end they would be a lot more comfortable.

Mrs. Robert A. Taft

Why is it when we talk to God, we're said to be praying—but when God talks to us, we're schizophrenic?

Lily Tomlin

Religion without humanity is poor human stuff.

Sojourner Truth

God gave us courage to make us daring,
Hope to smother despair;
Faith to inspire us to loving and sharing,
Joy to balance all care.

Helen Marie Walden

Tell the truth, have you ever found God in church? I never did. I just found a bunch of folks hoping for him to show. Any God I ever felt in church I brought in with me. And I think all the other folks did too. They come to church to *share* God, not find God.

Alice Walker

There are two things to do about the gospel: believe it and behave it.

Susannah Wesley

So many gods, so many creeds,
So many paths that wind and wind,
When just the art of being kind
Is all this sad world needs.

Ella Wheeler Wilcox

The good Pastor said, "Nearly everyone is in favor of going to heaven but too many are hoping they'll live long enough to see an easing of the entrance requirements."

Anon.

Chapter 32

RESPONSIBILITY

Take your life in your own hands, and what happens? A terrible thing: no one to blame.

Erica Jong

❦

RESPONSIBILITY is one of those words that really doesn't stand alone. Only when it is paired with its companion—freedom—does responsibility take on its true significance.

I have come to believe that life is a balance between these two concepts, and only when they are in balance can individuals, organizations, and even nations, creatively participate in the flow of events.

This is true because freedom without its counterbalance of responsibility can quickly become license. Unrestrained, anchorless freedom is a danger. The best comparison I can think of is the condition of an automobile with its tires skidding on ice, spinning out of control. That is a form of freedom without responsibility. It is the traction, the friction of restraint (responsibility) that enables controlled, orderly, planned movement to occur.

I hope no one confuses my advocacy of this kind of social traction with some sort of a yearning for the order in which responsibility comes to mean the *absence* of freedom. Certainly not. But no more than I would want to live in a society without freedom would I want to live in a society without responsibility.

Thank God we live in a society in which we are free to speak and to think unfettered by governmental controls. In this country in these times, most social controls are essentially voluntary. The speaker can help her listeners understand these principles and to see how they apply in their personal and organizational lives—at least within the context of the topic being discussed.

I find it helpful to connect the concepts of freedom as a triad: *rights* and *respect* as well as *responsibility*. People often find respect to be something of a quaint notion these days, but it is inherent in the concept of responsibility just as much as rights (freedom).

Each of us has the responsibility to respect the rights of others. We have the responsibility to be respectful of the beliefs of others. And we have the responsibility to respect the beings with whom we share the planet. We must not only have a responsibility in all these things, we must actively work to ensure their preservation and advancement.

Many organizations today focus on their ability to advocate for what they perceive to be *rights*, but forget their need to advocate for those same rights in others and to be respectful of those rights. It is this latter concept that embodies the essence of responsibility, and the presenter must especially be aware of this obligation. As speakers, we should never confuse our right to advocate with our responsibility to help bring balance and perspective to an issue.

It is a cliché about the platform being a "bully pulpit," but it's a cliché because it's true. When you are presenting you do, indeed, have the power of that podium. But you have a tremendous responsibility to use that power wisely and to lead your listeners in the same spirit.

I have written frequently in these chapter introductions about the need for the speaker to *empower* her listeners. It's important to emphasize in this chapter the need to bring a sense of responsibility along with a sense of empowerment. If you can achieve both, you have done something truly remarkable to and for any group before which you speak.

That same sense of empowerment, coupled with responsibility, is just as important for the speaker herself. The power of the bully pulpit can also be the power to *mis*lead, to point people toward *wrong* choices. So it is incumbent upon you to understand your power, its effect, and the responsibility that keeps this power in check.

Quotations about responsibility help a speaker validate her points and her principles. It is easy enough for an audience to sit back and, at least mentally, ask, "Who are you to tell me what we're responsible for?" These quotations are designed to help you reinforce your own convictions about responsibility with the convictions of other respected voices and perspectives. I hope every reader will use these quotations as thought stimulators to seek out her own quotations about responsibility. It is a concept that is universal in its applicability and powerful in its application.

❦

Woman must not depend upon the protection of man, but must be taught to protect herself.

Susan B. Anthony

This conflict is one thing I've been waiting for. I'm well and strong and young— young enough to go to the front. If I can't be a soldier, I'll help soldiers.

Clara Barton

Look twice before you leap.

Charlotte Brontë

If a woman doesn't vote, she doesn't have a right to complain about anything.

Bess Brown

I see that one of my opponents claims to have the ear of the President, while another says he has the ear of the Democratic nominee. I am making no collection of ears myself, but I have two good ones of my own, and if you return me to the Senate, I promise you they will always be attuned to your needs.

Hattie W. Caraway

We mothered this nation. Are we to be penalized for it forever? We have no intention of abandoning our roles as nurturer or wife, mother, loving daughter, tax-paying citizen, homemaker, breadwinner.

Liz Carpenter

Much misconstruction and bitterness are spared to him who thinks naturally upon what he owes to others rather on what he ought to expect from them.

Elizabeth de Guizot

The willingness to accept responsibility for one's own life is the source from which self-respect springs.

Joan Didion

Service is the rent you pay for being.

Marian Wright Edelman

I let Ike run the country and I ran the home.

Mamie Eisenhower

The reward of one duty is the power to fulfill another.

George Eliot

You can bear anything if it isn't your own fault.

Katherine Fullerton Gerould

Hath the spirit of all beauty
Kissed you in the path of duty?

Anna Katherine Green

Responsibility is the price every man must pay for freedom.

Edith Hamilton

I can remember walking as a child. It was not customary to say you were fatigued. It was customary to complete the goal of the expedition.

Katharine Hepburn

There is a fine line between healthy dissent and arrogant disregard for authority.

Pamela Herr

We read the papers and hear on the air,
Of killing and stealing and crime everywhere.
We sigh and say as we notice the trend,
"This young generation, where will it end?"
But can we be sure that it's their fault alone,
That maybe a part of it, isn't our own?

Are we less guilty, who place in their way
Too many things that lead them astray:
Too much money, too much idle time,
Too many movies of passion and crime,
Too many books not fit to be read,
Too much evil in what they hear said,
Too many children encouraged to roam,
Too many parents who won't stay home?

Kids don't make the movies, they don't write the books,
They don't paint gay pictures of gangsters and crooks,

They don't make the liquor, they don't run the bars,
They don't make the law and they don't sell the cars,
They don't peddle the drugs that addle the brain,
That's all done by older folks greedy for gain.

Delinquent teenagers, Oh how we condemn
The sins of the nation and blame it on them.
By the laws of the blameless the Savior made known,
Who is there among us to cast the first stone?
For in so many cases (it's sad but it's true),
The title "delinquent" fits older folks too.

Margaret Hogan

I slept and dreamed that life was Beauty;
I woke and found that life was Duty.

Ellen Sturgis Hooper

Education is a loan to be repaid with gift of self.

Lady Bird Johnson

Until the great mass of the people shall be filled with the sense of responsibility for each other's welfare, social justice can never be attained.

Helen Keller

We were individuals with highly responsible roles in a partnership that yielded rewards which we shared. (on her marriage)

Rose Fitzgerald Kennedy

Champions take responsibility. When the ball is coming over the net, you can be sure I want the ball.

Billie Jean King

My evil genius Procrastination has whispered me to tarry 'til a more convenient season.

Mary Todd Lincoln

There is nothing in the universe that I fear, but that I shall not know all my duty, or shall fail to do it.

Mary Lyon

People are no longer sinful, they are only immature or underprivileged or frightened or, more particularly, sick.

Phyllis McGinley

We are apt to mistake our vocation by looking out of the way for occasions to exercise great and rare virtues, and by stepping over the ordinary ones that lie directly in the road before us.

Hannah More

Remember always that you have not only the right to be an individual, you have an obligation to be one. You cannot make any useful contribution in life unless you do this.

Eleanor Roosevelt

Are we willing to give up some things we like to do, to move on to those things we must do?

Satenig St. Marie

Sometimes the Devil proposes to us great desires, so that we shall not put our hand to what we have to do, and serve our lord in possible things, but stay content with having desired impossible ones.

St. Theresa of Jesus

Experience shows us Wealth unchaperoned by Virtue is never an innocuous neighbor.

Sappho

I have a great responsibility because I can afford to be honest.

May Sarton

There are not good things enough in life, to indemnify us for the neglect of a single duty.

Anne Sophie Swetchine

Only yourself can heal you,
Only yourself can lead you.

Sara Teasdale

I will start afresh each new day
  with petty littleness freed;
I will cease to stand complaining
  of my ruthless neighbor's greed;
I will cease to sit repining
  while my duty's call is clear;
I will waste no moment whining,
  and my heart shall know no fear.

I will not be swayed by envy
  when my rival's strength is shown;
I will not deny his merit,
  but I'll try to prove my own;
I will try to see the beauty
  spread before me rain or shine;
I will cease to preach your duty
  and be more concerned with mine.

Author Unknown
"The Only Way"

A youth was questioning a lonely old man, "What is life's heaviest burden?"
  he asked.
The old fellow answered sadly, "To have nothing to carry."

Anon.

If a task is once begun
Never leave it till it's done.
Be the labor great or small
Do it well or not at all.

Anon.

Chapter 33

SELF-IMAGE

We don't see things as they are, we see them as we are.

Anaïs Nin

❧

One of the most blame-filled words in our vocabulary is *ego*. It is almost a pejorative, which is unfortunate. There is nothing wrong with a healthy ego. If you don't think well of yourself, who else will? Having an inner drive is not a sin; mis-using it probably is. As with many things, the existence and the excess tend to get confused.

One of the most powerful motivating forces in the world is a person's image of herself at her future best. That is what having a healthy SELF-IMAGE, a healthy ego, is all about. Self-image is the tool that either inhibits and holds us back or activates and elevates us to be and do our best.

The biblical admonition to "Love thy neighbor as thyself" presents an interesting spin on the concept of self-image. Perhaps that maxim is the reason one should have a positive self-image, for how can you extend to another something you yourself lack? Conversely, not *loving* yourself very readily translates into views, attitudes, and expectations of others that are equally limited and negative.

If you lack this positive self-image you will make a very poor presenter. On the other hand, if you give free rein to an ego larger than the hall in which you are speaking, your presentation may be artful, but it is not likely your content will equal the vessel from which it pours.

Quotations about self-image are designed to encourage you as surely as to encourage your audience. Reading the positive words of other women can have the effect of helping you see those positive qualities in yourself as much as it will help you bring an awareness of each of these qualities to your listeners.

These quotations by women and for women are especially important because we women tend to be harder on ourselves than anybody else is ever likely to be. We seem to work very hard to keep our self-image as subdued as possible. We aim for perfection and seldom forgive our inability to attain it. More than anything, I hope the quotations in this chapter help women focus less on being perfect and more on thinking well of who they are, as they are. You have to like yourself for your strengths and forgive yourself for your weaknesses—and do the same for others.

When you radiate a positive self-image from the platform, you can then help your listeners do the same. If you believe that you are a person of consequence, you can lead an audience to the same conclusion about themselves. And that is the first step in getting them to take positive action.

You will often find that one of your first tasks is to explain to your audience that they are, indeed, people of consequence. No matter who they are or what they do, they are human beings and, therefore, capable of making a difference. What better quality to help people identify and bring out their positive traits? As you help people re-shape or at least re-think themselves, you are leading them to a sense of personal empowerment. And when you do that, you have started them on the road to action, then to achievement. It all comes full circle.

The energizing force of a positive self-image is contagious. You have it; you transmit it to your listeners. They catch it; they carry it back to their workplace or home or wherever they can make a difference. Women are good at this. We just so seldom give ourselves the chance.

❦

I have been a selfish being all my life, in practice, though not in principle.

Jane Austen

If our people are to fight their way out of bondage we must arm them with the sword and the shield and the buckler of pride.

Mary McLeod Bethune

Let the world know you as you are, not as you think you should be—because sooner or later, if you are posing, you will forget the pose and then where are you?

Fanny Brice

An individual's self-concept is the core of his personality. It affects every aspect of human behavior: the ability to learn, the capacity to grow and change, the choice of friends, mates and careers. It is no exaggeration to say that a strong, positive self-image is the best possible preparation for success in life.

Dr. Joyce Brothers

I believe that when all the dreams are dead, you're left only with yourself. You'd better like yourself a lot.

Rita Mae Brown

To do good things in the world, first you must know who you are and what gives meaning in your life.

Paula P. Brownlee

When you're young and someone tells you what you are and shows you how to be proud, you've got a head start.

Vikki Carr

I think it's one of the scars in our culture that we have too high an opinion of ourselves. We align ourselves with the angels instead of the higher primates.

Angela Carter

Tact is the ability to describe others as they see themselves.

Eleanor Chaffee

Have you ever felt like nobody?
Just a tiny speck of air.
When everyone's around you,
And you are just not there.

Karen Crawford, age 9

Seek not outside yourself, heaven is within.

Mary Lou Cook

Advances are made by those with at least a touch of irrational confidence in what they can do.

Joan L. Curcio

We are indeed much more than we eat, but what we eat can nevertheless help us to be much more than what we are.

Adele Davis

I have always been driven by some distant music—a battle hymn no doubt—for I have been at war from the beginning. I've never looked back before. I've never had the time and it has always seemed so dangerous. To look back is to relax one's vigil.

Bette Davis

"Ah! if only there were two of me," she thought, "one who spoke and the other who listened, one who lived and the other who watched, how I would love myself! I'd envy no one."

Simone de Beauvoir

To have the sense of one's own intrinsic worth which constitutes self-respect is potentially to have everything: the ability to discriminate, to love and to remain indifferent. To lack it is to be locked within oneself, paradoxically incapable of either love or indifference.

Joan Didion

While we are young the idea of death or failure is intolerable to us; even the possibility of ridicule we cannot bear.

Isak Dinesen

One loses many laughs by not laughing at oneself.

Sara Jeannette Duncan

I seem to have an awful lot of people inside me.

Dame Edith Evans

I am practical or I am nothing.

Rebecca L. Felton

No wonder young people are confused. Half are urged to find themselves; the other half are told to get lost.

June Flynn

Fear is a question. What are you afraid of and why? Our fears are a treasure house of self knowledge if we explore them.

Marilyn French

I now know all the people worth knowing in America and I find no intellect comparable to my own.

Margaret Fuller

Humility is not my forte, and whenever I dwell for any length of time on my own shortcomings, they gradually begin to seem mild, harmless, rather engaging little things, not at all like the startling defects in other people's characters.

Margaret Halsey

Everyone thought I was bold and fearless and even arrogant, but inside I was always quaking.

Katharine Hepburn

A perfectly normal person is rare in our civilization.

Karen Horney

I went for years not finishing anything. Because, of course, when you finish something you can be judged. I had poems which were re-written so many times I suspect it was just a way of avoiding sending them out.

Erica Jong

I never intended to become a run-of-the-mill person.

Barbara Jordan

A world stretched out before me,
  dimly seen, by just the set sun,
Lord, show me my task, my talent,
  my share in the great undone.

Stella Grace Julian

I seldom think about my limitations, and they never make me sad. Perhaps there is just a touch of yearning at times; but it is vague, like a breeze among flowers.

Helen Keller

I'm just a loud-mouthed middle-aged colored lady . . . and a lot of people think I'm crazy. Maybe you do too, but I never stop to wonder why I'm not like other people. The mystery to me is why more people aren't like me.

Florynce Kennedy

When alone I am not aware of my race or my sex, both in need of social contexts for definition.

Maxine Hong Kingston

It is terrible to destroy a person's picture of himself in the interests of truth or some other abstraction.

Doris Lessing

I feel we are all islands—in a common sea.

Anne Morrow Lindbergh

He who devotes sixteen hours a day to hard study may become as wise at sixty as he thought himself at twenty.

Mary Wilson Little

Believing in yourself and liking yourself is all a part of good looks.

Shirley Lord

Nine-tenths of our suffering is caused by others not thinking so much of us as we think they ought.

Mary Lyon

It's this no-nonsense side of women that is pleasant to deal with. They are the real sportsmen. They don't have to be constantly building up frail egos by large public performances like over-tipping the hat-check girl, speaking fluent French to the Hungarian waiter, and sending back the wine to be recooled.

Phyllis McGinley

Research on the links between achievement, motivation and self-image suggests that possible selves—future selves—are part of one's present self-image and are keys to success or failure.

Hazel Markus

You need to claim the events of your life to make yourself yours. When you truly possess all you have been and done, which may take some time, you are fierce with reality.

Florida Scott Maxwell

Humiliating oneself is never fatal, unless one commits suicide thereafter.
Jinx Melia and Pauline Lyttle

To put it bluntly, I seem to be a whole superstructure with no foundation. But I'm working on the foundation.
Marilyn Monroe

It's a great satisfaction knowing that for a brief point in time you made a difference.
Irene Natividad

A certain amount of distrust is wholesome, but not so much of others as of ourselves; neither vanity nor conceit can exist in the same atmosphere with it.
Susanne Curchod Necker

Now that I've got the name I may as well play the game.
Anita O'Day

Poor self-image is the number one problem for women. And it is the Indian's biggest problem and that of teenagers too. It used to be my biggest problem until the day I suddenly decided that I don't care if I impress people or not because if I make friends with people I don't need to impress them.
Princess Pale Moon

For a long time the only time I felt beautiful—in the sense of being complete as a woman, as a human being—was when I was singing.
Leontyne Price

Ultimately, love is self-approval.
Sondra Ray

There were two ducks; the female with the brown head and the other with the green head—the unfemale.
Danielle Rettinger, age 5

The psychic scars caused by believing that you are ugly leave a permanent mark on your personality.
Joan Rivers

No one can make you feel inferior without your consent.
Eleanor Roosevelt

Nothing is more certain of destroying any good feelings that may be cherished toward us than to show distrust. On the contrary confidence leads us naturally to act kindly; we are affected by the good opinions others entertain of us, and are not easily induced to lose it.

La Marquise de Sévigné

In a dream you are never eighty.

Anne Sexton

The delights of self-discovery are always available.

Gail Sheehy

Being powerful is like being a lady. If you have to tell people you are, you aren't.
Margaret Thatcher

Just remember, we're all in this alone.

Lily Tomlin

If you have your language and you have your culture, and you're not ashamed of it, then you know who you are.

Maria Urquides

It's not that I lack ambition. I *am* ambitious in the sense that I want to be more than I am now. But if I were truly ambitious, I think I'd already *be* more than I am now.

Jane Wagner

To feel valued, to know, even if only once in a while, that you can do a job well is an absolutely marvelous feeling.

Barbara Walters

It is very easy to forgive others their mistakes; it takes more grit and gumption to forgive them for having witnessed your own.

Jessamyn West

I have long felt that the trouble with discrimination is not discrimination *per se*, but rather that the people who are discriminated against think of themselves as second-class.

Rosalyn Yalow

Chapter 34

SPEECH

Blessed is the man who, having nothing to say, abstains from giving us wordy evidence of the fact.

George Eliot

❦

Quotations by women about SPEECH in a book of quotations for women speakers might sound like a double-redundancy. But it isn't, it isn't.

Somebody once said that three things matter in a speech: what is said, how it is said, who said it—and, of the three, the latter is of greatest importance. In making and preparing a speech, it is essential to keep these three points in mind and to keep them in their proper perspective.

Think of these three points—what, how, who—as being like the elements that go into presenting a play.

The *how* is the equivalent of everything that goes on backstage: the costuming, sound, lighting, etc.

The *what* involves the words and their meaning.

The *who* is what the audience focuses on. For a speaker, the *who* is you. When delivering public remarks, however, you are not only the speaker (the actor in the play), you are also the writer and the director and the producer.

The quotations in this chapter fall into the same three general classifications as that imaginary stage play:

Some of them deal with the *how*'s of research, presentation, dress, and the other "backstage" work of the public presenter.

Others deal with the *what*'s of your presentations—content and concept.

Still others address the *who*'s of speaking, the notion of the woman as public speaker, thinker, and activator.

Taken as a whole, these quotations are insights and tips from women of consequence—of consequence for who they are, for what they said, and for how they said it.

Quotations concerning speech are designed to enliven your thoughts and to enlighten your audiences, and to help you throughout the process of conceiving, building, and presenting your remarks. They are intended to help you understand the various goals of public speaking and to give you some perspective on the various goals of your presentation. Some are "how to's" but most are "how come's"—the *why*'s that undergird the *how*, *what*, and *who* of your presentation.

It is said that creativity can be defined as old truths told from a new vantage point. In developing your speaking skills, nothing can be more helpful than drawing from the common sense of other women, incorporating your own unique perspective, and enriching your audience with this combined wisdom.

ॐ

There shall never be another season of silence until women have the same rights men have on this green earth.

Susan B. Anthony

People fighting their aloneness will do almost anything to avoid silence.

Myrtle Barker

A kiss is a lovely trick designed by nature to stop speech when words become superfluous.

Ingrid Bergman

God wove a web of loveliness, of clouds and stars and birds, but made not anything at all so beautiful as words.

Anna Hempstead Branch

The human heart has hidden treasure,
In secret kept, in silence sealed;
The thoughts, the hopes, the dreams, the pleasure,
Whose charms were broken if revealed.

Charlotte Brontë

My mother once defined me as "someone who never has an unexpressed thought." She gave me what I've always considered excellent advice when she said, "There is a difference between telling the truth and telling everything you know."

Kathryn Carpenter

Love is the merest look, the lightest touch,
The thought almost too subtle to recall,
When love is deepest, words may be too much.

Kathi Coolidge

A word is dead
When it is said,
Some say.
I say it just
Begins to live.

Emily Dickinson

One of the lessons of history is that nothing is often a good thing to do and always a clever thing to say.

Ariel and Will Durant

Falsehood is so easy, truth so difficult! Examine your words well and you will find that even when you have no motive to be false, it is very hard to say the exact truth, even about your own immediate feelings—much harder than to say something fine about them which is not the exact truth.

George Eliot

He talks with more claret than clarity.

Susan Ertz

When a man gets up to speak, people listen then look. When a woman gets up, people *look*; then, if they like what they see, they listen.

Pauline Frederick

Strange, isn't it, that when a man expresses a conviction fearlessly, he is reported as having made a trenchant and forceful statement, but when a woman speaks thus earnestly, she is reported as a lady who has lost her temper.

Jessie B. Fremont

We cannot have expression till there is something to be expressed.

Margaret Fuller

He knows so little and knows it so fluently.

Ellen Glasgow

I like people who refuse to speak until they are ready to speak.

Lillian Hellman

Somewhere in your presentation, the audience stops thinking of you as a 5- foot, 6-inch woman with freckles on your nose. If people think you are immersed, are serious, have done your homework, then they take you seriously.

Carla Hills

God preserve us from the destructive power of words! There are words which can separate hearts sooner than sharp swords. There are words whose sting can remain through a whole life.

Mary Botham Howitt

Gossip is the opiate of the oppressed.

Erica Jong

Next to family affection, health, and the love of work, does anything contribute so much to the pleasantness of life, restoring and raising our self-esteem as the traffic in kind speeches?

Lucy Elliot Keeler

There is nothing more beautiful, I think, than the evanescent fleeting images and sentiments presented by a language one is just becoming familiar with—ideas that flit across the mental sky, shaped and tinted by capricious fancy.

Helen Keller

A gossip is someone who talks to you about others, a bore is one who talks to you about himself, and a brilliant conversationalist is one who talks to you about yourself.

Lisa Kirk

A person who talks fast often says things she hasn't thought of yet.

Caron Warner Lieber

If one talks to more than four people it is an audience, and one cannot really think or exchange thoughts with an audience.

Anne Morrow Lindbergh

My swords are tempered for every speech,
For fencing wit, or to carve a breach
Through old abuses the world condones.

Amy Lowell

There are very few people who don't become more interesting when they stop talking.

Mary Lowry

It's useless to hold a person to anything he says while he's in love, drunk, or running for office.

Shirley MacLaine

Sticks and stones are hard on bones
Aimed with angry art,
Words can sting like anything
But silence breaks the heart.

Phyllis McGinley

I would rather fight with my hands than my tongue.

Dolley Madison

Wit has a deadly aim and it is possible to prick a large pretense with a small pin.

Marya Mannes

Verbal Felicity is the fruit of art and diligence and refusing to be false.

Mariane Moore

A whisper can be stronger, [just as] an atom can be stronger, than a whole mountain.

Louise Nevelson

There's a helluva distance between wisecracking and wit. Wit has some truth in it; wisecracking is simply calisthenics with words.

Dorothy Parker

A world of vested interests is not a world which welcomes the disruptive force of candor.

Agnes Repplier

Lying is done with words and also with silence.

Adrienne Rich

Never assert anything without first being certain of it.

St. Theresa of Jesus

Man . . . is only too glad to have woman hold strictly to the Christian principle of suffering in silence.

George Sand

The more articulate one is, the more dangerous words become.

May Sarton

I find intellectuals are more interested in gossip than anybody else.

Dorothy Schiff

When we have the courage to speak out—to break our silence—we inspire the rest of the "moderates" in our communities to speak up and to vote their views.

Sharon Schuster

Remarks are not literature.

Gertrude Stein

Silent gratitude isn't much use to anyone.

Gladys Browyn Stern

The most likely place to have your idea pocket picked is at a meeting. Here an idea becomes public property the moment it hits the airwaves.

Jane Trahey

Harry may not be as silver-tongued as Churchill. But I honestly believe the people understand him lots better!

Bess Truman

Show me someone who never gossips, and I'll show you someone who isn't interested in people.

Barbara Walters

The tongue is more to be feared than the sword.

Japanese proverb

You have allowed me 30 minutes to speak. That's the same amount of time that it takes for:
—Paint to dry on a wall
—A level of deep sleep to be reached
—Aspirin to be absorbed into the blood
—Spinal anesthetic to take effect

Anon.

A preacher who was popular with his congregation explained his success as the result of a silent prayer which he offered each time he took the pulpit. It ran thus: "Lord, fill my mouth with worthwhile stuff, and nudge me when I've said enough."

Anon.

If you don't strike oil in the first ten minutes, stop boring.

Anon.

A speech should be as long as a piece of string—long enough to wrap up the package.

Anon.

A poor speaker quits talking when he is tired. A good speaker quits before the audience is tired.

Anon.

Everyone has at least one sermon in him.

Anon.

He had nothing to say—and said it endlessly.

Anon.

Before I start speaking, I'd like to say something.

Anon.

Chapter 35

STYLE

Civility costs nothing and buys everything.

Lady Mary Wortley Montague

❦

Some will find it appropriate, others amusing, that a book of quotations by women, compiled by a woman, contains a chapter titled STYLE. I suppose the assumption is that these pages contain a collection of quotations about fashion or "dressing for success" or some other such set of sex-biased quotations. Wrong on all counts!

Although this chapter contains quotations that I have at various times categorized as *Grace, Class, Elegance, Beauty, Charm,* or *Manners,* I have chosen to title it *Style* because the overall concepts I want to convey in these quotations encompass the qualities enumerated above—and more.

A concept of style is especially important for a speaker—whether male or female—because it communicates to those who see and hear you the essence of who you are. From the platform, you should embody all the positive qualities inherent in having grace, class, elegance, charm, and manners. The way you manifest those things defines your *style,* so that is the word I have used in a comprehensive sense to tie it all together.

All these attributes also relate to your individuality. And they all start with good manners, in the broadest sense of that term. It has been said that manners are the oil that lubricates the machinery of society.

For the speaker, good manners—and good style—begin with how you look—and looking good doesn't mean the number of dollar signs on your clothing bill. It doesn't mean out-dressing your audience or being a fashion plate. It means dressing with a sense of appropriateness, presenting yourself in a way that reflects your responsibility as a speaker. It means conducting yourself in a way that brings credit to those who invited you to speak, preparing your remarks and delivering them in a way that communicates your best thoughts and efforts. A speaker with style will recognize a cohesion in all these elements and will respond accordingly.

Visible manifestations reflect your external style—the fact that you knew enough and cared enough to publicly manifest them reflects your internal style. Style is not just how you look; it is how you think.

These elements of style reflect your individuality. This is in no way an I-centered concept. Rather it demonstrates the speaker's other-centeredness because it shows regard for your listeners. It says, "I respect you and your purpose, and I have done my very best to indicate that in how I look and what I have to say." Nothing says more about self-respect than the demonstration of it through consideration for others.

For the speaker, who and what you are is reflected in what you share. An understanding of style, as expressed in these quotations, can provide a richness and variety to both how you think and what you say.

These quotations are intended to help the speaker identify—if only by exclusion—her own (and perhaps her listeners') collective style. Some are classics, some aren't; some are funny, some are profound. I hope that they will in some way allow the speaker to help the audience relate to her and to each other.

By using this type of quotation, but employing somebody else's words, the speaker can demonstrate her personal difference with an attitude or a behavior without sounding or appearing pompous or pontifical. She can allow her audience to accept or reject a concept without automatically linking *herself* to the behavior or attitude in question. Everyone involved can agree or disagree with her, with the concept, with both or neither—and still accept the independent authority of the speaker.

The speaker who communicates this sense of both fairness and respect, through style, has just taken several giant strides toward becoming a true professional. She has also moved closer to bringing out the totality that makes each one in her audience feel like a very special person.

❦

Love is a great beautifier.

Louisa May Alcott

Beauty comes in all sizes—not just size 5.

Roseanne Barr Arnold

It's a strenuous job everyday of your life to live up to the way you look on screen.
Jean Arthur

So many women just don't know how great they really are. They come to us all vogue outside and vague on the inside.

Mary Kay Ash

You don't have to be dowdy to be a Christian.

Tammy Faye Bakker

Loveliness—a beautiful envelope for mortality, presenting a glittering and polished exterior, the appearance of which gives no certain indication of the real value of what is contained therein.

Clara Balfour

I think knowing what you can *not* do is more important than knowing what you can do. In fact, that's good taste.

Lucille Ball

Character contributes to beauty. It fortifies a woman as her youth fades. A mode of conduct, a standard of courage, discipline, fortitude, and integrity can do a great deal to make a woman beautiful.

Jacqueline Bisset

Who has not experienced how, on nearer acquaintance, plainness becomes beautified and beauty loses its charm, according to the quality of the heart and mind?
Fredrika Bremer

Nearly every glamorous, wealthy, successful career woman you might envy *now* started out as some kind of schlep.

Helen Gurley Brown

Fashion is made to become unfashionable.

Coco Chanel

I kill myself for my body.

Cher

It is wise to apply the refined oil of politeness to the mechanism of friendship.

Colette

I never go out unless I look like Joan Crawford the movie star. If you want to see the girl next door, go next door.

Joan Crawford

I was the only star they allowed to come out of the water looking wet.

Bette Davis

Modesty is the polite concession *worth* makes to *inferiority*.

Comtesse de Diane

Good taste is the modesty of the mind; that is why it cannot be either imitated or acquired.

Delphine de Girardin

A woman would be in despair if nature had formed her as fashion makes her appear.

Mlle. Julie de Lespinasse

How intoxicating is the triumph of beauty, and how right it is to name it queen of the universe! How many courtiers, how many slaves, have submitted to it! But alas! why must it be that what flatters our senses almost always deceives our souls?

Mme. de Surin

It is the personality of the mistress that the home expresses. Men are forever guests in our homes, no matter how much happiness they may find there.

Elsie De Wolfe

How dreary to be somebody!
How public, like a frog
To tell your name the livelong day
To an admiring bog.

Emily Dickinson

A good face is the best letter of recommendation.

Queen Elizabeth I

Dreck is dreck and no amount of fancy polish is going to make it anything else.

Linda Ellerbee

Next to beauty is the power of appreciating beauty.

Margaret Fuller

It appears that the current stairway to heaven is lined with celery sticks. Everyone wants to be Born Again—three sizes smaller.

Ellen Goodman

Beauty depends more upon the movement of the face than upon the form of the features when at rest. Thus a countenance habitually under the influence of amiable feeling acquires a beauty of the highest order.

Mrs. S. C. Hall

The Avon Lady called this morning and asked me not to tell anyone where I buy my cosmetics.

Margaret Hance

Beauty seemed to the Greeks the visible sign of an inward grace, and an expression of divine good-will.

Mrs. H. R. Haweis

Show me an actress who isn't a personality and I'll show you a woman who isn't a star.

Katharine Hepburn

True delicacy, that most beautiful heart-leaf of humanity, exhibits itself most significantly in little things.

Mary Botham Howitt

Etiquette is what you are doing when people are looking and listening. What you are thinking is your business.

Virginia Cary Hudson

A market stall, a fine Bokhara rug, a scrap of Chinese embroidery—food for the eye is to be found almost everywhere.

Jocasta Innes

Now and then one sees a face which has kept its smile pure and undefiled. It is a woman's face usually; often a face which has a trace of great sorrow over it, till the smile breaks. Such a smile transfigures; such a smile, if the artful but know it, is the greatest weapon a face can have.

Helen Hunt Jackson

Tact is after all a kind of mind reading.

Sarah Orne Jewett

I'm tired of all this nonsense about beauty being only skin deep. That's deep enough. What do you want, an adorable pancreas?

Jean Kerr

Class is an aura of confidence that is being sure without being cocky. Class has nothing to do with money. Class never runs scared. It is self-discipline and self-knowledge. It's the sure-footedness that comes with having proved you can meet life.

Ann Landers

The skilled woman can invent beauty over and over again with extraordinary effect. The art of inventing beauty transcends class, intellect, age, profession, geography—virtually every cultural and economic barrier.

Estee Lauder

Humility is no substitute for a good personality.

Fran Leibowitz

Sex appeal is 50 per cent what you've got and 50 per cent what people think you've got.

Sophia Loren

The sign of intelligent people is their ability to control emotions by the application of reason.

Marya Mannes

Since the masses have always known we are far from impoverished, it would have been a terrible mistake for me to have appeared before them in old or shabby clothes just because they dress shabbily. . . . They would have thought I was belittling them. On the other hand, it flattered them to no end to see that I always took the trouble to wear my best.

Imelda Marcos

Monsieur, I beg your pardon. (to the executioner after she stepped on his foot)

Marie Antoinette

Don't be humble; you're not that great.

Golda Meir

I wouldn't say I invented tacky, but I definitely brought it to its present high popularity.

Bette Midler

How goodness heightens beauty.

Hannah More

With her whole heart's welcome in her smile.

Caroline Norton

Good dressing includes a suggestion of poetry. One nowhere more quickly detects sentiment than in dress. A well-dressed woman in a room should fill it with poetic sense, like the perfume of a flower.

Miss Oakley

Cosmetics is a boon to every woman, but a girl's *best* beauty aid is still a near-sighted man.

Yoko Ono

I require only three things of a man: he must be handsome, ruthless, and stupid.

Dorothy Parker

You'd be surprised how much it costs to look this cheap.

Dolly Parton

Beauty of form affects the mind, but then it must be understood that it is not the mere shell that we admire; we are attracted by the idea that this shell is only a beautiful case adjusted to the shape and value of a still more beautiful pearl within. The perfection of outward loveliness is the soul shining through its crystalline covering.

Jane Porter

I base my fashion taste on what doesn't itch.

Gilda Radner

The chief excitement in a woman's life is spotting women who are fatter than she is.

Helen Rowland

Men are just as vain as women, and sometimes even more so.

Helena Rubinstein

The great thing about fads is that they fade away.

Debra J. Saunders

Ideal beauty is a fugitive which is never located.

La Marquise de Sévigné

You can't be too rich or too thin.

Wallis Simpson, Duchess of Windsor

The trouble about most Englishwomen is that they will dress as if they had been a mouse in a previous incarnation or hope to be one in the next.

Dame Edith Sitwell

My creed is that public service must be more than doing a job efficiently and honestly. It must be a complete dedication to the people and to the nation with full recognition that every human being is entitled to courtesy and consideration, that constructive criticism is not only to be expected but sought, that smears are not only to be expected but fought, that honor is to be earned but not bought.

Margaret Chase Smith

Social science affirms that a woman's place in society marks the level of civilization.

Elizabeth Cady Stanton

Being a sex symbol has to do with an attitude, not looks. Most men think it's looks, most women know otherwise.

Kathleen Turner

You don't have to signal a social conscience by looking like a frump. Lace knickers won't hasten the holocaust, you can ban the bomb in a feather boa just as well without, and a mild interest in hemlines doesn't necessarily disqualify you from reading *Das Kapital* and agreeing with every word.

Jill Tweedie

Good manners have much to do with the emotions. To make them ring true, one must feel them, not merely exhibit them.

Amy Vanderbilt

Money has nothing to do with style at all, but naturally it helps every situation.

Diana Vreeland

Modesty is the graceful, calm virtue of maturity; bashfulness the charm of vivacious youth.

Mary Wollstonecraft

If all good people were clever,
And all clever people were good,
The world would be nicer than ever
We thought that it possibly could.
But somehow, 'tis seldom or never
The two hit it off as they should;
The good are so harsh to the clever,
The clever so rude to the good.

Elizabeth Wordsworth

There is no cosmetic for beauty like happiness.

Anon.

Chapter 36

SUCCESS

We are not interested in the possibilities of defeat.

Queen Victoria

❦

SUCCESS can be a fact, an attitude, or a sort of mental ambiance. When standing before an audience (of five or fifty or five hundred) it is essential that you radiate all three.

Being a success doesn't mean being a household word. Being a success as a speaker means having the attitudinal comfort, the positive self-image, and the absolute certainty of preparedness that allows you to be and do your very best. If you *are* those things, you will be perceived that way—and *you will be a success*!

My favorite definition of success is that it is a state of mind combined with a state of readiness. You can have *one* and be a flop; if you have *both*, you'll win every time. And as a speaker, when you win, your audience wins, too.

As with so many things, it is impossible for the speaker to encourage her audience to be what she herself is not. If people don't perceive success in you, there is no way they will follow your lead. (They may decide they have it and you *don't*—certainly not a recipe for success as a speaker.)

When you appear before an audience you have a certain set of goals in mind. You may want to encourage people to work through a challenge or a problem, you may want them to initiate a certain course of action, you may want them to increase their sales. Whatever it is, you want to encourage them to experience a positive outcome—in other words, you want them to be a success.

In order to lead audiences toward this goal, you must always remember that your job, as a speaker, is to help your listeners focus on outcomes.

The first manifestation of success as an outcome begins with *you*. Do you stand tall, radiate, reach out, greet warmly? Do you look, sound, act, and think successful—and successfully? Do you generate an attitude of achievement? Do you radiate a belief in what you are doing and saying? If you can look yourself in the mirror and answer "Yes" to all these, then the odds are good that you'll be able to generate the same answers from, and for, your listeners.

Remember: you must embody success in order to help others generate it. These quotations about success approach it from every perspective: personal, organizational, and attitudinal. The women quoted in this chapter have approached life and achievement from many different perspectives and standings. The commonality is that they have achieved success—or in some cases have "achieved" the kind of failure that illuminates success—in their own worlds and in their own ways.

As a woman speaker, especially before predominantly female audiences, it is crucial that you use the words of other women—all kinds of women—to define success.

Success is clearly not always material. Often it can only be recognized by the owner. It is not necessarily even fully attainable. It is generally more sought after than achieved. But it is part of an attitudinal achievement level. You and your listeners should be able to use the definitions and descriptions of other women as you each seek your own path to success.

The excellent becomes the permanent.

Jane Addams

Children's talent to endure stems from their ignorance of alternatives.

Maya Angelou

Failure is impossible.

Susan B. Anthony

It made me feel as if I'd made a contribution. We just can't be cold automatons all our lives. Anyway, I made a difference. I made a small, little difference.

Carol Bellamy

I've never sought success in order to get fame and money; it's the talent and the passion that count in success.

Ingrid Bergman

It's very important to define success for *yourself*. If you really want to reach for the brass ring, just remember that there are sacrifices that go along.

Cathleen Black

I stopped believing in Santa Claus when I was six. Mother took me to see him in a department store and he asked for my autograph.

Shirley Temple Black

Figure out what your most magnificent qualities are and make them indispensable to the people you want to work with. Notice that I didn't say "work for."

Linda Bloodworth-Thomason

I hope I have convinced you—the only thing that separates successful people from the ones who aren't is the willingness to work very, very hard.

Helen Gurley Brown

Success is important only to the extent that it puts one in a position to do more things one likes to do.

Sarah Caldwell

You must accept that you might fail; then, if you do your best and still don't win, at least you can be satisfied that you've tried. If you don't accept failure as a possibility, you don't set high goals, you don't branch out, you don't try—you don't take the risk.

Rosalynn Carter

The only people who never fail are those who never try.

Ilka Chase

Dynasty was the opportunity to take charge of my career rather than waiting around like a library book waiting to be loaned out.

Joan Collins

The object in business is not to make others comfortable, but to make them successful.

Laurel Cutler

The process of empowerment cannot be simplistically defined in accordance with our own particular class interests. We must learn to lift as we climb.

Angela Davis

This became a credo of mine: attempt the impossible in order to improve your work.

Bette Davis

Success in the modern world takes far more than knowledge. It takes stability, stamina, level-headedness, courage, a desire to learn, and the ability to make good use of one's learning.

Alice L. Dement

Success is counted sweetest by those who ne'er succeed.

Emily Dickinson

Women share with men the need for personal success, even the taste for power, and no longer are we willing to satisfy those needs through the achievements of surrogates, whether husbands, children or merely role models.

Elizabeth Dole

You're only as good as your last picture.

Marie Dressler

There is no sorrow I have thought about more than that—to love what is great, and try to reach it, and yet to fail.

George Eliot

The great high of winning Wimbledon lasts for about a week. You go down in the record books, but you don't have anything tangible to hold on to. But having a baby—there just isn't any comparison.

Chris Evert

Any pretty girl can be a model; but not any pretty girl can be a star.

Eileen Ford

Until recently, the "old girls" did not know how the "old boys" network operated. Women didn't know they needed to have a network to capture a top-level position in an institution or organization. They thought that all it took was hard work; eventually the organization would recognize worth and promote able people. Women now know that, besides hard work and lots of skill, the move to the top requires a supportive network.

June E. Gabler

This is what it's like being a successful woman in America. You get to be treated as the second sex by an ever-more-elite class of men.

Ellen Goodman

Success isn't everything but it makes a man stand straight.

Lillian Hellman

I was fortunate to be born with a set of characteristics that were in public vogue.

Katharine Hepburn

Financial success comes second. My greatest accomplishment is raising my children to be caring, contributing members of the world.

Caroline Rose Hunt

Behind every man who achieves success
Stand a mother, a wife and the IRS.

Ethel Jacobson

Power is the ability not to have to please.

Elizabeth Janeway

Life is a succession of moments. To live each one is to succeed.

Corita Kent

I think success has no rules, but you can learn a lot from failure.

Jean Kerr

When you do nothing, you feel overwhelmed and powerless. But when you get involved, you feel the sense of hope and accomplishment that comes from knowing you are working to make things better.

Pauline R. Kezer

Success and failure are both greatly overrated. But failure gives you a whole lot more to talk about.

Hildegard Knef

The penalty of success is to be bored by the attentions of people who formerly snubbed you.

Mary Wilson Little

To be successful, the first thing to do is fall in love with your work.

Sister Mary Lauretta

It is with many enterprises as with striking fire; we do not meet with success except by reiterated efforts, and often at the instant when we despaired of success.

Françoise d'Aubigné Maintenon

To be successful, a woman has to be better at her job than a man.

Golda Meir

The worst part of success is to try to find someone who is happy for you.

Bette Midler

Develop an institutional memory, which can be valuable to you as you strive not to repeat mistakes of the past.

Lorraine Mintzmyer

No modest man ever did or will make a fortune.

Lady Mary Wortley Montague

Life's an open book and an education helps you write success stories.

Joyce A. Myers

Worship your heroes from afar; contact withers them.

Susanne Curchod Necker

We have to confound them with competence.

Constance Newman

Unfortunately, there are still many women in the business world who refuse to support women. I call them "Honorary Males"—women who think that power is to be had only in the company of men. Women must realize they have power—economic and political. Don't give your power away; use it for yourself and for the benefit of other women.

Ginger Purdy

Integrity is so perishable in the summer months of success.

Vanessa Redgrave

Choose to have a career early and a family late. Or choose to have a family early and a career late—but plan a long life.

Dr. Janet Davison Rowley

Success is a public affair. Failure is a private funeral.

Rosalind Russell

Success is never a destination—it's a journey.

Satenig St. Marie

Human successes, like human failures, are composed of one action at a time and achieved by one person at a time.

Patsy H. Sampson

Getting to the top isn't bad, and it's probably best done as an afterthought.

Anne Wilson Shaef

You may be disappointed if you fail, but you are doomed if you don't try.

Beverly Sills

It's time to take a look at my failures and stop calling them successes. Now I can start working at something that can use me best.

Nina Simone

The only place you find success before work is in the dictionary.

May V. Smith

My expectations—which I extended whenever I came close to accomplishing my goals—made it impossible ever to feel satisfied with my success.

Ellen Sue Stern

The world has been busy for some centuries in shutting and locking every door through which a woman could step into wealth, except the door of marriage.

Harriet Beecher Stowe

There's no deodorant like success.

Elizabeth Taylor

Success is having a flair for the thing that you are doing; knowing that is not enough, that you have got to have hard work and a certain sense of purpose.

Margaret Thatcher

Sometimes I worry about being a success in a mediocre world.

Lily Tomlin

Success in show business depends on your ability to make and keep friends.

Sophie Tucker

A successful man is one who makes more money than his wife can spend. A successful woman is one who can find such a man.

Lana Turner

If you want a place in the sun, you have to put up with a few blisters.

Abigail Van Buren

I like earning money. I like it when companies seek me out and sign me up to design no matter what—sheets, yard goods, glassware, scarves, wallpaper, table linen, valentines. I like being every year in greater demand. I like having to face week after week my all but impossible deadlines. The fame you earn has a different taste from the fame that is forced upon you.

Gloria Vanderbilt

All my life I've wanted to *be* somebody.
But I see now I should have been more specific.

Jane Wagner

Success can make you go one of two ways. It can make you a prima donna—or it can smooth the edges, take away the insecurities, let the nice things come out.

Barbara Walters

I very sinearly [sic] wish you would exert yourself so as to keep all your matters in order your self without depending on others as that is the only way to be happy to have all your business in your own hands.

Martha Washington

She's the kind of woman who climbed the ladder of success, wrong by wrong.

Mae West

The best career advice to give the young is "Find out what you like doing best and get someone to pay you for doing it."

Katherine Whitehorn

I really believe that if you know what you're doing, if you believe in what you're doing, you can make it—in any business.

Riva Yares

Success is a failure turned inside out.

Anon.

Experience is what you get when you don't get what you want.

Anon.

To hit mark, aim above it.

Anon.

Chapter **37**

TIME

I must govern the clock, not be governed by it.

Golda Meir

❦

TIME is the most valuable commodity there is. This is obviously true for everyone; it is doubly true for the speaker. You give it to your audience and they give it to you. The "time of our life" is all any of us have to give anybody.

Time is also one of the most useful tools in a speaker's repertoire. It allows you to frame an issue, a problem, a concept, or a challenge into a perspective within which both you and your audience can work.

In using quotations about time, I find it useful to divide the notion into three segments:

1. *Time as a concept.*

    A very useful device is to use the concept of time as a way to frame a point. For example: the United States is the world's oldest continuous democracy, yet the lifetimes of only four Presidents—from Thomas Jefferson to Abraham Lincoln to Woodrow Wilson to George Bush—span the history of the nation. Such an illustration can cause time to be a manageable, conceivable concept.

    Similarly, you can relate the age of an organization or a company to events that have transpired during a certain period of time. Putting things in perspective not only helps to make them more understandable, it also creates something memorable for your listeners to take away with them, helping them remember you as well as what you said.

2. *Time as a reality.*

Sometimes it isn't enough to simply frame your points within a time concept. Occasionally you need to place issues within a context of "Do we do it now, do we do it later, or do we do it at all?" This is a concept that can be brought to any presentation. You can help your listeners grapple with the reality of not only doing something, but of doing it within a realistic time frame. It is important, when discussing issues or abstractions, to quantify as much as possible *when* something can or should be done.

There is another point about time as a reality that the speaker must consider: that is the fact that what you have to say should be worth your listeners' time. I will reiterate this point because it is so crucial: your audience is giving you the most valuable thing they have—their time; you have a moral obligation to use it wisely.

One effective way to help your audience, as well as yourself, is to frame your remarks as much as possible in some sort of a sequential order that your audience can easily follow—*and let them know what that order is.*

The last point about time as a reality is that you should begin on time and end on time. Of those two points, the *second* is more important than the first!

3. *Time as an imperative.*

Underlying the two preceding concepts is the fact that, whether as an idea or as a decision-making reality, time is an issue of urgency. The degree of urgency may vary, but it is (or should be) a major factor. As a speaker, you need to help your listeners focus on this imperative.

Attitude is never a substitute for action, and thinking about something is never a substitute for doing it. If your audience thinks a topic is important enough to ask you to speak to them about it, and if you think it is important enough to accept the invitation, then you certainly want to help the listeners reach an outcome regarding that topic. Even when talking about abstract concepts or the worthiness of a cause, never fail to frame some element of your remarks around the necessity to act.

Among the most effective ways to illustrate the importance of these three concepts of time are with quotations. Some deal with time as an abstraction and some deal with it as a reality. But all will help bring substance and support to the points you wish to make. In their own way, each quotation is timely.

❦

Patience with ills you can cure is the greatest evil.

Margery Ashby

Years ago I thought old age would be dreadful, because I should not be able to do things I would want to do. Now I find there is nothing I want to do.

Lady Nancy Astor

There is a way to look at the past. Don't hide from it. It will not catch you—if you don't repeat it.

Pearl Bailey

From the sad years of life we sometimes do short hours, yea, minutes strike, keen, blissful, bright, never to be forgotten; which, through the dreary gloom of time o'er past, shine like fair sunny spots on a wild waste.

Joanna Baillie

Time is a dressmaker specializing in alterations.

Faith Baldwin

The only thing I regret about my past is the length of it. If I had to live my life again, I'd make the same mistakes, only sooner.

Tallulah Bankhead

I cannot sing the old songs
I sang long years ago
For heart and voice would fail me
And foolish tears would flow.

Charlotte Barnard

Our faith in the present dies out long before our faith in the future.

Ruth Benedict

I am so tired and I am crabby. There are enough nights when my husband and I are reduced to eating cheese rinds and tuna fish out of the can because we don't have anything in the refrigerator. I can't get the energy to cook, and I think, I'm going to lose this man over a tuna sandwich!

Candice Bergen

The clock would never let him forget the amount of time he was wasting.

Sallie Bingham

Forget the past and live the present hour.

Sarah Knowles Bolton

A memory without blot of contamination must be an exquisite treasure, an inexhaustible source of pure refreshment.

Charlotte Brontë

I believe you are your work. Don't trade the very stuff of your life, time, for nothing more than dollars. That's a rotten bargain.

Rita Mae Brown

Celebrity was a long time in coming; it will go away. Everything goes away.

Carol Burnett

At the end of your life, you will never regret not having passed one more test, not winning one more verdict or not closing one more deal. You will regret time not spent with a husband, a friend, a child or a parent.

Barbara Bush

Never does one feel oneself so utterly helpless as in trying to speak comfort for great bereavement. Time is the only comforter for the loss of a mother.

Jane Welsh Carlyle

Little drops of water, little grains of sand,
Make the mighty ocean and the pleasant land;
Thus the little minutes, humble though they be,
Make the mighty ages
Of eternity.

Julia Fletcher Carney

In every outthrust headland, in every curving beach, in every grain of sand there is a story of the earth.

Rachel Carson

A committee takes hours to put into minutes what can be done in seconds.

Judy Castrina

There is no time for cut-and-dried monotony. There is time for work. And time for love. That leaves no other time.

Coco Chanel

My hands were busy through the day,
I didn't have much time to play
The little games you asked me to,
I didn't have much time for you.
I'd wash your clothes, I'd sew and cook
But when you'd bring your picture book
And ask me please to share your fun,
I'd say, "A little later, Son."
But life is short, the years rush past,
A little boy grows up so fast!

Now the picture books are put away,
There aren't any games to play
No good night kiss, no prayers to hear;
That all belongs to yesteryear.
My hands once busy, now lie still,
The days are long and hard to fill.
I wish I might go back and do
The little things you asked me to!

Alice Chase

The very fact that we make such a to-do over golden weddings indicates our amazement at human endurance.

Ilka Chase

Love is the emblem of eternity; it confounds all notion of time; effaces all memory of beginning, all fear of an end.

Mme. de Staël

There are few husbands whom the wife cannot win, in the long run, by patience and love.

Marguerite de Valois

I have only to take up this or that to flood my soul with memories.

Dorothée DeLuzy

That it will never come again is what makes life so sweet.

Emily Dickinson

Most of us spend too much time on the last twenty-four hours and too little on the last six thousand years.

Ariel and Will Durant

I desire no future that will break the ties of the past.

George Eliot

All my possessions for one moment of time.

Queen Elizabeth I

To be somebody you must last.

Ruth Gordon

I believe one thing: that today is yesterday and tomorrow is today and you can't stop.

Martha Graham

Experience joined with common sense, to mortals is a providence.

Mary A. E. Green

It is a mark of many famous people that they cannot part with their brightest hour.

Lillian Hellman

Though the past haunt me as a spirit, I do not ask to forget.

Felicia Hemans

These are my daughters, I suppose. But where in the world did the children vanish?

Phyllis McGinley

Most of us become parents long before we have stopped being children.

Mignon McLaughlin

Old age is like a plane flying through a storm. Once you're aboard, there's nothing you can do.

Golda Meir

A thousand years from this tonight
When Orion climbs the sky,
The same swift snow will still the roofs,
The same mad stars run by.

And who will know of China's war,
Or poison gas in Spain?
The dead, they'll be forgotten, lost
Whether they lose or gain.

Of all the brilliant strategies
Or war-lords now alive,
Perhaps a Chinese iris vase
Of porcelain, may survive.

Perhaps a prayer, perhaps a song,
Fashioned of love and tears,
But only beauty, only truth
Will last a thousand years.

Margaret Moore Meuttman

Death and taxes and childbirth! There's never a convenient time for any of them.
Margaret Mitchell

Life is a short day; but it is a working day. Activity may lead to evil, but inactivity cannot lead to good.

Hannah More

Nobody sees a flower really; it is so small. We haven't time, and to see takes time—like to have a friend takes time.

Georgia O'Keeffe

In youth we learn how little we can do for ourselves; in age how little we can do for others. The wisdom of experience is incommunicable.

Isabel Patterson

Life is entirely too time-consuming.

Irene Peter

One wastes so much time, one is so prodigal of life, at twenty! Our days of winter count for double. That is the compensation of the old.

George Sand

Time—our youth—it never really goes, does it? It is all held in our minds.
Helen Hoover Santmyer

If we could have a little patience, we should escape much mortification; time takes away as much as it gives.

La Marquise de Sévigné

We're always being told that time is running out; it is and getting things done won't stop it.

Joan Silber

Lost
yesterday
somewhere between sunrise and sunset
two golden hours
each set with sixty diamond minutes.
No reward is offered
for they are gone forever.

Lydia H. Sigourney

How pleasant it is, at the end of the day,
No follies to have to repent;
But to reflect on the past, and be able to say,
That my time has been properly spent.

Anne Taylor

It was a spring that never came, but we have lived enough to know what we have never had remains. It is the things we have that go.

Sara Teasdale

Oh! How impatience gains upon the soul, when the long promised hour of joy draws near. How slow the tardy moments seem then to roll.

Mary B. Tighe

Only you can know how much you can give to every aspect of your life. Try to decide what is the most important. And if you do, then only occasionally will you resent or regret the demands of the marriage, the career, or the child, or the staying.

Barbara Walters

The past is written! Close the book
  On pages sad and gay;
Within the future do not look,
  But live today today.

Lydia Avery Coonley Ward

The days grow shorter, the nights grow longer,
The headstones thicken along the way;
And life grows sadder, but love grows stronger
For those who walk with us day by day.

Ella Wheeler Wilcox

It doesn't happen all at once. You become. It takes a long time.

Margery Williams

Each has his past shut in him like the leaves of a book known to him by his heart, and his friends can only read the title.

Virginia Woolf

One generation plants the trees; another gets the shade.

Chinese proverb

When as a child I laughed and wept,
  Time crept;
When as a youth I dreamed and talked,
  Time walked;
When I became a full-grown man,
  Time ran;
When older still I daily grew,
  Time flew;
Soon shall I find in traveling on,
  Time gone.

Anon.

Every time history repeats itself the price goes up.

Anon.

Old years and new years
With all their pain and strife,
Are but the bricks and steel and stone
With which we fashion life.

Anon.

Chapter 38

VISION

Far away there in the sunshine are my highest aspirations. I may not reach them but I can look up and see their beauty, believe in them and try to follow them.

Louisa May Alcott

❧

One of the most meaningful passages in the Old Testament is in Chapter 29 of Proverbs: "Where there is no vision, the people perish."

In contemporary language we might use a word other then VISION. We might say *purpose*, or *goal*, or *focus*—and all of these would be correct. But each of these words simply describes one aspect of that overarching concept of vision. Each is useful to the extent that it helps to clarify, but it does not begin to supplant the larger concept.

As a speaker, you cannot succeed if you fail in some way to communicate a concept of vision. You have to have it in your own plans of what you are going to say and how you are going to say it, and you have to impart some sense of it to your listeners. But if you give them only glimpses of the parts and not the vision of the whole, you haven't done your job.

Sometimes it is useful for the speaker to communicate vision by talking about its antithesis. When you do this, you are driving with fear as well as leading with facts. This can sometimes be an effective motivational technique. You can show the serious consequences of no vision or of a diluted, distorted vision. Discussing the opposite effect of vision—hopelessness—can help to demonstrate the potential end result of an unsuccessful vision.

A clarity of vision is one of the absolute necessities for success in any endeavor, including making a speech or a presentation of any kind. Throughout history there have been few events of significance that have occurred purely by accident—and few truely influential political, social, religious, or corporate leaders have failed to have vision. That vision may be misguided or wrongly intentioned (Hitler, after all, had a very clear vision of what he wanted to accomplish), but vision is always present when history is made.

As a speaker, it is difficult to encourage people to take courageous steps, to make difficult decisions, or even decide to decide unless they can understand *why* the action is worth the doing. It is your job to convey or illuminate or clarify that *why*.

The greatest motivating component of a presentation is the definition or articulation of a vision. Even if it isn't really do-able, if it is shared it can cause people to move forward.

Quotations from women who were committed to a vision make excellent testimony. Their thoughts clarify both life and action. They help shed a verbal light that strengthens any presentation. At the beginning of your remarks, these words help focus your listeners; at the conclusion, they help inspire them. With those kinds of bookends, you should be able to build your own library of thoughts and concepts about vision.

ৼ

Imagination is the highest kite one can fly.

Lauren Bacall

There are people who put their dreams in a little box and say, "Yes, I've got dreams, of course, I've got dreams." Then they put the box away and bring it out once in awhile to look in it, and yep, they're still there. These are *great* dreams, but they never even get out of the box. It takes an uncommon amount of guts to put your dreams on the line, to hold them up and say, "How good or how bad am I?" That's where courage comes in.

Erma Bombeck

One can live in the shadow of an idea without grasping it.

Elizabeth Bowen

In communion with the highest, in striving for the best, in losing oneself in others, one is lifted above the common material furniture of life, above its gaudy trappings and encumbering paraphernalia, above its contentions and toils, its antagonisms and weariness into a realm of peace which passeth understanding.

Olympia Brown

Light tomorrow with today.

Elizabeth Barrett Browning

There are many ways of breaking a heart. Stories were full of hearts broken by love, but what really broke a heart was taking away its dream—whatever that dream might be.

Pearl S. Buck

Intensive training, they say,
Produced leaders.
Is it better to have five men
That are mental experts,
Or fifty thousand
That have had a glimpse
Of what life may mean?

Virginia Church

Don't be afraid of the space between your dreams and reality. If you can dream it, you can make it so.

Belva Davis

We are all of us imaginative in some form or other, for images are the brood of desire.

George Eliot

Man can never come up to his ideal standard. It is the nature of the immortal spirit to raise that standard higher and higher as it goes from strength to strength, still upward and onward. The wisest and greatest men are ever the most modest.

Margaret Fuller

I believe you rarely achieve more than you expect.

Carol Grosse

We must overcome the notion that we must be regular . . . it robs you of the chance to be extraordinary and leads you to the mediocre.

Uta Hagen

There is no shadow of protection to be had by sheltering behind the slender stockades of visionary speculation, or by hiding behind the wagon-wheels of pacific theories.

Madame Chiang Kai-Shek

The most pathetic person in the world is someone who has sight, but has no vision.

Helen Keller

Vision is of God. A vision comes in advance of any task well done.

Katherine Logan

The world stands out on either side
No wider than the heart is wide;
Above the world is stretched the sky,
No higher than the soul is high.

Edna St. Vincent Millay

If help and salvation are to come, they can only come from the children, for the children are the makers of men.

Maria Montessori

Oh, the joy of young ideas painted on the mind, in the warm, glowing colors fancy spreads on objects not yet known, when all is new and all is lovely!

Hannah More

A #2 pencil and a dream can take you anywhere.

Joyce A. Myers

Only when men are connected to large, universal goals are they really happy— and one result of their happiness is a rush of creative activity.

Joyce Carol Oates

Our griefs, as well as our joys, owe their strongest colors to our imaginations. There is nothing so grievous to be borne that pondering upon it will not make it heavier; and there is no pleasure so vivid that the animation of fancy cannot enliven it.

Jane Porter

To attempt to climb—to achieve—without a firm objective in life is to attain nothing.

Mary G. Roebling

The future belongs to those who believe in the beauty of their dreams.

Eleanor Roosevelt

Inquisitiveness and strength make me want to rise above my valley-bound brothers. I must reach the summit to see the truth.

Delores Seats

Twinkle, twinkle, little star,
How I wonder what you are,
Up above the world so high,
Like a diamond in the sky.

As your bright and tiny spark
Lights the traveler in the dark,
Though I know not what you are,
Twinkle, twinkle, little star.

Jane Taylor

It's easy, perhaps to die for a dream
With banners unfurled—and be forgiving!
It's the harder part to follow the gleam
When scorned by the world—and go on living!

Myra Brooks Welch

When I look at the future, it's so bright it burns my eyes.

Oprah Winfrey

So long as you write what you wish to write, that is all that matters, and whether it matters for ages or only for hours, nobody can say. But to sacrifice a hair of the head of your vision, a shade of its colour, in deference to some Headmaster with a silver pot in his hand or to some professor with a measuring-rod up his sleeve, is the most abject treachery.

Virginia Woolf

He who has imagination without learning has wings but no feet.

Anon.

Chapter **39**

WOMEN

The eye that directs a needle in the delicate meshes of embroidery will equally well bisect a star with the spider web of the micrometer.

Maria Mitchell

❦

WOMEN have said so much *about* women that it is difficult not to build an entire book of quotations around just this topic. The quotations in this chapter are just a sampling of what we have said about each other. They were selected to illuminate and illustrate the variety of those perspectives.

Many of these quotations, not surprisingly, exalt women and women's contributions. Many do so by contrasting—sometimes humorously, sometimes not—women with men. And, though there is a certain amount of it, there is very little of the moaning, "poor me" attitude about the lot or the fate of women. Happily, most women who have something to say also say it with a sense of exhilaration, of expectation, of determination, often of joy.

Much of this exhilaration is because, in large measure, women have had to define themselves. Women throughout history have had a considerably different view of themselves than have men, and it has caused us to think a great deal about just what it means to be a woman. In today's society it has led far too many of us to decide that it has to mean everything. We have to be super-mom, super-wife, super-executive, super-chauffeur, super-cook, or super-volunteer—and generally all at the same time. Somewhere along the way we decided that super had to be a prefix for everything that we did.

Women have been perfectly willing to allow men to define themselves in the most tolerant, accepting terms possible, and we have been perfectly willing to accept those definitions. But we certainly haven't been willing to define ourselves in those same terms.

It is fascinating to note the varying stages of self-definition revealed by the quotations in this chapter. Some women are still desperately struggling, unwilling or unable to become "unhyphenated." Many others have made it into a newer, freer reality. There is a place for the words of both in the woman speaker's vocabulary.

As you read these words and collect quotations of your own, I encourage you to think about your own progress along this path of self-definition.

Some of us have learned to accept a standard of less-than-perfection, both in ourselves and in other women. Some of us have gotten to the point of "ego-comfort" where we can accept who we are, figurative warts and all.

As you speak to women, and to men, use these quotations to help humanize yourself and them. Help them, as you help yourself, exchange guilt for comfort, a positive self-image for self-doubt or deprecation. As a woman presenter, give your listeners a sense of perspective, a sense of a woman, a person, who is imperfect but competent; one who is imperfectable, knows it, and can laugh at it. Be a woman. Be a real person. That's all you have to be.

I long to hear that you have declared an independency. And, by the way, in the new code of laws which I suppose it will be necessary for you to make, I would desire you would remember the ladies and be more generous and favorable to them than your ancestors.

Abigail Smith Adams

Whenever serious intellectuals, psychologists, sociologists, practicing physicians, Nobel Prize novelists take time off from their normal pursuits to scrutinize and appraise the Modern American Woman, they turn in unanimously dreary reports.

Grace Adams

The only question left to be settled now is: are women persons?

Susan B. Anthony

It has often been said that [Ferdinand] Marcos was the first male chauvinist to underestimate me.

Corazon Aquino

In passing, also, I would like to say that the first time Adam had a chance he laid the blame on woman.

Lady Nancy Astor

Mr. President, I don't know why it took 200 years for one of us to get the job [of ambassador].

Shirley Temple Black

I'm real ambivalent about [working mothers]. Those of us who have been in the women's movement for a long time know that we've talked a good game of 'go out and fulfill your dreams' and 'be everything you were meant to be.' But by the same token, we want daughters-in-law who are going to stay home and raise our grandchildren.

Erma Bombeck

Women observe subconsciously a thousand little details, without knowing they are doing so. Their subconscious mind adds these little things together—and they call the result intuition.

Agatha Christie

The majority of women commit the strategic error of attempting to excel in a maximum of fields in order to satisfy all their customers' needs. This phenomenon is particularly true of working wives. Through a mixture of guilt and vanity they wear themselves out trying to combine their roles of working women and perfect housewives. Thus they run the risk of compromising part of the capital essential to the smooth running of their business—their health.

Christiane Collange

I know God is not a woman—no woman would have created men with so many imperfections.

Jill M. Consideine

One is not born a woman, one becomes one.

Simone de Beauvoir

I like viable women who are out there doing. I don't mean in terms of the working woman vs. the non-working woman, because we all know that ALL women are working, each in their own way. I like women who are very involved with living and who haven't pulled out from life.

Colleen Dewhurst

The entire being of a woman is a secret which should be kept.

Isak Dinesen

Until women learn to want economic independence, i.e., the ability to earn their own living independently of husbands, fathers, brothers or lovers,—and until they work out a way to get this independence without denying themselves the joys of love and motherhood, it seems to me feminism has no roots.

Crystal Eastman

A girl should not expect special privileges because of her sex but neither should she adjust to prejudice and discrimination.

Betty Friedan

There is no female mind. The brain is not an organ of sex. Might as well speak of a female liver.

Charlotte Perkins Gilman

People have been writing premature obituaries on the women's movement since its beginning.

Ellen Goodman

The thing women must do to rise to power is redefine their femininity. Once, power was considered a masculine attribute. In fact power has no sex.

Katherine Graham

I never realized until lately that women were supposed to be the inferior sex.

Katharine Hepburn

When women help women they help themselves.

Wilhelmina Cole Holladay

We do not understand the psychology of women because women have not articulated their experience.

Karen Horney

We haven't come a long way, we've come a short way. If we hadn't come a short way, no one would be calling us "baby."

Elizabeth Janeway

No matter the fight, don't be ladylike! God almighty made women and the Rockefeller gang of thieves made the ladies.

"Mother" Mary Jones

Any girl can be glamorous. All you have to do is stand still and look stupid.

Hedy Lamarr

I believe that what a woman resents is not so much giving herself in pieces as giving herself purposelessly.

Anne Morrow Lindbergh

The people I'm furious with are the women's liberationists. They keep getting up on soap boxes and proclaiming that women are brighter than men. It's true but it should be kept quiet or it ruins the whole racket.

Anita Loos

Male supremacy has kept woman down. It has not knocked her out.

Clare Boothe Luce

Nobody objects to a woman being a good writer or sculptor or geneticist if at the same time she manages to be a good wife, good mother, good-looking, good-tempered, well-groomed and unaggressive.

Leslie M. McIntyre

Some people still think women are supposed to have a sixth sense. Listen, I don't even know what my birth sign is.

Lorraine Mintzmyer

Women through all ages could have had physical strength and mental creativity and still have been called feminine. The fact that these things have been suppressed is the fault of society.

Louise Nevelson

Being a woman has only bothered me in climbing trees.

Frances Perkins

So many women have chosen lives of seeming contradictions. I remember mentioning the baby sitter in a column once and receiving outraged letters from readers who could not understand how anyone who could write feelingly of her children would hire help with their care. When did those people think I was writing? In the checkout line at the supermarket?

Anna Quindlen

No woman is all sweetness; even the rose has thorns.

Mme. Recamier

I am woman, hear me roar.
In numbers too big to ignore
And I know too much to go back and pretend
'Cause I've heard it all before
And I've been down there on the floor
And no-one's ever gonna keep me down again.

Helen Reddy and Ray Burton

Today's women
Born yesterday
Dealing with tomorrow
Not yet where we're going
But not still where we were.

Adrienne Rich

A good woman inspires a man; a brilliant woman interests him; a beautiful woman fascinates him; and a sympathetic woman gets him.

Helen Rowland

After all, God made man and then said: I can do better than that—and made woman.

Adele Rogers St. Johns

Women are going to learn how to be providers. I don't mean *workers*; we're already workers. The difference is taking responsibility not only for your economic present, but for your future. That's a big change. Up to this point, women have been expected to be contributors and helpmates. But relationships and marriage are not predictable anymore, so women are starting to pick careers and think about money, lifestyle, location, how many children to have—everything from A to Z in terms of what they alone can support.

Pepper Schwartz

To think that all in me of which my father would have felt proper pride had I been a man, is deeply mortifying to him because I am a woman.

Elizabeth Cady Stanton

If women want any rights they had better take them, and say nothing about it.

Harriet Beecher Stowe

If you want anything said, ask a man. If you want anything done, ask a woman.

Margaret Thatcher

A man has to be Joe McCarthy to be called ruthless. All a woman has to do is put you on hold.

Marlo Thomas

The men who espoused unpopular causes may have been considered misguided, but they were rarely attacked for their morals or their masculinity. Women who did the same thing were apt to be denounced as harlots or condemned for being *unfeminine*—an all-purpose word that was used to describe almost any category of female behavior of which men disapproved.

Margaret Truman

From birth to age eighteen a girl needs good parents. From eighteen to thirty-five she needs good looks. From thirty-five to fifty-five she needs a good personality. From fifty-five on she needs good cash.

attributed to Sophie Tucker

When women go wrong, men go right after them.

Mae West

People call me feminist whenever I express sentiments that differentiate me from a doormat or a prostitute.

Dame Rebecca West

Whatever women do they must do twice as well as men in order to be thought half as good. Luckily this is not difficult.

Charlotte Whitton

It is fatal for anyone who writes to think of their sex. It is fatal to be a man or woman pure and simple; one must be woman-manly or man-womanly.

Virginia Woolf

The full and complete development of the world and the cause of peace requires the maximum participation of women as well as men in all fields.

United Nations Declaration on
Elimination of Discrimination Against Women

If the hours are long enough and the pay is short enough, someone will say it's women's work.

Anon.

Chapter **40**

WORK

Opportunities are usually disguised by hard work, so most people don't recognize them.

Ann Landers

WORK is perhaps my favorite word. I know why I'm possessed of this aberrant quality. It is because I grew up a "Depression baby" in the Oklahoma Dust Bowl when the only things that stood between many folks and survival was hard work. Even if you didn't like it that way, the economy and Mother Nature didn't give you much choice. So the value of work was ingrained in me from birth.

Women as a whole tend to be a medium, a fertile culture in which the concept of work has always been able to grow. This seems to have been true throughout history because women have often identified their worth as persons by the quality and quantity of the work they could do. This has certainly been true in the history and development of the United States from a few tiny colonies to a dynamic, booming nation. Women were always there, publicly or privately, toiling away. The images that confront us—from Betsy Ross and Sojourner Truth, from Clara Barton and that wonderful statue of the "Pioneer Woman," to Eleanor Roosevelt and Sally Ride—all bear out our view of women working at or for something.

This reality, and this image and self-image, are why the dangers of the *glass ceiling* are so great. For people who will do whatever work is available to them and required of them, and who will do it well, and then to be denied the *opportunity* to do that work, there is a devastating effect. The repercussion is a diminishing of both self-worth and self-image.

The quotations chosen for this chapter are designed to illustrate women's words that exalt work in all its manifestations. In putting this chapter together, I seldom came across a single quotation by a woman disparaging or diminishing the value or concept of work. The fact that work is so large a component in the lives of women comes through on every page. To a person, they have focused on the reality and the satisfaction of a job well done.

As a woman speaker, you will have all sorts of audiences. You may sometimes speak to groups—of both sexes—in which the concept of work is essentially missing. There are folks out there who believe that achievement is possible without work; that recognition and riches, if not happiness, are attainable without effort. The women who speak from these pages deny that mistaken view. They demonstrate that the avoidance of work is not an achievement, but that doing something, that making a difference, *is* an achievement.

It is important that you help your listeners, especially your women listeners, differentiate between drudgery (mindless labor) and genuine effort that leads to accomplishing something. Work well done is a joy. You can use the quotations from women whose lives demonstrate this fact to help your audiences see that purposeful work can lead to good things. You can help them understand the law of cause and effect.

As you transmit enthusiasm for the concept of work, you will find that you are making a difference not only in the lives of your listeners, but in your own life as well. As a speaker you work hard. It is important to make your work both a contribution and a pleasure.

❧

Shock is bad enough. But the aftershock is worse. Work is the only answer. (on the death of her husband)

Lo Abshier

Perfection consists not in doing extraordinary things, but in doing ordinary things extraordinarily well. Neglect nothing; the most trivial action may be performed to God.

Angelique Arnauld

The only thing I like about being an actress is acting.

Elizabeth Ashley

Making peace is the most difficult work of all.

Hanan Mikhail Ashrawi

People should tell your children what life is about—it's about work.

Lauren Bacall

I don't know anything about luck. I've never banked on it, and I'm afraid of people who do. Luck to me is something else: hard work and realizing what *is* opportunity and what *isn't*.

Lucille Ball

When it comes to getting things done, we need fewer architects and more brick layers.

Colleen C. Barrett

The prosecution of modern wars rests completely upon the operation of labor in mines, mills and factories, so that labor fights there just as truly as the soldiers do in the trenches.

Mary Ritter Beard

Work, alternated with needful rest, is the salvation of man or woman.

Antoinette Brown Blackwell

Measure not the work until the day's out and the labor done.

Elizabeth Barrett Browning

Build a little fence of trust
Around today;
Fill the space with loving work,
And therein stay.

Mary Frances Butts

I have worked all my life, wanted to work all my life, needed to work all my life.
Liz Carpenter

You always feel when you look it straight in the eye that you could have put more into it, could have let yourself go and dug harder.
Emily Carr

With hand on the spade and heart in the sky
Dress the ground and till it;
Turn in the little seed, brown and dry,
Turn out the golden millet.
Work, and your house shall be duly fed:
Work, and rest shall be won;
I hold that a man had better be dead
Than alive when his work is done.
Alice Cary

I don't think necessity is the mother of invention. Invention, in my opinion, arises directly from idleness, possibly also from laziness—to save oneself trouble.
Agatha Christie

Never learn to do anything. If you don't learn you'll always find someone else to do it.
Jane Clemens

Who said you should be happy? Do your work.
Colette

Because of the nature of my career, the constant striving, I never feel that I have arrived. There's always so much more to do. I'm constantly amazed at how much the body can do—much more than anyone thinks. Each step opens whole new doors. Other dancers ask me if I get bored. I don't, I don't get bored. There's always another possibility.
Eleanor D'Antuono

Employment and ennui are simply incompatible.
Dorothée DeLuzy

All play and no work makes Jack a mere toy.
Maria Edgeworth

God has no hands but our hands and no tongue but our tongue.

Annie Johnson Flint

Laziness may appear attractive, but work gives satisfaction.

Anne Frank

I am a marvelous housekeeper. Every time I leave a man I keep his house.

Zsa Zsa Gabor

My grandfather once told me that there were two kinds of people: those who do the work and those who take the credit. He told me to try to be in the first group; there was much less competition.

Indira Gandhi

The most popular labor-saving device is still money.

Phyllis George

Work, the object of which to serve one's self is the lowest. Work, the object of which is merely to serve one's family is the next lowest. Work, the object of which is to serve more and more people, in widening range . . . is social service in the fullest sense, and the highest form of service we can reach.

Charlotte Perkins Gilman

My parents always told me that people will never know how long it takes you to do something. They will only know how well it is done.

Nancy Hanks

I think housework is the reason most women go to the office.

Heloise

Men see work as a series of tasks to be completed, all adding up to something; women often look at a job as an endless stream of work, with no beginning, middle or end.

Margaret Henning and Anne Jardin

As for me, prizes mean nothing. My prize is my work.

Katharine Hepburn

My epitaph should read: "She worked herself into this ground."

Kay Bailey Hutchinson

I long to accomplish a great and noble task, but it is my chief duty to accomplish small tasks as if they were great and noble.

Helen Keller

For the last third of life there remains only work. It alone is always stimulating, rejuvenating, exciting and satisfying.

Käthe Kollwitz

You can get lonesome—being that busy.

Isabel Lennart

My kids were only babies when their Daddy went away.
So I hung up my apron and went out to work for pay.
They put me on the night-shift working on a big machine;
That was the last of normal life my kids and I have seen.

Marilyn Major

There is a type of woman who cannot remain at home. In spite of the place her children and family fill in her life, her nature demands something more; she cannot divorce herself from the larger social life. She cannot let her children narrow her horizon. For such a woman there is no rest.

Golda Meir

Father, I beg of Thee a little task
to dignify my days, 'tis all I ask.

Edna St. Vincent Millay

The fruit that falls without shaking, indeed, is too mellow for me.

Lady Mary Wortley Montague

It's not so much how busy you are, but why you are busy. The bee is praised; the mosquito is swatted.

Marie O'Conner

Nighttime is really the best time to work. All the ideas are there to be yours because everyone else is asleep.

Catherine O'Hara

What is sad for women of my generation is that they weren't supposed to work if they had families. What were they to do when the children were grown—watch the raindrops coming down the windowpane?

Jacqueline Kennedy Onassis

Labor is life! 'Tis the still water faileth;
Idleness ever despaireth, bewaileth;
Keep the watch wound, for the dark rusty assaileth.

Frances S. Osgood

This is a country where women have won the right to be terminally exhausted. But we can start to say things to ourselves and our employers like "Two of us can share a job" and "Why do we have to go to an office?" There really isn't as much reason anymore. The day the FAX machine came into our lives, everything changed. We can work in a closet or anywhere.

Sally Jessy Raphael

Does the road wind up-hill all the way?
Yes, to the very end.
Will the day's journey take the whole long day?
From morn to night, my friend.

Christina Rossetti

Career is too pompous a word. It was a job, and I have always felt privileged to be paid for what I love doing.

Barbara Stanwyck

The business end of things interested him far less than the Natural Beauty and the manual labor necessary to maintain it.

Danielle Steel

You'll be old and you never lived, and you kind of feel silly to lie down and die and to never have lived, to have been a job chaser and never have lived.

Gertrude Stein

Everyone confesses in the abstract that exertion which brings out all the powers of body and mind is the best thing for us all; but practically most people do all they can to get rid of it, and as a general rule nobody does much more than circumstances drive them to do.

Harriet Beecher Stowe

It is amazing how much people can get done if they do not worry about who gets the credit.

Sandra Swinney

We can do no great things—only small things with great love.

Mother Teresa

Leisure for men of business, and business for men of leisure, would cure many complaints.

Esther L.S. Thrale

A job is not a career. I think I started out with a job. It turned into a career and changed my life. A career means long hours, travel, frustration and plain hard work, and finally perhaps a realization that you can't have it all.

Barbara Walters

The two kinds of people on earth that I mean
Are the people who lift and the people who lean.

Ella Wheeler Wilcox

Too many people are ready to carry the stool when the piano needs to be moved.

Anon.

Man may work from sun to sun, but women's work is never done.

Anon.

BIOGRAPHICAL INDEX

A

Abbott, Berenice (b. 1898) Am. photographer

Abrams, Alice (b. 1931) Am. jewelry designer, goldsmith

Abshier, Lo (b. 1910) Am. educator

Abzug, Bella (b. 1920) Am. feminist, N.Y. Congresswoman

Adams, Abigail Smith (1744–1818) Am. First Lady, writer

Adams, Grace (b. 1900) Am. psychologist

Addams, Jane (1860–1935) Am. social reformer, author

Alcott, Louisa May (1832–1888) Am. novelist

Alexander, Mrs. [pseud. of Annie Hector] (1825–1902) Am. novelist

Allen, Elizabeth Akers (1832–1911) Am. poet, author

Allen, Gracie (1906–1964) Am. comedienne

Alther, Lisa (b. 1944) Am. novelist

Anders, Valerie

Anderson, Margaret (1893–1973) Am. writer, musician

Anderson, Marian (b. 1902) Am. singer

Andrews, Julie (b. 1934) Br. singer, actress

Andrews, Lynn V. (contemporary) Am. author

Andrus, Ethel Percy (1884–1967) Am. social activist

Angelou, Maya (b. 1928) Am. writer

Anne of Austria (1601–1666) Fr., consort of Louis XIII

Anthony, Susan B. (1820–1906) Am. suffragist

Antrim, Minna (1861–d.?) Am. writer

Aquino, Corazon (b. 1933) President of the Philippine Islands

Arden, Elizabeth (1878–1966) Can./Am. cosmetics executive

Arendt, Hannah (1906–1975) Ger./Am. political philosopher

Arendt, Leah (1898–1989) Am. businesswoman

Arnauld, Angelique (1624–1684) Fr. abbess

Arnold, Roseanne Barr (b. 1953) Am. actress, comedienne

Arthur, Jean (1905–1991) Am. actress

Ash, Mary Kay (b. 1918) Am. cosmetics executive

Ashby, Margery [m. Corbett] (1882–1981) feminist

Ashford, Jan (b. 1932) Am. businesswoman

Ashley, Elizabeth (b. 1941) Am. actress

Ashley, Katherine (1840–1916)

Ashrawi, Hanan Mikhail (b. 1950) Palestinian diplomat

Ashton-Warner, Sylvia (b. 1908) Br. educator, author

Asphasia (c. 431 B.C.) Greek writer, common-law wife of Pericles

Astor, Lady Nancy (1879–1964) Br., first woman Member of Parliament

Atherton, Gertrude Franklin (1857–1948) Am. novelist

Atwood, Margaret (b. 1939) Am. novelist

Auel, Jean (b. 1936) Am. novelist

Austen, Jane (1775–1817) Br. novelist

Austin, Mary Hunter (1868–1934) Am. novelist, suffragist

B

Babbitt, Lorraine Ussher (c. 1958) Am. poet, writer, publisher

Bacall, Lauren (b. 1924) Am. actress

Baez, Joan (b. 1941) Am. folk singer

Bailey, Pearl Mae (1918–1990) Am. singer

Baillie, Joanna (1762–1851) Scot. dramatist, poet

Bakker, Tammy Faye (b. 1942) Am. religious leader

Baldwin, Faith (1893–1978) Am. writer

Balfour, Clara Lucas (1808–1878) Br. temperance leader

Ball, Lucille (1911–1989) Am. comedienne, actress

Bankhead, Tallulah (1903–1968) Am. actress

Banuelos, Romana (b. 1925) Am., U.S. Treasurer

Barbauld, Anna Letitia (1743–1825) Br. poet

Barker, Myrtle Lillian (b. 1910) Am. journalist, writer

Barnard, Charlotte Alington (1830–1869) Br. ballad writer

Barrett, Colleen C. (b. 1944) Am. businesswoman

Barrymore, Ethel (1879–1959) Am. actress

Barton, Clara (1821–1912) Am. nurse, founder of Red Cross

Bates, Katherine Lee (1859–1929) Am. poet, educator

Beard, Mary Ritter (1876–1958) Am. historian

Becker, Mary Lamberton (1873–1958) Am. critic, author

Bellamy, Carol (b. 1942) Am. businesswoman

Benedict, Agnes Elizabeth Beard (d. 1950)

Benedict, Ruth (1887–1948) Am. anthropologist

Bensley, Jill (b. 1946) Am. businesswoman

Bergen, Candice (b. 1946) Am. actress

Berger, Sally (b. 1933) Am. businesswoman

Bergman, Ingrid (1915–1982) Swed./Am. actress

Bernard, Dorothy (1890–1955) Am. actress

Bernhardt, Sarah (1844–1923) Fr. actress

Bethune, Mary McLeod (1875–1955) Am. educator, writer

Bingham, Sallie (b. 1937) Am. writer

Birch, Alison Wyrley (b. 1922) Am. writer, journalist

Bisset, Jacqueline (b. 1944) Br. actress

Black, Cathleen (b. 1944) Am. publisher

Black, Shirley Temple (b. 1928) Am. actress, diplomat

Blackwell, Alice Stone (1857–1950) Am. writer

Blackwell, Antoinette Brown (1825–1921) Am. feminist, writer

Blandford, Linda (b. 1942) Br. journalist, broadcaster

Blessington, Lady Marguerite [nee Power] (1789–1849) Irish writer

Bloodworth-Thomason, Linda (contemporary) Am. writer, TV producer

Bly, Mary

Bogan, Louise (1897–1970) Am. poet

Bolton, Sarah Knowles (1841–1916) Am. poet, editor, social reformer

Bombeck, Erma (b. 1927) Am. humorist, writer

Bosone, Reva Beck (1895–1983) Am., Utah Congresswoman

Bottome, Phyliss (1882–1963) Br. novelist, writer

Bowen, Catherine Drinker (1897–1973) Am. writer, historian

Bowen, Elizabeth (1899–1973) Irish/Br. writer

Bowring, Eva (b. 1892) U.S. Senator from Nebraska

Bracken, Peg (b. 1918) Am. writer, humorist

Bradley, Amanda (d. 1916) Am. actress

Bradley, Marion Zimmer (b. 1930) Am. writer

Bradstreet, Anne (1612–1672) Am. writer

Braiker, Harriet Beryl (b. 1948) Am. psychologist

Branch, Anna Hempsted (1875–1973) Am. poet, social worker

Braverman, Kate (b. 1950) Am. poet, novelist, editor

Bray, Ann Eliza (1790–1883) Br. novelist

Bregnard, Edythe E.

Bremer, Fredrika (1801–1865) Swed. writer

Brice, Fanny (1891–1951) Am. comedienne, singer

Bridges, Madeline S. [nee Mary Ainge De Vere] (1844–1920) Am. poet

Brittain, Vera (1893–1970) Br. writer, poet

Brontë, Charlotte (1816–1855) Br. novelist

Brontë, Emily (1818–1848) Br. novelist

Brothers, Dr. Joyce (b. 1925) Am. psychologist, writer, TV personality

Brown, Bess (1871–d.?) Am. political activist

Brown, Helen Gurley (b. 1922) Am. publisher, author

Brown, Olympia (1835–1900) Am. minister, suffragist

Brown, Rita Mae (b. 1944) Am. feminist, writer, educator

Felkin, Ellen Thornycroft Fowler (1860–1929) Br. writer

Felton, Rebecca Latimer (1835–1930) Am. author

Fenwick, Millicent (b. 1910) Am. editor, N.J. Congresswoman

Ferber, Edna (1887–1968) Am. novelist

Ferguson, Marilyn (b. 1938) Am. publisher

Ferraro, Geraldine (b. 1935) Am. Vice Pres. candidate, N.Y. Congresswoman

Firstenberg, Jean (b. 1936) Am. businesswoman

Fisher, Carrie (b. 1956) Am. actress, writer

Fisher, Dorothy Canfield (1879–1958) Am. novelist

Fitzgerald, Ella (b. 1918) Am. singer

Fitzgerald, Zelda (1900–1948) Am. writer; m. F. Scott Fitzgerald

Flint, Annie Johnson (1866–1932) Am. poet

Flynn, June

Fonda, Jane (b. 1937) Am. actress, political activist

Fonteyn, Dame Margot (1919–1991) Br. ballerina

Ford, Betty [nee Elizabeth Bloomer] (b. 1918) Am. First Lady

Ford, Eileen (b. 1922) Am. businesswoman

Fordyce, Kelly

Fosdick, Dorothy (b. 1913) Am. author

Frank, Anne (1929–1945) Ger. diarist

Fraser, Antonia (b. 1932) Br. author

Frederick, Pauline (1883–1938) Am. actress

Fremont, Jessie B. (1824–1902) Am. writer, political activist

French, Marilyn (b. 1929) Am. novelist

Freud, Anna (1895–1983) Austrian psychologist; dgt. of Sigmund Freud

Fried, SuEllen (b. 1928) Am. social activist

Friedan, Betty (b. 1921) Am. feminist author

Fuldheim, Dorothy (b. 1893)

Fuller, Margaret [m. Ossoli] (1810–1850) Am. writer, social critic

G

Gabler, June E. (b. 1930) Am. educator

Gabor, Zsa Zsa (b. 1919) Hungar./Am. actress

Gandhi, Indira (1917–1984) Prime Minister of India

Garland, Judy (1922–1969) Am. singer, actress

Gaskell, Elizabeth (1810–1865) Br. novelist

Gasparin, Catherine Valerie, Comtesse de (1813–1894) Fr. author

Gatty, Margaret (1809–1873) Br. author

George, Phyllis (b. 1949) Am. TV personality

Gerould, Katherine Fullerton (1879–1944) Am. writer

Getty, Estelle (b. 1923) Am. actress

Geyer, Georgie Ann (b. 1935) Am. columnist, author

Gilman, Charlotte Perkins (1860–1935) Am. author, social critic

Gingold, Hermione (1897–1987) Br. actress, comedienne

Giroud, Françoise (b. 1916) Fr. writer, publisher

Girzartis, Loretta (b. 1920) Am. educator, writer

Glaser, Susan (contemporary) Am. educator, writer

Glasgow, Ellen (1874–1945) Am. novelist

Godwin, Gail (b. 1937) Am. writer, journalist, educator

Goldberg, Whoopi (b. 1955) Am. actress, comedienne

Goldman, Emma (1869–1940) Rus./Am. anarchist, writer

Goodall, Jane (b. 1934) Br. ethologist, writer

Goodman, Ellen (b. 1941) Am. columnist

Gorbachev, Raisa (b. 1932) Rus., USSR First Lady

Gordon, Ruth (1896–1985) Am. actress

Gordon, Suzanne (b. 1920) Am. writer

Gould, Hannah Flagg (1789–1865) Am. poet

Grace, Princess of Monaco [nee Kelly] (1928–1982) Am. film actress

Graham, Katherine (b. 1917) Am. newspaper publisher

Graham, Martha (1894–1991) Am. dancer, choreographer

Grant, Lee (b. 1929) Am. actress

Grasso, Ella T. (1919–1981) Am., Gov. of Conn., U.S. Congresswoman

Green, Anna Katherine (1846–1935) Am. writer

Green, Edith Starrett (b. 1910) Am., Oregon Congresswoman

Green, Mary Anne Everett (1818–1895) Br. writer, historian, editor

Green, Thelma (b. 1906) Am. businesswoman

Greenfield, Meg (b. 1930) Am. journalist

Greer, Germaine (b. 1939) Austral. feminist, writer

Greer, Jackie M. (b. 1909) Am. columnist

Greeson, Janet (contemporary) Am. author

Greschel, Ramona (b. 1939) Am. educator

Grey, Lita [nee McMurphy] (b. 1908) Am. actress; m. Charlie Chaplin

Grimké, Sarah (1792–1873) Am. suffragist, abolitionist

Grosse, Carol (b. 1948) Am. educator

Guggenheimer, Elinor (b. 1912) Am. city planner, writer

H

Haberli, Iris (c. 1971) Urug. social activist

Hagen, Uta (b. 1919) Ger./Am. actress, educator

Haight, Dorothy (b. 1912) Am. social activist

Hale, Sarah Josepha (1788–1879) Am. author, editor

Hall, Anna Maria [Mrs. S. C.] (1800–1881) Br. novelist

Halsey, Margaret (b. 1910) Am. writer

Hamer, Fannie Lou (1917–1977) Am. social reformer

Hamilton, Edith (1867–1963) Am. writer, scholar

Hamilton, Gail (1833–1896) Am. writer

McClintock, Barbara (1902–1992) Am. scientist

McCormick, Anne O'Hare (1882–1954) Am. journalist

McCullers, Carson (1917–1967) Am. author, playwright

McGillis, Kelly (b. 1958) Am. actress

McGinley, Phyllis (1905–1978) Am. author

McIntyre, Leslie M.

McLaughlin, Mignon Bushell (contemporary) Am. author, journalist

Mead, Margaret (1901–1978) Am. anthropologist, writer

Meir, Golda (1898–1978) Rus./Am. Prime Minister of Israel

Melia, Jinx (b. 1936) Am. writer, educator

Merman, Ethel (1908–1984) Am. singer, actress

Metalious, Grace (1924–1964) Am. author

Meuttman, Margaret Moore

Meyer, Agnes (1887–1970) Am. writer, journalist, social worker

Michaelis, Aline Triplett (1885–d.?) Am. journalist, poet

Michaud, Fay (contemporary) Am. educator

Midler, Bette (b. 1945) Am. singer, actress

Mikulski, Barbara (b. 1936) U.S. Senator from Maryland

Millay, Edna St. Vincent (1892–1950) Am. poet, author

Mills, Joan

Minnelli, Liza (b. 1946) Am. singer, actress

Mintzmyer, Lorraine (b. 1935) Am. government official

Miss Piggy muppet created by Jim Henson

Mitchell, Marcia (b. 1942) Am. writer

Mitchell, Margaret (1900–1949) Am. novelist

Mitchell, Maria (1818–1889) Am. astronomer, educator

Mitchell, Marion (b. 1929) Am. educator

Mitford, Nancy (1904–1973) Br. novelist, biographer

Mondale, Joan Adams (b. 1930) Am. Second Lady

Monroe, Marilyn (1926–1962) Am. actress

Montague, Lady Mary Wortley (1689–1762) Br. poet, writer

Montessori, Maria (1870–1952) Ital. educator, writer

Moody, Helen Wills (b. 1906) Am. tennis champion

Moore, Mariane (1887–1972) Am. poet

Moore, Mary Tyler (b. 1937) Am. actress

More, Hannah (1745–1833) Br. writer, social reformer

Moreau, Jeanne (b. 1929) Fr. actress

Mosala, Bernadette (contemporary) S. Afr. feminist

Moses, Grandma [nee Anna Mary Robertson] (1860–1961) Am. artist

Mother Goose Nursery rhyme character

Mother Teresa (b. 1910) Yugos. Roman Catholic nun, humanitarian

Motoni, Nomura (1806–1867) Jap. political activist, poet

Ono, Yoko (b. 1933) Jap./Am. artist; m. singer John Lennon

Orlock, Carol Gibson (b. 1947) Am. novelist, poet

Orr, Kay Stark (b. 1939) Am., Governor of Nebraska

Orwig, Barbara (b. 1947) Am. businesswoman

Osgood, Frances S. (1811–1850) Am. poet

Ouida [pseud. for Marie Louise de la Ramee] (1838–1908) Br. novelist

P

Paddleford, Clementine (1900–1968) Am. food editor, columnist

Pale Moon, Princess (contemporary) Am. Cherokee/Ojibwa performer; foundation executive

Paley, Grace (b. 1922) Am. writer

Pandit, Vijaya Lakshmi (1900–1991) India; Pres. of U.N. General Assembly

Pankhurst, Cristabel (1880–1958) Br. suffragist, evangelist

Pankhurst, Emmeline (1858–1928) Br. suffragist

Parker, Dorothy (1893–1967) Am. humorist, writer, poet

Parks, Rosa (b. 1913) Am. civil rights activist

Parton, Dolly (b. 1946) Am. singer, songwriter, actress

Patterson, Isabel (contemporary) Am. novelist, journalist

Pearson, Maryon (1897–1972) Can.; m. Prime Minister Lester Pearson

Pepper, Mildred Webster (d. 1979) Am.; m. Fla. Congressman Claude Pepper

Pepple, Connie Warner (b. 1955) Am. homemaker

Perkins, Frances (1882–1965) Am. writer; U.S. Secty. of Labor

Perón, Eva [nee Duarte] (1919–1952) Argen.; m. Juan Perón; acting president of Argentina

Peter, Irene (contemporary) Am. writer; m. Laurence J. Peter 1967

Peyser, Joan (b. 1931) Am. musicologist, author

Pfost, Gracie Bowers (1906–1965) Am., Idaho Congresswoman

Phelps, Elizabeth Stuart (1815–1852) Am. novelist

Pickford, Mary (1893–1979) Can./Am. silent film actress, businesswoman

Plath, Sylvia (1932–1963) Am. poet, writer

Porter, Anna Maria (1781–1850) Br. novelist

Porter, Jane (1776–1850) Br. novelist

Porter, Katherine Anne (1890–1980) Am. author

Porter, Sylvia (b. 1913) Am. economist, writer

Post, Emily (1873–1960) Am. authority on etiquette, writer

Potter, Beatrix (1866–1943) Br. writer, illustrator

Preston, Maude V. Am. writer, poet

Price, Leontyne (b. 1927) Am. opera singer

Priest, Ivy Baker (1905–1975) U.S. Treasurer

Purdy, Ginger (b. 1926) Am. women's advocate

Rowland, Helen (1876–1950) Am. humorist, writer

Rowley, Janet Davison (b. 1925) Am. physician

Rubinstein, Helena (1870?-1965) Pol./Am. cosmetics executive

Ruckelshaus, Jill (b. 1937) Am. government official, lecturer

Rudner, Rita (b. 1955) Am. comedienne

Rukeyser, Muriel (1913–1980) Am. poet, biographer

Ruman, Marilyn

Runbeck, Margaret Lee (1905–1956) Am. author

Russell, Dora (1894–1986) Br. author, political activist

Russell, Lady Rachel (1636–1723) Br. noblewoman

Russell, Rebecca (b. 1905)

Russell, Rosalind (1911–1976) Am. actress

S

Sadler, Lena Kellogg (1875–1939) Am. physician

Sagan, Françoise (b. 1935) Fr. writer

Sampsell, Susan (b. 1945) Am. businesswoman

Sampson, Patsy H. (b. 1932) Am. university president

Sand, George [pseud. for Amandine Dupin] (1804–1876) Fr. novelist

Sanger, Margaret (1883–1966) Am. social reformer

Santmyer, Helen Hoover (1895–1986) Am. writer

Sappho (c. 612 B.C.) Greek poet

Sarraute, Nathalie (b. 1900) Rus./Fr. novelist, essayist

Sarton, May (b. 1912) Belgium/Am. writer, poet

Saunders, Debra J. (contemporary) Am. columnist

Schaefer, Mary (b. 1913)

Schaffer, Gloria (b. 1930) Am. political activist

Schiff, Dorothy (1903–1989) Am. newspaper publisher

Schlafly, Phyllis (b. 1924) Am. political activist, writer

Schroeder, Patricia (b. 1940) Am., Colorado Congresswoman

Schuster, Sharon Lee (b. 1939) Am. association executive

Schwartz, Pepper (b. 1945) Am. educator, writer

Scott, Hazel (1920–1981) W. Ind./Am. pianist, singer, actress

Scats, Delores (b. 1928) Am. poet, playwright

Sedgwick, Catherine M. (1789–1867) Am. author

Seton, Julia (b. 1889) Am. historian, writer, lecturer

Seton-Thompson, Grace (1872–1959) Am. writer, feminist, lecturer

Sévigné, La Marquise de [nee Marie de Rabutin-Chantal] (1626–1696) Fr. letter writer

Sexton, Anne (1928–1974) Am. poet

Shaef, Anne Wilson (b. 1934) Am. writer

Shanahan, June N. (contemporary) poet

Shaw, Anne (d. 1680) Br. poet; m. Robert Shaw

Sheehy, Gail (b. 1937) Am. author, social critic

Sherwood, Margaret (1864–1955) Am. author, poet

Shore, Dinah (b. 1920) Am. singer, TV personality

Sigourney, Lydia Huntley (1791–1865) Am. author

Silber, Joan (b. 1945) Am. writer

Sills, Beverly (b. 1929) Am. opera singer

Simone, Nina (b. 1933) Am. singer, songwriter, pianist

Simpson, Inice (b. 1911) Am. businesswoman

Simpson, Wallis Warfield (1896–1986) Am./Br.; Duchess of Windsor

Sinclair, Carole (b. 1942) Am. businesswoman, publisher

Sitwell, Dame Edith (1887–1964) Br. writer, poet, critic

Sizemore, Barbara (b. 1927) Am. civil rights activist

Skinner, Cornelia Otis (1901–1979) Am. actress, writer

Slick, Grace (b. 1939) Am. rock singer, songwriter

Small, Jacquelyn

Smeltzer, Ruth

Smith, Dodie [pseud. C. L. Anthony] (b. 1896) Br. playwright

Smith, Elizabeth Oakes (1806–1893) Am. writer, suffragist, lecturer

Smith, Lillian (1897–1966) Am. educator, novelist, social activist

Smith, Margaret Chase (b. 1897) U.S. Senator from Maine

Smith, May V. (b. 1922) Am. government worker

Snow, Carrie (b. 1914)

Snow, Phoebe (b. 1951) Am. singer, songwriter

Sontag, Susan (b. 1933) Am. author, social critic

Spacek, Sissy (b. 1949) Am. actress

St. Catherine of Siena (1347–1380) Ital. mystic

St. George, Katherine Price Collier (1896–1983) Am., N.Y. Congresswoman

St. Johns, Adele Rogers (1894–1988) Am. writer, journalist

St. Marie, Satenig (b. 1927) Am. businesswoman, writer

St. Theresa of Jesus [Theresa de Avila] (1515–1582) Span. nun

Stair, Nadine Am. writer

Stanton, Elizabeth Cady (1815–1902) Am. suffragist, social reformer

Stanwyck, Barbara (1907–1990) Am. actress

Staubus, Kristi (contemporary) Am. student

Steel, Danielle (b. 1947) Am. author

Stein, Gertrude (1874–1946) Am./Fr. author

Steinbaum, Rosemary Konner (b. 1952) Am. educator

Steinem, Gloria (b. 1934) Am. feminist, writer, editor

Stern, Ellen Sue

Stern, Gladys Browyn (1890–1973) Br. novelist

Stewart, Judy Lynn (contemporary) Am. student

Stewart, Mary W. (1803–1879) Am. civil rights activist

Stokes, Rose Pastor (1879–1933) Rus./Br. social worker

Stone, Nan (b. 1925) Am. editor

Stout, Juanita Kidd (b. 1919) Am. jurist

Stowe, Harriet Beecher (1811–1896) Am. author, abolitionist, social critic

U

Ueland, Brenda (1891–1986) Am. writer

Urquides, Maria (b. 1908) Am. educator

V

Van Buren, Abigail (b. 1918) Am. advice columnist

Van Doren, Mamie (b. 1933) Am. actress

Vance, Eleanor Graham (b. 1908) Am. poet; songwriter

Vance, Patricia H. (b. 1936) Am., Pennsylvania legislator

Vanderbilt, Amy (1908–1974) Am. authority on etiquette

Vanderbilt, Gloria (b. 1924) Am. fashion designer

Varda, Agnes (b. 1928) Fr. filmmaker

Vaught, Brig. Gen. Wilma L. (b. 1930) Am. USAF officer

Victoria, Queen of the British Empire (1819–1901)

Voillez, Mme.

Von Furstenberg, Diane (b. 1946) Am. fashion designer

von Krüdener, Baroness Barbara (1764–1824) Latvian religious mystic

Von Suttner, Bertha

Vorse, Mary Heaton (1881–1966) Am. writer

Vreeland, Diana (1903?-1989) Am. journalist, fashion editor

W

Wagner, Jane (b. 1935) Am. humorist, writer

Walden, Helen Marie

Walker, Alice (b. 1944) Am. author

Walters, Barbara (b. 1931) Am. broadcast journalist

Ward, Barbara [Lady Jackson] (1914–1981) Br. writer, educator

Ward, Lydia Avery Coonley (d. 1924) Am. author

Warford, Rita

Warner, Carolyn (b. 1930) Am. lecturer, Ariz. Supt. of Public Instruction

Warner, Christi Mary (b. 1961) Am. businesswoman

Washington, Martha Dandridge Custis (1732–1802) Am. First Lady

Wattleton, Faye (b. 1943) Am. social/political activist

Wauneka, Annie Dodge (b. 1910) Am. Navajo leader

Wayne, June (b. 1918) Am. artist, writer

Weatherford, Cathy Warner (b. 1951) Am. homemaker, educator

Webb, Mary Gladys (1882?-1927) Scot. religious leader, writer, poet

Weil, Simone (1909–1943) Fr. writer, revolutionary

Welch, Myra Brooks

Wells, Corrine V.

Welshimer, Helen Louise (d. 1954) Am. writer

Welty, Eudora (b. 1909) Am. author, photographer

Wesley, Susannah (c. 1700) Br.; mother of John Wesley

West, Dame Rebecca [nee Cicily Isabel Fairfield] (1892–1983) Br. writer

INDEX